D1564624

EVELYN UNDERHILL

EVELYN UNDERHILL
(1875-1941)

An Introduction to her Life and Writings

by

CHRISTOPHER J. R. ARMSTRONG

William B. Eerdmans Publishing Company
Grand Rapids, Michigan

© 1975, A. R. Mowbray & Co. Limited

First published 1975 by A. R. Mowbray & Co. Limited,
The Alden Press, Osney Mead, Oxford OX₂ OEG.

First American edition January 1976, by
special arrangement with Mowbrays.

Library of Congress Cataloging in Publication Data

Armstrong, Christopher J R 1935–
   Evelyn Underhill, 1875–1941.

   Bibliography: p. 293
   Includes index.
   1. Underhill, Evelyn, 1875–1941.
BV5095.U5A75 1976   248'.22'0924 [B]   75-33401
ISBN 0-8028-3474-4

Contents

The world is finding out, as it has often done before, and more or less forgotten, that it cannot do without religion. Love is the first thing to wither under its loss. What love does in transfiguring life, religion does in transfiguring love. . . . Love is sure to be something less than human if it is not something more. Coventry Patmore, *Love and Poetry*, XIX.

Foreword

by Lord Ramsey of Canterbury

Evelyn Underhill had considerable religious influence in the years between the wars, as one who did more than others to diffuse and interpret the influence of Baron von Hugel and to guide the revival of interest in mysticism along the paths of Christian theology. Like others of her time—or indeed of any time—she came to be regarded as "dated" and in the decades after her death her name went through a phase both of apathy and antipathy. Now that thirty-five years have passed, the time is ripe for a new assessment in a larger perspective: I believe that this book provides such an assessment with sympathy, critical discernment and a sense of history.

Evelyn Underhill's writings were numerous and they cover a long period. They include works which seem naive and immature, reflecting the weaknesses of the revival of mystical religion in her early years of this century; and they include others which show her development into a deep, theological understanding. If she had written only the books which are now judged to be her best she would be known as a powerful exponent of Christian spirituality. As it is, her books show not only that but also the way in which her ideas and indeed her own character was deepened immeasurably by the influence of the Baron and by a grasp of the Christian doctrine of the Incarnation. This new study recalls both her mature teaching and, with much sensitivity, the spiritual pilgrimage which led to it. It is a story valuable for our own time, as we need not only to commend Christian spirituality, but to be sensitive to the contemporary spiritual hunger with the many hazards and pitfalls which face it on the road to the wisdom of the saints.

I think that in the twenties and thirties there were few, if indeed any, in the Church of England who did more to help people to grasp the priority of prayer in the Christian life and the place of the contemplative element within it. If there was a 'cosy' or 'middle class' tinge in her style and language the same may no doubt be said of St Francis de Sales and other spiritual guides. But I would deny the charge of 'preciousness' in reference to her mature writings, for 'preciousness' implies the enjoyment of an idea as a phrase without regard to the wider human context, and Evelyn Underhill was acutely aware that you cannot know God without a concern for God's world, a world which she both saw and felt as it moved towards the horrors of war. In our efforts to follow the Christian way in our own times we can learn both from her pilgrimage and her teaching. The serenity of the latter grew from the painful conflicts of the former, and this book will help us to learn how God works, and uses his servants to work, in human lives.

15 July 1975   ✠ *Michael Ramsey*

Introduction

TRUTH is said to be the daughter of time: a true saying no doubt in the long term, that is the point of it. But in the short term? There can be little doubt that time hitherto has not been kind to the reputation of Evelyn Underhill, born 1875, died 1941. While the enigmatic powers which decide such matters have decreed that she should be granted a place in the *Dictionary of National Biography* and in such a standard work of reference as the *Oxford Dictionary of the Christian Church*, no one could say that she has been smothered with interest and, despite her very considerable literary output, she is still far from generating a research 'industry'. To find historians who give her substantial attention even in the context of her own church one has to turn back a number of years, for example to the relatively 'old-fashioned' history of the Church of England of Roger Lloyd. Lloyd links her with Dean Inge and the Catholic, Friedrich von Hugel, as one of the main architects of the 'mystical revival' of the years immediately preceding the war of 1914–18.

Why turn again to so remote a personage? Have we not had enough of idle gossip about the ecclesiastical personalities of a by-gone age, enough praise of past theological achievements and of a virtue which we can no longer honestly say we aspire to? Is there anything special about Evelyn Underhill that she should be drawn from the decent limbo of oblivion into which the deserving but unremarkable moral tutors of every age inevitably fall? Such questions can only be answered in the light of her particular history.

Evelyn Underhill is still remembered by many as a serene and

loving person gifted with a sense of humour and a large generosity. She is remembered also as a person who was reticent and
slow to speak about what most concerned her, alert of intelligence and decisive in giving advice. Many who heard her retreats
recall the spell she was able to cast through her combination of
personal charm, skill with words and calming serenity. Such is
the late image as one may call it, of Evelyn Underhill as she is
generally remembered today and especially by Anglicans. For
these she is the unobtrusive shrewdly articulate guide of souls,
rather asthmatic, in a long skirt and button shoes, a person whom
since she nearly became Roman Catholic and didn't, then sat at
the feet of von Hugel and still didn't, it was re-assuring to have
about in a Church always prone to be unsure of its own credentials. She at least could be trusted to *know* about prayer and the
spiritual life: steeped in Catholic principles she had learnt her
trade from von Hugel, the man Charles Gore described in 1912 as
'perhaps the most learned man of living men'—she too who was
the friend of Abbot Chapman, Cuthbert Butler and E. I. Watkin,
quoted Jacques Maritain, de Caussade and Henri Brémond as
though to the manner born, seemed to many in her lifetime and since
the authentic representative of a spiritual tradition to which they
knew they belonged but from which too often they felt isolated.

But there was also another side to Evelyn Underhill. Her friend
of later years, Margaret Cropper, said that she 'always wore her
Anglicanism with a difference', an interesting remark which
reflects one suspects the reaction to her and her work of a fair
number of her fellow-communicants in the Anglican Church
and may also help to explain the somewhat uneven course of her
subsequent reputation.

For Evelyn was that on the whole rare phenomenon, a person
of a certain intellectual fame, achievement and maturity who
actually *became* an Anglican. True, she had been born into the
Church of England and was confirmed by one of its bishops; it is

even possible that she attended church for a little while after confirmation. But she did not remain in that body and her religious awakening took place under very different auspices. When she returned to the fold she was in every way far more the creature of her extra-Anglican religious career than of her sheltered 'Sunday-school' Christian childhood. Evelyn was indeed a 'cradle' Anglican but when the time came she was happy enough to bid farewell to 'childish things' and certainly did not spare her scorn for the institution in which her school if not her parents had brought her up. When she returned at the age of forty-six, a major part of her achievement behind her, it was certainly not the security of cradle life that she was seeking.

To understand the religious courses of Evelyn Underhill in the closing years of the last century and in what we now call the 'Edwardian era' it is necessary to know something of the philosophical and cultural atmosphere of the time, not necessarily in depth or at the level of carefully researched monographs, but in its general impact on society and as it might be expected to affect a wide-awake intelligent person in her early twenties with—like most of her contemporaries before and since—a decided romantic bent. Some taste of this atmosphere we have attempted to give in the pages which follow, some glimpse of the enormous excitement impalpably everywhere in the air in those days, mysteriously compounded of the psychic, the psychological, the occult, the mystical, the medieval, the advance of science, the self-unfolding of the Absolute, the apotheosis of Art, the re-discovery of the feminine and an infatuation simultaneously with both the most unashamedly sensuous and the most ethereally 'spiritual'. Anglicanism for better or worse seemed to the Evelyn of those days out-of-key with this, her world. The orotund periods of theological dons, the diligent labours of tens of thousands of parish clergyman up and down the country, failed to impress her. She sought, as we now say, 'the place where the action was', the heart

and centre of life as she and, it seems, many of her generation
conceived it, not in the state religion, but in experience and the
heart. It was indeed the age of 'the soul', one of those periods
when a sudden easing, apparently, of social taboos brings on, or
is brought on by, a great sense of personal emancipation and a
desire for an El Dorado apparently cold-shouldered and despised
by an older, more morose and insensitive generation.

Such an El Dorado was for Evelyn the sphere of the mystical.
Her exploration is plotted in the following pages to the extent
that our information allows. The 'mystic quest' led to her encounter with the Neoplatonists and the honey-toned Plotinus
with his lyrical exaltation of divine and earthly beauty, who also
had first won the youthful St Augustine to spiritual loves, then to
the practical mystics, the occultists, explorers of mystery in dark
places, in innocuous looking suburban homes in London and
elsewhere. She came next upon the Roman Church with its
apparent genius for both harnessing and satisfying man's mystical
passion—but at how great a price? Then she came into religious solitude and learnt from the Bible of the trees, the birds, the flowers
and the fields. This lasted some years until finally, with a growing
awareness of the inadequacies of a purely individualistic religious
orientation, however mitigated by acts of unselfish love and compassion, she accepted a fresh encounter with institutional religion
and asked to be reintegrated within the Anglican communion.

Such at least is the external history. For much of the internal
history of Evelyn Underhill we have little more to go on than her
published work which is in many respects as, if not more, revealing, than those few private documents which survive. This study
is largely if not wholly concerned to recount as accurately as
possible under the circumstances 'the story of a soul' i.e. not the
public or even the social career of a fairly well-known personality,
but the development of ideas, feeling and general outlook which
led her to propose and to undertake the works and tasks which

made her famous. From this point of view her story has seemed to emerge more and more as a process of what one can only call progressive incarnation, a gradual mitigation then transmutation of her early other-worldly mystical values, until we find in her at the end someone whom experience has taught the triviality of seeking Experience, a woman whom life has taught the lesson of the expendability of life if living values are to be adequately served. Not that the incarnational and sacrificial idea is not present from near the beginning: it is, and strongly. But, as Coventry Patmore put it, 'impatience for vision is one of the last faults to be cured' and it took Evelyn many years to see how in practice the satisfaction of the 'metaphysical thirst' at the heart of all living religion, as both she and von Hugel saw it, could be reconciled with the renunciation of such satisfaction for the higher value of 'an overflowing love to all in common'.

There are therefore a number of aspects of the career and personality of Evelyn Underhill which make her interesting for our times. For in these days also there is a renewed interest in the value of authentic personal experience in religion and a corresponding depreciation of authoritarian institutional religious forms. Evelyn's life, if it does no more, illustrates how one devoted and critical seeker found an answer to this problem. In these days too, much interest is shown in esoteric forms of religion and established religious bodies find themselves challenged as to their efficacy to 'mediate the vision'. Evelyn knew the efforts of both the one and the other from the inside. The old theology of clearly defined concepts and *a prioristic* reasoning is out of favour: it is hard to find a writer on mysticism who had less use for what she called, in Barth's phrase, 'the dreadful prattle of the theologians', and almost to the end of her days put the word 'grace' in quotation marks or escorted it with a periphrasis to show what she meant by it. Again, though the vision seems to beckon us anew, nevertheless at the same time never have the pressures of

incarnational religion seemed stronger upon its adherents to ex-
ecrate the way of retreat, tranquility and recollection, and to count
the vision well lost if but one ounce of deprivation and suffering
can be lifted from the human burden. Such a conflict was one might
say the very warp and woof of Evelyn Underhill's existence,
made all the more urgent by the fact that she was no lonely hermit
but the wife of a professional lawyer living in London, who had
freely and deliberately chosen so to be.

This book does not purport to record all Evelyn's utterances
nor to relate all her doings. The external events of her life have
been to some extent recorded in the *Life of Evelyn Underhill* by
Margaret Cropper (London: Mowbrays, 1958). Fresh light is
however cast here on her early quest for mystical enlightenment
and, in particular, attention has been devoted to her early short
stories and novels, both for the sake of their intrinsic interest and
for the light they shed on her developing religious outlook.
Throughout it has been all but impossible to keep a just balance
between the amount of attention which should be paid to the
'life' and that due to the 'works': if the balance seems to tilt
heavily in favour of the latter this is largely because no coherent
account of them has hitherto been published, a fact lamented as
long ago as 1959 by Mr E. I. Watkin. Certain aspects of Evelyn's
thought have had to be passed over in silence, largely for lack of
space and time. There is for example the topic of mysticism and
art, to which Evelyn devoted a good deal of attention: there is
also the topic of the ministry of women to which she devoted a
paper in 1932 (published in *Mixed Pasture*, pp. 113ff). It may be
said in parenthesis that proponents of the ordination of women
cannot claim her as a pioneer of their cause. It has not indeed been
possible to devote nearly enough space to many subjects which
Evelyn touched upon, usually with sense and ability, in the course
of her immensely prolific life. Once again it seemed best to try to
disengage the earlier and less well-known figure who gave us

Mysticism (1911) rather than the still remembered if equally mis-understood writer of *Worship* (1936). Finally her relations with von Hugel may seem inadequately summarized; one understands that further work is proceeding on this point. But, in general, Evelyn Underhill does stand in some need of defence from her detractors, chiefly Anglican. Is it that Anglicans find it scarcely credible that anyone should whole-heartedly wish to join their ranks? Or is it the case that when Rome sneezes, the Church of England catches a cold and an Evelyn Underhill labelled 'modern-ist' by some Catholics had inevitably to be kept at arm's length by her own Church? The fact remains that, with the exception of Roger Lloyd, who goes to an opposite extreme in erroneously claiming Evelyn as an Anglican when she wrote and published *Mysticism*, and of her previous biographer, Margaret Cropper, Evelyn has not had a good press from Anglicans. This tendency was duly noted at the time of her death by Fr Geoffrey Curtis and has been confirmed of recent years. The two most sympa-thetic short studies of her are by Mr E. I. Watkin, a Roman Catho-lic, and Bishop Lumsden Barkway of the Episcopal Church of Scotland. The foundation of all subsequent biographies was laid by her friend and disciple, Lucy Menzies, for most of her life a Scottish Presbyterian, and the only Ph.D. thesis so far to study her life's work is the achievement of a Roman Catholic nun, Sister Mary Xavier Kirby, now President of Chestnut Hill College, Phila-delphia.

It is not simply a matter of neglect. As we turn to the scant previous criticism of Evelyn's life and works inside and outside the Church of England we find a curious mixture of attitudes. For the Catholic historian, Professor David Knowles, for example (in his Introduction to Cuthbert Butler's *Western Mysticism* and elsewhere), Evelyn Underhill, whom he appears to classify as an 'agnostic', belongs to a kind of stone age in the history of mystical studies, being tainted with an excessive empiricism and found

impervious if not hostile to the attractions of theological speculation in such matters. For Miss Pitt, an Anglican, on the other hand,
writing a vitriolic piece on Miss Cropper's *Life* in the June 1959
number of *Prism*, Evelyn appears cast in the role of scape-goat for
all Miss Pitt likes, or liked, least about the Anglican Church: cosi-
ness, privilege, amateurishness, sloppy pseudo-mystical chit-chat
over the tea-cups, ignorance, spiritual clichés, self-interested
charity, 'esoteric groups of devotees' and allied phenomena. Is
Miss Pitt partly responsible for the Anglican coldness about
Evelyn? It seems possible. Fr Martin Thornton, certainly, in his
English Spirituality (London: S.P.C.K., 1963) seconds her comments, adding his own rider that Evelyn was, among others, the
representative of a 'spiritual theology' both 'obsolete' and 'out-
dated and incompatible with present trends'. She is, he implies,
guilty of fostering 'almost puerile enthusiasm for the more obscure
and exotic forms of mysticism, and of a debasement of the mystical coinage such that 'practically any Christian who said his
prayers affectively, was a "mystic" '. This last comment is in
striking contrast to the more usual criticism of Evelyn among
those contemporaries who had read her books that she over-
restricted mystical experience to a few 'special types'. Fr Thornton
concludes his remarks by observing that pastorally 'the whole
thing' became 'very unhealthy indeed' when and wherever
Evelyn Underhill's influence was operative.

The truth and accuracy of such statements and judgements may
appear more clearly in the light of what follows though any considered opinion will have to be based on the *whole* life and written
oeuvre. The reader is simply invited at this point to keep in mind
the prevailing predominantly unfavourable judgement on Evelyn
Underhill. The merest outline of a defence must suffice for the
present, based on three points only. First, with regard to Fr
Knowles, it may be enough to appeal to that section of Evelyn's
actual or potential public for whom the constructive labours of

the inter-war neoscholastics are not the last word in ascetico-mystical professionalism. Evelyn believed profoundly that mystical doctrines were about actual human experiences, or they were about nothing. But if anyone chooses to say that such doctrines are uniquely concerned with supernatural grace which by definition is imperceptible to intellect and feeling, so be it, Evelyn Underhill is not his writer. Reconciliation of two views so opposed is in any case possible only at the cost of laying aside polemical and exclusive attitudes.

With regard to Miss Pitt and Fr Thornton, it has to be said that Evelyn has not always been very well served even by her best-meaning friends. Miss Cropper would be the first to admit that she had not dealt adequately with Evelyn's published work. Indeed, she made no pretence of doing so. Yet it seems unjust of Miss Pitt to seize upon the small change of friendly intercourse in a bygone idiom, very much *not* intended for publication, and to use it as a stick to beat a woman so dedicated, so productive and by many so highly regarded as Evelyn Underhill. For how many of us would stand up to such treatment? But in some things Miss Pitt seems especially difficult to satisfy. Edith Stein, with whom she compares Evelyn unfavourably, ended her days in a Nazi concentration camp and earned no doubt a peculiar right to be heard at her preaching of the Cross. And Evelyn? Married to a London barrister of no mystical or even mildly devotional proclivities what should she have done that she did not to do earn such a right? Miss Pitt does not tell us. Again, how many of Christ's preachers have earned such a right in the extreme sense demanded by Miss Pitt?

Did Evelyn 'debase' or over-vulgarize mysticism? Much depends on which periods of her work one chooses to look at. Arguably she presented too 'human' a picture of mystical experience in *Mysticism*; but if her book was a great success why should *she* be blamed? Later, while she keeps a special much revered corner for 'the mystics' and always feels them to be relevant, she did not in fact unduly emphasise the availability of mystical experience to all and sundry. On the contrary. Nor, despite Bishop Lumsden Barkway's contrary assertion, did she greatly emphasize in her later period the old three-fold division of the spiritual life according to purgative, illuminative and unitive stages. The consecrated three-fold scheme she found useful especially in her early period and in *Mysticism*. It is referred to once in her *Collected Papers* and is insignificant in comparison with the three-fold non-progressive, non-evolutionary scheme she owed to M. Olier: adoration, communion, cooperation.

It would be possible to continue, to carry the war into the camp of Evelyn's hostile critics, to point out how singularly free she was of polemical oppositions, how little, once she had learned her lesson by about 1915, she was a prey to fashionable metaphysics, how little she needed to be taught that 'to see a tree is to unite with a being let-be by Being rather than to see a creature made by the Father, redeemed by the Son, and somehow indwelled by the Spirit'—in Fr Thornton's words (*Prayer—A New Encounter*, London: Mowbrays, p. 125).

Still more tempting would be the task of comparing her with such latter-day English proponents of mysticism as Gerald Heard and Aldous Huxley, who rampage into the mystical arena long after Evelyn had to a large extent freed herself from its spell. Nowhere perhaps does Charles Moeller's excellent observation that the English spirit ('l'esprit anglais') is a 'curious mixture of naive idealism and cynical empiricism' seem more apt than in considering these two apostles of a 'third way' for whom the incarnate Godhead of the Christian was an 'anthropocentric projection' (Heard, *The Third Morality*) and man an angel fallen into 'the slime of personal and emotional love' (Huxley, *The Perennial Philosophy*). Evelyn Underhill has much both directly and indirectly to say about such attitudes and the related doctrines of non-dualism and immanence. Let it suffice here to remember that Evelyn Underhill was enraptured by, and frequently quoted, some forty years before Huxley, Blake's dictum in *The Marriage of Heaven and Hell* that 'if the doors of perception were cleansed everything would appear to man as it is, Infinite'. It seems no less than the truth to add that Evelyn had already thought her way through and out of most of the attitudes much later arrived at by that soaring 'pilot without a cargo', as Moeller calls Huxley, some time before the latter had left Eton.

The sources for this study have been found chiefly in Evelyn Underhill's well-nigh uncountable publications of which a representative sample of well over one hundred items is given in the bibliography. Other printed sources include the valuable biography of Miss Cropper, the collection of letters edited by Charles Williams and several appreciations written by those who knew her, including Bishop Lumsden Barkway, Fr Geoffrey Curtis, E. I. Watkin, Olive Wyon, Lucy Menzies. The chief group of unpublished material is in the possession of Mr William Wilkinson, her literary executor, to whom the writer of this study is deeply indebted for many services. It consists mainly of early letters between Evelyn and her fiancé, later her husband, a considerable heap of publisher's accounts, ms. notebooks of retreats, review cuttings, typescript copies of the correspondence with Tagore, some unpublished letters of von Hugel, etc. With this material is also a handsome bundle of Evelyn's bindings. The originals of most of the letters edited by Charles Williams with the help of Lucy Menzies appear to be either destroyed or irrecoverable, notably those of her correspondence with Lucy Menzies and Abbot Chapman. This is especially regrettable in that the editing of the *Letters* seems to have been rather heavy handed, judging by the exception to this rule to be seen in the correspondence with Margaret Robinson in the library of St Andrews University, Scotland. At St Andrews also is the valuable typescript copy of the later correspondence between Evelyn and von Hugel. Two items from this in Evelyn's hand survive in the care of her literary excutor. Also at St Andrews is the partially completed biography of her by Lucy Menzies, made use of by Miss Cropper. In addition, other unpublished letters and an especially valuable manuscript notebook containing some of Evelyn's personal reflections in the twenties have been used. I am indebted for one or two points to the Ph.D. thesis of Sister Mary Xavier Kirby already referred to and deposited in the University of Pennsylvania.

Finally a word should be said about the circumstances in which this study was undertaken. The present writer was foolhardy enough to accept an invitation to write a centenary study of Evelyn Underhill's life and work some eighteen months ago. Such a period is not generous for the study of a writer so prolific and in several respects complex as Evelyn Underhill and if this work falls short in certain respects both of scholarship and of judgement the writer can only beg a certain indulgence on the part of the reader. The book is offered to recall and appraise the achievement of an interesting and underrated personality, and in the hope that others may be encouraged to explore further and correct its errors where necessary. The writing of the book has itself been a voyage of discovery, a task repaid in previously unsuspected ways. For the past can indeed speak to the present and to listen is not necessarily to retreat. The circular movement of history has made a number of key issues in Evelyn Underhill's life as actual now as they ever were. She and her work may survive longer than was imagined by the generation of her immediate successors.

Whatever its defects, for which the writer alone is responsible, this work could not have been completed without the cooperation of many helpers. I owe a particular debt of gratitude to Mr William Wilkinson for making available the documents in his charge. Others to whom I am deeply grateful for personal reminiscences, for the loan of documents or for permission to use quotations include Miss Margaret Cropper, Miss Agatha Norman, Fr Geoffrey Curtis, c.r., Miss Hetty Wyon, Sister Mary Xavier Kirby, s.s.j., Mrs R. Tickell, Mrs W. Surrey Dane. For crucial information concerning Evelyn's membership of The Golden Dawn I am indebted to Mr R. A. Gilbert, and to Mrs A. J. Swainston I owe the invaluable account of Evelyn's last illness. For various items of information, helps and suggestions it is a pleasure to thank Bishop Colin James, my father: Professor A. H. Armstrong, Professor Geoffrey Parrinder and Professor J. A. W. Bennett; Canon William Purcell, Brian Carter, John Stockdale, Ellic Howe, F. Brocard Sewell O. Carm, Dr Allan Macfarlan, Miss Mary Every. To the Bishop of Hereford and my Rector, Richard Hill, I owe thanks for a vital fortnight 'off work' to get on with writing; to the Principal and staff of the Edinburgh Theological College and to the Warden of Hawarden Library, gratitude for time spent happily in their midst. The libraries of Aberdeen and St Andrews, the National Library of Scotland and the Bodleian, the British Library and Dr Williams's Library have all at different times and in different ways lent their accustomed and friendly aid. To them also my thanks are due.

All references to Evelyn Underhill's works are given by short title, full details being provided in the bibliography. Similarly, references to other frequently quoted books are abbreviated and given in the bibliography, e.g. *Life* refers to *The Life of Evelyn Underhill* by Margaret Cropper, *Letters* refers to *The Letters of Evelyn Underhill* edited by Charles Williams, etc. Passages from letters for which no reference is given may be assumed unpublished.

Ledbury C. J. R. Armstrong
15 April 1975

I
An Eligible Child

IT is no exaggeration to say that Evelyn Underhill has been one of the most widely read writers on prayer and the spiritual life in the first fifty years of the twentieth century. Thanks to the diligent secretarial work of her husband, Hubert Stuart Moore, it would even now be possible to compute almost exactly how many of each of the thirty or so titles which she published were sold and at what stage of their history in print. Probably no book of its type has had such success as her *Mysticism*, published in 1911, unless it be Aldous Huxley's *Perennial Philosophy* of 1946. And even *Mysticism* seemed for a time to be threatened in its supremacy by its shorter and more easily digestible sister work, *Practical Mysticism*, which Evelyn first published some three years later.

The dates are important. Evelyn was born in Wolverhampton on 6 December 1875. *Mysticism* therefore, the book by which she is best known, was published in her thirty-sixth year. To one familiar with the whole of her life and works it seems to make a peak in her activity, the climax of some eight years of ever-increasing energy and application during which, in her love and enthusiasm, her utter devotion to and belief in the excellence of what she called 'the mystic way of life', she sought through her writing to express and convince others of the truths she had discovered. Thereafter, although she remained well-known and was indeed honoured by learned bodies and her church, the image she projects is no longer that of the excited herald of little known countries of the spirit but rather that of the wise, experienced and lucid traveller who recollects in tranquility and deepens insight by reflection rather than experiment.

Those who remember Evelyn best in her later years, before her death on Sunday, 15 June 1941, insist upon her marvellous serenity of manner and the atmosphere of calm and reassurance which she radiated. Those familiar with her later published addresses or even the somewhat earlier lectures of the twenties are struck by her command of her material, her logic, her lucidity. The greatest work of her later period, *Worship* (1936), is in its way a masterpiece of clear exposition and balanced discrimination in a field where pedantic scholarship and fanciful speculation, tub-thumping and platitude, are almost respectable vices. But what will probably most strike any who have followed her career and her work *from the beginning* is her extraordinary consistency, the sense which she communicates of singleness of purpose and faith-fulness to her vision. Such a career does not have to be unwavering to be impressive; nor is sheer fidelity the greatest of virtues. But a steady adherence to original and personal insights of general importance, deepened and widened in their application over the years so as to embrace as many aspects as possible of life in its fullness, that is or can be impressive. But to follow Evelyn's mental and spiritual development coherently we must begin at the beginning.

Evelyn was born on 6 December 1875 in the hey-day of the Victorian era. Her father, Arthur Underhill, a Wolverhampton lawyer like his father, was at the time she was born on the point of leaving the North Midlands for a highly successful career at the bar and as an academic legal figure in London where the family established itself first in Pembridge Place, then in Campden Hill Place. He described himself in his *Memoirs* as a 'Victorian *pur sang*' and his judgements on the world as he saw it in 1938 reflect the outlook one would expect after so frank a declaration. His causes for complaint include 'the eccentric collection of discords, squeals and bangs to which the B.B.C. has sought to accustom us', 'the glorification of crooks and gangsters', speeds above 30 m.p.h., the 'disgusting word "pal" ', and the 'hideous bowler'. In spite of not being, in his own admission, by inclination and belief a devout Christian and regular church-goer, he also laments what he calls the 'decay of orthodox religious belief'. His references to religion reveal him as one who believes himself to have been inoculated against it early in life by excessive school services in chapel at Hurstpierpoint, a Woodward school insisting strongly on religious training. This notwithstanding, his autobiography discloses a certain interest in philosophy and a firm adherence to the argument from design for the existence of God.

There is some point in dwelling on the career and character of Evelyn's father since we can without too much difficulty adopt his suggestion that she did in some respects take after him. In his *Memoirs* he describes a bookish youth in which he developed a taste for solitude; he also lays some stress on the taste which he acquired at Trinity College, Dublin, for philosophy and astronomy:

> 'It is curious,' he wrote, 'that my interest in philosophy and metaphysics has been emphasized in my daughter (known in literature as "Evelyn Underhill"). I do not know of any other member of the family having a like taste, but whether she would have become distinguished in these subjects if I had never been introduced to them at T[rinity] C[ollege] D[ublin] is a question with which I have sometimes flirted.'

No doubt he flattered himself in such moments and yet there are points of contact even at the philosophical level. Evelyn's rather liberal approach to Holy Writ not improbably reflects Arthur Underhill's own liberal-critical views. He suggests in his book that the Church should undertake a 'revision' of the Old Testament rather on the lines, one suspects, of his own successful revisions of English property law. His proposal is introduced by his observation:

I suppose that for some years no educated person has seriously considered the Old Testmant as literally true, and still less as inspired (p. 154).

Evelyn in any case was sufficiently interested in these subjects in her early school days to clip out a paragraph from a newspaper headed *Anglican Reactionaries* in which numerous points are made in defence of 'the tendencies of modern criticism' and in condemnation of 'the reactionary Dean and Archdeacons who signed the singular document concerning the inspiration of the Scriptures to which we called attention briefly in our last issue.'[2]

It is always difficult to pinpoint parental influences. In Evelyn's case one is most struck by a certain down-to-earth practicality and efficiency which she shares with her father. One is also impressed in both by their relentless energy and addiction to hard work. For Arthur Underhill was very much a self-made leader of his profession in much the same way as, *mutatis mutandis*, Evelyn became of the world of religious literature. Her father's career proper began with his call to the bar on 6 June 1872 at the age of twenty-one and culminated in his being created a knight bachelor by King George V (with whom he found it 'extraordinarily easy to get on') on 13 December 1922. Although Evelyn published a greater variety of titles than her father the editions and re-editions of his standard legal works such as *A Treatise on the Law of Torts* (1875) and *A Treatise on Private Trusts* (1878) leave her some way behind in terms of column inches in the British Museum Catalogue of Printed Books. Evelyn dedicated to him her first volume of collected poems, *Immanence* (1912). When not writing or practising his profession Arthur Underhill found an outlet for his energies in sailing. His memoirs give an exhaustive account of the successive yachts in which the family spent their holidays. He

1. This was all part of the furore which followed the publication of advanced views on biblical inspiration in *Lux Mundi* (1889).

sat for the Board of Trade's Certificate of Competency and was mainly responsible for founding the Cruising Club, later the Royal Cruising Club, in 1879. He became its first Commodore, a title which became the family name for him. The letters of Evelyn's maturity generally refer to him as 'the Commodore'.

If the masterful figure of 'the Commodore' loomed fairly large in Evelyn's life the personality of her mother, Lucy Iremonger, is less distinct. It is possible that, like other Victorian mothers, she allowed the nursery door to divide her and her daughter for, although Evelyn never seems to have had a nursemaid or nanny to look after her, the relationship of mother and daughter appears not to have been close and may even, especially after her marriage, have become somewhat oppressive. Even in her girlhood there is a note of insecurity in Evelyn's repeated plea not to be left to last or unvisited on some occasion or other at school; possibly a similar fear that her mother would neglect her or her interests prompted the plaintive little postscript to a letter of June 1890: 'have they [their prospective hosts at a party] got an eligible child for a companion for me? If so *mind* you let me know her'. There is a suggestion in a small piece of Evelyn's doggerel verse surviving from this period that her mother tended to be heavy-handed in punishment. The spirit in these rhymes suggests, it is true, that Evelyn was far from being unduly cast down by such treatment.

We know very little of Evelyn's early home life and not very much about her school-life. The family did enjoy the country and outdoor exercise. Arthur Underhill claimed that he and his uncle were the first people to ride bicycles in the town of Wolverhampton in 1867. Arthur Underhill's younger brother, uncle Ernest to Evelyn, went to Cambridge and became a priest of the Church of England. Evelyn does not seem to have seen a great deal of him if a letter of 15 February 1891 is anything to go by. It reads: 'I have written to Uncle Ernest, I generally do every six

months or so. ...' On the other hand a reference in a letter of
30 December 1907 suggests that she later came to know him
better for she then writes to a friend:

> I have always meant to ask you whether you have come across
> my very High Anglican uncle in Liverpool? He is the vicar of
> St Thomas, Toxteth: a delightful person, & always at war with
> the bishop.

Since Evelyn in 1907 had no use for Anglicans as such and thought
High Anglicans especially regrettable, this praise of uncle Ernest
must have been merited.

When she was thirteen Evelyn was sent away for school terms
to a small boarding establishment called Sandgate House, in the
village of Sandgate near Folkstone, where she spent some three
years. The surviving evidence of her life and ideas begins in these
years in the form of a handful of letters home, some notebooks
the precise whereabouts of which is unclear but which have been
previously quoted, and a little book of crumbling clippings from
newspapers and periodicals, many of which contain items of her
own composition. Though this material is exiguous it does enable
the searcher who has the benefit of hindsight to piece together a
picture of the way Evelyn's interests began to focus in her early
life and the sorts of influence to which she was exposed.

Evelyn's letters home reveal her as in every respect an affectionate, home-loving, high-spirited and intelligent person. An
early example to her mother dated 13 July 1888 opens:

> Dearest Mudgie
> Thank you very much for your nice letter. It took me nearly
> ¼ of an hour to read the part from My Darling [presumably
> her father], but you need not tell him so all the same. On
> Wednesday we did not go out, so I wrote to Mary, & Uncle
> Ernest, & yesterday I wrote to My Darling, & addressed my
> letter to the Salisbury Club.

The rest of the letter, written in a painstakingly regular copper-plate hand with flourishes, conveys vividly the girlish enjoyment of such school activities as inventing languages and hiding secrets with her friends. Towards the close a great longing overtakes her to be fetched home in good time at the end of term so as not to be left high and dry after her friends have gone:

> *please* darling Mummie fetch me on the 25 or 26, the former if possible because we should not do very many lessons and it is *not* nice to be the last left.

This particular letter also reveals that she is doing particularly well at Scripture, Conduct and Sums, reasonably well in Grammer [sic] and poorly in 'Order'. She adds a 'new riddle'—'What King had most cause to complain of his laundress?' Such riddles are a recurring feature of these letters and include one dated 10 February 1891, 'What English river is what Daddy is always ready to do?'.

There can be no doubt that her mind was stimulated by her schooling, though not always necessarily in ways intended by her teachers. A name which crops up frequently is that of 'Mr Wakefield' who can be identified as Russell Wakefield, later Dean of Norwich (1909–11) and Bishop of Birmingham (1911–24). At this period of his career Mr Wakefield combined the offices of vicar of Sandgate and 'Lecturer on English Philology and Literature at the Crystal Palace School of Literature'. This gentleman evidently delivered what she calls 'lectures in church', either additional to or instead of sermons, and the occasions of these lectures were christened by the Sandgate House children as 'Wakeys'. One letter, dated 4 June 1890, having thanked 'my darling mother' for the 'scarlet doll at Burton's' and described 'some lovely sensational moral stories for Sunday reading' which she had just bought from 'the colporter', continues 'Oh! please can you tell me who Spinoza was, he was mentioned in the sermon last Sunday; he seems to have been a not very nice person from what Mr Wakefield said'. Another letter of 21 June 1889, having thanked her mother for the 'scrumtious [sic] strawberries', reads:

> Last Sunday we went to a lecture in the church it was on Milton's Paradise Lost and was *horribly* uninteresting, all about dogmas & conclusions to be drawn from the poem & such stuff & what Satan was like, just as though Mr Wakefield had seen him.

But Mr Wakefield seems to have done better on Sunday, 6 July 1890, when he contributed his ruminations on Luke 11. 37–39 to an evensong service described by the future author of *Mysticism* and *Worship* as 'most lovely'. Mr Wakefield also presided over Evelyn's preparation for confirmation. This took place on 11 March 1891 at Christchurch, Folkstone. The occasion was chiefly looked upon by Evelyn as an additional opportunity to see her parents: 'Only 28 days tomorrow till the 11th of March', runs one letter, 'I *wonder* if I'll see you then mother dearest'. This letter ends 'Your internally frisky kiddy' and carries a postscript or rather *Nota Bene*: 'If I were you I wouldn't call me "kid" any more, it is conclusive evidence that you consider yourself not on the side of the sheep, but with the goats. Humble but not cheering! (Matt. 25)'.

Evelyn's letters home may not betray a habit of introspection but other documents do. There is in particular a small black notebook described by Miss Cropper but which has since disappeared from view, containing prayers, hymns and self-examinations prior to her confirmation. Included is a list of 'sins' composed, according to Lucy Menzies, when she was fifteen years old. It runs:

> Selfishness, pride, conceit, disorder, moral cowardice, self-deceit, scepticism, thoughtlessness, revengefulness, exaggeration, want

of truth, changeableness, double-dealing, teasing, unkindness, disobedience, dishonourableness, profanity, idleness.

There is no point in labouring the significance of such a collection of failings although it does seem worth remarking that they have a consistency and freshness which gives them the ring of truth and that they add up to quite an attractive character. To be capable of so many disorders, to be capable of thus marshalling them and of being regretful on top of that, does suggest a certain depth and resilience of character. It would be rash in any case not to take Evelyn at her word when she examines her conscience. She was not a fool.

A complementary self-portrait concentrating on the highlights rather than the shadows is to be found in the pages of the little black book, written on the eve of her seventeenth birthday in 1892. The account is given in full by Miss Cropper from whom we here transcribe it:

I am going to write down this short account of my own feelings and opinions because I think that tomorrow will close a period of my life, and I want to preserve some memory of it before it quite goes away.

First as to ideals. My ideal of a man is that he should be true, strong, intellectual, and considerate; not an adherent of any extreme party, but always ready to help the poor and oppressed. It does not matter if he is not good-looking or is shy and brusque, for those are outside things. I have never read or seen a man who comes up to my ideal. In real life I most admire Mahomet, because he was sincere, Giordano Bruno, because he was strong for the truth, and Jesus Christ because ethically He was perfect, and always thought of the weak ones first.

In fiction I admire Milton's Satan for his strength, Tennyson's King Arthur for his goodness, and Shakespeare's Romeo for his personal charms.

My ideal of a woman is that she should be clever, vivacious, accurately but not priggishly informed, gentle, truthful, tactful and tolerant, and should have a due sense of proportion. I have never met or read of anyone exactly like this, but in real life my own mother comes nearest to it. I think in fiction, Angela Messenger in *All Sorts and Conditions of Men*.

My favourite heroines in real life are Joan of Arc for her sincerity, and Caroline Herschel for her unselfish love of knowledge. In fiction I like Hypatia, Portia and Princess Ida, for their mental qualities, Milton's Eve for her womanliness, and Angela Messenger for herself.

My favourite prose writers are Matthew Arnold, Hallam, and Huxley for their style, Carlyle for his Philosophy, Besant for his characters. Amongst the poets I prefer Shakespeare for general excellence, Milton for majesty, Tennyson and Keats for beautiful thoughts, musically set, and Calverley and Austin Dobson for *vers de société*.

Amongst animals I prefer the cat, because when off duty in a zoological capacity it makes an excellent muff.

In politics I am a Socialist. I think it is the only fair form of government, and it gives every class an equal status, and does away with the incentive to many sorts of crime.

As to religion, I don't quite know, except that I believe in a God, and think it is better to love and help the poor people round me than go on saying that I love an abstract Spirit whom I have never seen. If I can do both, all the better, but it is best to begin with the nearest. I do not think anything is gained by being orthodox, and a great deal of the beauty and sweetness of things is lost by being bigoted and dogmatic. If we are to see God at all it must be through nature and our fellow men. Science holds a lamp up to heaven, not down to the Churches.

I don't believe in worrying God with prayers for things we want. If He is omnipotent He knows we want them, and if He isn't, He can't give them to us. I think it is an insult to Him to repeat the same prayers every day. It is as much as to say He is deaf, or very slow of comprehension.

I do not believe the Bible is inspired, but I think nevertheless that it is one of the best and wisest books the world has ever seen.

My favourite occupations are literature and art, though I do not think I have much taste for the latter. When I grow up I should like to be an author because you can influence people more widely by books than pictures. If I had been a rich man, I would have been a doctor, and lived among the poor, and attended them for nothing. I think that would be one of the noblest careers open to any man. My motto at the present time:

> Be noble men of noble deeds,
> For love is holier than creeds.

Goodbye sixteen years old. I hope my mind will not grow tall to look down on things, but wide to embrace all sorts of things in the coming year.[2]

Many points could be picked out of this description by Evelyn of her likes and dislikes, her aims, ambitions and ideals. Her love of cats, for example, is clearly established although in no sentimental tone. It remained with her all her life. Her literary preferences speak for themselves though the admiration for Milton's Satan might have surprised Mr Wakefield. Her father's influence can be detected in her attitude to the Bible and probably also in her matter-of-fact remarks about dogmatism and 'worrying God with prayers for things we want'. A less easily accountable theme in this document, one might almost describe it as a leitmotiv, is the insistence on compassion. Her ideal of a man demands that he be 'always ready to help the poor and oppressed'. Jesus Christ

2. *Life*, pp. 4–6.

is admired not only because he was perfect but because he 'always thought of the weak ones first'. The affirmation of a Socialist adherence in politics together with her statement of faith in both God and practical love to 'poor people' speak of the same pre-occupation as does her statement that had she been a man and rich she would have become a doctor, lived among the poor, and tended them for nothing.

It is possible that this girlish idealism was more than just a passing whim. Evelyn's father describes in his *Memoirs* how Evelyn attempted to win over his deck-hand, Bill Gailey, to the tenets of socialism. Arthur Underhill records with evident satis-faction how Bill got the best of the argument with the apparently knock-down observation, 'No missy, it wouldn't do. I'll lay that if it [socialism] came in I'd have Jack's daily share out of him by before tea-time.' Wherever Evelyn caught her socialism from, it wasn't from her father. As to what kind of socialism she sub-scribed to—apart from a general sense of sympathy for the less well-off in society—we have only the slender clue provided by a cutting in her scrap-book from *The Times* of London, dated 22 February 1894. In this a correspondent, one J. Hunter Watts, who describes himself as a 'revolutionary socialist', is at great pains to distinguish his group from the Anarchists. It seems that Bill Gailey was not alone in supposing that socialism and anarchy were one and the same thing, and one can only speculate whether Evelyn's argument with him took place before or after the date of this letter and whether Arthur Underhill's account really does justice to his daughter's side in the dispute. Our evidence is at least sufficient to show that she retained an interest in 'socialism' of some sort for approximately three years, and this despite a home environment unfavourable to such notions.

Did Evelyn then revolt against the solid middle-class world in which she was brought up? The answer is certainly not, at least not in the normal way in which such revolt is understood. Her attitude to such emancipation is humorously expressed in *An Imaginary Dialogue Between Two Dolls* printed in *The Children's Salon* of 26 May 1894 which, since it has the additional advantage of displaying her talent for writing at this time, deserves lengthy quotation; the exchange takes place between Dolly, a wax doll, and Dodo, a Jumeau ditto:

DODO: By the way have you revolted?

DOLLY: What's that mean?

DODO: Emanicpation from the despotism of nursery conventionalities. Do you see this? (*pointing to a small key fastened to her waist*).

DOLLY: Yes, what is it?

DODO: A skeleton key for our toy-cupboard and one of the chief Symbols of the Revolt of the Playthings.

DOLLY: And what do you use it for?

DODO: What for? Why, for my Wanderjahr, of course.

DOLLY (*much mystified*): But why do you want to wander?

DODO: If you read the *Nursery Newsman* you would not need to ask such a question.

DOLLY: We take *The Toybox Times*. Did *The Newsman* teach you how to revolt?

DODO: It first awoke me to the knowledge of the slavery in which I lived, and led me to begin the work of my own emancipation. Why should the doll life of the nation be crushed between the sticky fingers of the tyrant child? Why should we be locked in a cupboard all night when the rocking horse stays outside? Answer me that!

DOLLY (*puzzled*): I suppose because he's too big to go inside. But you haven't told me yet what you wander for.

DODO: In search of excitement, the only diversions of the fin-de-siècle doll. If I could but find a sensation which thrilled my

composition to its core, I should feel that life had been
worth living, and break without a groan.

The dialogue concludes with Dodo being 'seized by her mistress
and stuffed head first into a basket to be conveyed home', upon
which Dolly reflects ('meditatively') that the revolted doll is
ultimately as powerless as the unrevolted, and 'Old ways are
best, after all!' Such a piece would no doubt have a solid moral
for the readers of *The Children's Salon* but it also expresses
Evelyn's conviction that home *is* best in the end. If revolt there
had to be then it should be of a kind to leave one better rather
than less able to cope with the actual circumstances of life. The
little fable of the two dolls already suggests that it is the nature
of the restless subject rather than the surrounding circumstances
which stand most in need of change. One could on Evelyn's
youthful and her mature view lead an outwardly conventional
life while living at a far from conventional intensity below the
surface.

A number of Evelyn's permanent interests emerge already in
the scrapbook. We find for example a cutting which directly
associates the wonders of nature and religious experience in a
way which even the late Victorians would have called 'mystical'
and which has curious similarities in tone with Evelyn's more
popular works such as those published just before the first World
War under the pseudonym of John Cordelier or *Practical Mysticism*. The anonymous piece dating from about 1892 and entitled
A Woman's Thoughts about Silence reads in part:

Yes, leave for a while that crowded gas-lit room, that young
man in spectacles, who is about to read a botanical paper (and
of its erudition who would doubt?), yes, leave him. Take one
flower with you and muse over its exquisite construction, its
delicate stamens and slender pistil, its pure calyx, and fairy-like
petals; and when you have realized its beauty and marvellous

formation, you shall hear within your soul a still small voice whisper, 'Is is not very good?' Or go out under the solemn stars, and strive to think of Infinite Love which guides and governs them in their courses from the least to the greatest, which is so guiding these poor human lives of ours, each to fulfil a Divinely appointed purpose.

We do not know just how impressed Evelyn was by such rhapsodizing but clearly enough to preserve this example in her book. Certainly this type of interest did not exclude a more prosaic type of enthusiasm for nature. The cuttings include a number describing the wonders revealed by telescope or microscope. It would be no exaggeration to say that at some stage in her mid-teens Evelyn 'discovered' nature, perhaps some time between the 1892 pre-seventeenth birthday document with its preference for Walter Besant's heroine, Angela Messenger and his novel *All Sorts and Conditions of Men*, and the prize essay contributed to *The Lady* of 24 April 1893, in which she comes down firmly in favour of R. D. Blackmore's *Lorna Doone*. The final remarks of this essay show a love of natural sights, sounds, and scenes which remained with Evelyn to her dying day: 'The book', she concludes:

> will teach you to love and notice all the sights and sounds of Nature; the deep green ditch in the ash-copse where the tiny ferns grow, and the loaches that sport in the dark, cold pools of the Bagworthy stream; so that at length you will be forced to echo the hero's observation that 'Since he came to love Lorna, he learnt to love Nature too.'

Evelyn for most of her life cultivated this love of nature and expeditions abroad or into the English countryside, especially later in life, usually contained a good deal of botanizing and observation of birds. She was a nature-lover who knew the names of the creatures at which she wondered.

There seem to have been no special *coups de foudre* or extra-ordinary revelations in Evelyn's youth. Any she did experience occurred later in her life. She herself attributes no particular importance to the rather peculiar and not uncommon semi-conscious states which she described in a letter to Mrs Meyrick Heath in 1911 but which one supposes may have afflicted her in her teens. In this letter she is commenting on a reference of Mrs Heath to the 'anaesthetic revelation' (of which the correspondence gives no further details) and goes on:

> At one time of my life I used to have abrupt fainting fits, and in those I used to plunge into some wonderful peaceful but quite 'undifferentiated' plane of consciousness, in which everything was quite simple and comprehended. I always resented being restored to what is ordinarily called 'consciousness' intensely.

A phrase of J. A. Stewart in *The Myths of Plato* seemed, she wrote, a good oblique description of the state: a 'solemn sense of Timeless Being'. Evelyn continues in this letter of 1911:

> I've never seen any chain of cause and effect as you say—but rather felt happy *within* a quiet peaceful Reality, like the 'still desert' of the mystics—where there was no multiplicity and no need of explanations. Personally I doubt whether this is a very *high* way of apprehending reality, though no doubt it is *a* way (*Letters*, pp. 122-3).

One curiosity of this account of her early experience is the inconsistent writing of the word 'reality'—if Charles Williams has accurately transcribed it. This is probably an additional indication of Evelyn's doubts about the status of what she experienced.

It is tempting but would be tedious to exploit in greater detail the contents of Evelyn's scrap-book. This provides what one must suppose is an exhaustive collection of her printed work up to her twentieth year. The items, of which there are some twenty-seven in all, range from doggerel and alliterative verse published by such periodicals as *The Children's Salon*, to reviews of art exhibitions written up for *The Midland Weekly News*. *The Lady* of 6 April 1893 printed *Some Verses on Easter*, five verses and forty lines to be exact, which may be Evelyn's first published contribution to 'mystical verse' and are too conventional to merit further comment. The best reading are the lively imaginative little tales, of which the first to be given a prize and published is *A Literary 'At Home'* published in *Hearth and Home* for 10 March 1892. This simply makes the most of unlikely encounters between well-known fictional characters assembled for a party; it is all good fun. The same periodical also published on 27 July 1893 Evelyn's contribution to the theme *How Should a Girl Prepare Herself for a Worthy Womanhood*. Her sentiments are naturally irreproachable and if anything distinguishes her opinion it is her insistence that:

in order to become widely and generally sympathetic, a girl should try to cultivate a habit of, and an interest in, everything: not only her fellow creatures and immediate surroundings, but all the beauties of nature and art with which she is brought in contact.

Sympathy is necessary because it confers what Watson calls 'A sense of oneness with our kind' and enables one to be tactful and considerate to all human beings. For the same reason Evelyn insists that her well-prepared girl should have knowledge which is wide rather than deep. She should on no account become absorbed, introspective or a blue-stocking. On the other hand it is little use being able to discourse on every subject 'from metaphysics to penny novelettes' if one can't darn a stocking or peel a potato. The mature Evelyn is certainly recognisable in this picture.

It may be best to leave the scrap-book there. Through its pages, in conjunction with the confidences of the little black notebook and the letters, we derive an impression of a bookish, sensitive person, open but fundamentally conservative in outlook, intellectual but determined to keep her feet on the ground, witty but not supercilious, self-aware but also loving. She tells us she believes in God but one has the impression that God is going to be believed in on her terms rather than his. She is unstuffy and humorous but not yet satirical; perhaps, as Lucy Menzies thought, rather young for her age—at least by nineteen. But perhaps most important of all she is already a writer full of curiosity about life and determined to embrace it in its wholeness—a balanced, poised person, then, not unlike the personality she wrote about in a piece dated 5 April 1894 which purports to describe a 'happy exception' to the general run of disgruntled 'modern womanhood'. This exceptional person Evelyn describes in terms which perhaps best sum up finally her own attitudes, as:

the earnest unassuming student, to whom 'knowledge is no more as a fountain sealed' and in whom, to quote the words of another recent poet,

A thirst to know and understand
A large and liberal discontent,

has effectually quenched the feeble pessimism and querulous carpings at fate which are only too widely disseminated amongst her contemporaries.

Evelyn could hardly have expressed more succinctly the state of willingness to embark on spiritual and mental adventures which her subsequent career presupposes. Her very freedom from dissatisfaction with her physical circumstances is the counterpart of a very real dissatisfaction and 'divine discontent' at an altogether different level. We have a sense that even in her teens

Evelyn was set on the road which would lead to the writing of *Mysticism* rather than to attempt to emulate social pioneers such as Beatrice Webb or Sylvia Pankhurst.

2

An Enchanting Friend

NO account of Evelyn Underhill's life and achievements up to the publication of *Mysticism*, early in 1911, would be complete without a close examination of her stories and novels which we shall look at in the next chapter. These are perhaps an even better reflection of her attitudes and ideas at this time than our other main source of information, the fairly numerous letters which survive from the correspondence between her and her fiancé, Hubert Stuart Moore, whom she eventually married on 3 July 1907. The letters and the literary work complement and complete one another in a remarkable way. The former reveal the Evelyn Underhill of the family circle: keen on travel, arts, crafts, landscapes, cats, hats and dresses, a little gossipy, even cattish herself on occasions, loving, concerned and affectionately querulous. The latter, the Evelyn for whom all such matters are strictly—to use her own word—'illusion', whose heart and aim are resolutely fixed on the 'one thing necessary', whose vision, if her work is not one tissue of purest self-delusion and make-believe, pierces already the veil of space and time to seek its nourishment in a 'beyond' totally unknown, humanly speaking, to those with whom she was in closest contact.

These very distinct aspects of Evelyn's life at the time not only justify separate treatment of the respective sources but must raise the question of a real dichotomy in her outlook if not her personality. That she was aware of such a split in her existence seems undeniable and indeed the chief interest of both her biography and her writings consists in following her attempts to deal with the situation. For the split is not absolute; we are not here considering a paranoid personality; intellectually and emotionally it seems that Evelyn did finally establish a *modus vivendi*, a balance, the cost of which it is possible only to infer in the vaguest way from the hints available in both literary and personal material.

Hubert Stuart Moore was some four years older than Evelyn. He also outlived her by almost exactly ten years. They were friends at least from 1890 and sweethearts by 1895. Marriage was certainly in view before the end of the century. The letters which survive were chiefly occasioned by Evelyn's annual absences abroad with one or both of her parents from 1898, absences which also continue after the wedding, the old pattern prolonging itself in this respect until 1913.

The two sides of the correspondence are not equal. This is not simply because Evelyn was having all the fun while Hubert toiled away in chambers in King's Bench Walk trying to advance his career as a barrister. Perhaps it was Hubert's misfortune to have lighted upon a sweetheart who, able and more than willing herself to render her feelings and impressions in vivid words, looked for an equivalent literate zest in her lover. The fact is that Hubert's letters are more than once and at widely different times described by his sweetheart as either 'scrappy' or 'little letters', which, to judge from the remaining sample, was no less than the truth. Hubert, anxious to please, seems to have tried to make up for this at one stage by sending either postcards or short letters twice daily, an expedient which Evelyn unhelpfully found excessive.

These letters furnish valuable scraps of biographical information. They take us round Italy, France, Holland and Switzerland in Evelyn's vivacious company; they reveal her as the loving and attentive companion of the man with whom she shared her life. They tell us almost nothing about her evolution towards, and establishment in, a life of prayer and dedication to 'the finding of reality . . . the one thing that matters'. For the moment, then, it is necessary to follow Evelyn's account of herself almost in abstraction from what was really going on in her mind, 'really' that is, if we accept at face value the account of things given by her when quoting William Blake's 'a fool does not see the same tree that a wise man sees'. In this connection, though it may seem brutal, Evelyn's perspective requires us to say that Hubert was cast in the role of the fool, feasting on the small change of the world symbolical and transfigured which Evelyn felt herself powerless to convey to him but into which she was almost simultaneously, for much of the time, inviting others through her writing.

The Underhills were, by 1898, fairly well-off and could travel abroad in some style. Arthur Underhill's only relevant reference to his financial affairs—'I do not think that I earned four figures (even gross) in any year until I had been in practice at least four years'—suggests 1882 as the turning point of the family fortunes (he was called to the bar in 1872). But the letters also suggest that money was one of the principal reasons, if not the only one, for the protracted, if informal engagement between Evelyn and Hubert. There were certainly no other objections to Hubert that one can discover, he being the son of a close friend of the family and all the more a member of the Underhill family for having lost his mother early in life. Thus on 2 November 1900, in one of the rare letters written from home, Evelyn writes 'The air of chastened joy with which the missis (her mother) hears you are getting more work would please you. Like a warhorse, she scents Armageddon from afar'. It is in a letter from Blois, written on 4 May 1906 in a region where 'all the things here seem to be about silly kings and improper women, as far as I can make out ...' that we learn of what was almost certainly Hubert's final and successful attempt to have the wedding day fixed, for she goes on: 'This climate would make anyone's morals slack which reminds me that if you *do* attack the Commodore don't *ruffle* him & tell me *just* what he says.'

Most other references to their own particular and private affairs
tend to be cryptic. The letter of 1895 written from St Albans and
clearly only one in an on-going and affectionate correspondence
reveals that Evelyn Underhill had for her London Extension
Lecturer on book-binding no less a master than T. J. Cobden
Sanderson: 'I don't think I shall get to the 1st day of term show
this time as the second Cobden Sanderson [lecture] [is] that day.
The first was rather vapory all about ideals of craftsmanship &
reviving the old trade guilds & stuff like that but next time he is
going to bring his own tools and demonstrate'. Cobden Sanderson, the celebrated book-binder and craftsman, is later described
as a 'charming speaker' but the chairwoman 'is what Hamilton
used to call a cough drop'. Evelyn pursued her favourite craft of
bookbinding even when abroad and we read of her receiving
lessons in Siena from a Miss Bailey, and giving them to her hostess
in Alassio, both in 1904. Fine craftsmanship was an interest she
and Hubert had in common and many letters describe and sometimes sketch the rare and wonderful achievements of mediaeval
carvers, sculptors, intarsia-workers, forgers and enamelists. Especially the last, for Hubert's great interest in life was enamel work,
to which he seems to have moved from metal work, and for
which he eventually set up his own workshop complete with
furnace. Examples of his work survive and photographs of Evelyn
often show her wearing his creations.

Evelyn was not above needling her 'retriever' sometimes, as,
for example, when she writes on 15 April 1902 (from Perugia)
'The enamelled poppies sound nice but why don't you make a
real *thing* not all these horrid little show pieces in frames and trays?
It's so amateurish to make "nothings". What about that wonderful matchbox?' Hubert's reaction to this may be judged from
the fact that by 29 April 1904 we find him working on a cross and
a casket simultaneously. The 1902 letter is also of some interest in
revealing that they took The Artist, a periodical which in that

year suffered enough of a change in editorial policy for Evelyn to wonder whether they should not change to The Architectural Review.

Evelyn rarely broaches the topic of religion to her finacé. It is of some interest that already in 1901 Hubert is susceptible to gentle teasing on the subject of the Catholic Church. Thus in a letter from Chartres of 17 April 1901 (Letters, p. 48), 'I wish you were here, and I think you would like it, though the place swarms with priests who would set your Protestant teeth on edge'. Again, in a letter from Lugano of 26 March 1902, the Underhills made an expedition by water to the Grota Orrida. As they passed through it 'the boat swirled from side to side, and the missis gave little yells'; as they continued however, they passed 'lots of nice little towns some built into the face of the cliff, & some perched on the tops, & lots of nice nouveau—art trees & each with its own naughty wicked Catholic church.' It is clear from one or two other allusions that Hubert has no love of church services in general and of funerals in particular. Evelyn does nevertheless describe her attendance at various church occasions. In a letter of 10 April 1899 she writes that on Sunday she went to the baptistry of the cathedral in Florence where she was led to believe every Florentine infant since the time of Dante had been baptised at four o'clock on Sunday afternoon. 'We arrived about half-way through the ceremony & watched two or three turned off, but it was horrid to see the way the fat old priest gabbled over the service looking about him all the time & not displaying the least interest in the matter.' On another holiday she managed by dint of suitable largesse to get a seat in the choir of San Marco in Venice for the Easter Mass (letter of April 1905, Easter Monday). Indeed, she writes that that Easter she has had 'a perfect orgy of splendid church ceremonies' and feels she will 'never be able to bear English services again' (letter of 6 May 1905). It is hardly necessary to say that 'the Commodore' did not share his daughter's tastes and she reflects somewhat ruefully in a letter dating from the end of this holiday that there were 'too many churches and pictures for his taste, I think. He said on his last day that he hoped he should never see a Virgin or a child again as long as he lived' (letter of 29 April 1905). Next time the family came to Venice, two years later, the paterfamilias firmly asserted his own preferences and hired a large motor-boat.

Evelyn dearly loved Italy, the landscapes, the towns, the churches, the libraries, the saints, the people, the monks. Her descriptions of the places she visited were published posthumously with a selection from the considerable number of sketches she made of landscapes and architectural detail. (See bibliography: *Shrines and Cities*.) She also took a great many photographs, only relatively few of which now survive. Italy is above all for her the land of the middle ages, the home of Dante and Francis and Catherine, the 'primitive' painters and the craftsmen. After perusing her letters for a while it is not difficult to fall into step with this 'superficial' Evelyn. Thus (21 April 1899) from Florence 'There is an old Franciscan monastery up there but they will not let girls go in. However, two sweet Monks [sic] in brown robes with rope tied round them, & lovely but slightly dirty faces came in the electric train with us, & they were most charming to look at.' Again, at the Florence 'certosa', or Carthusian monastery, 'a perfectly sweet old monk, in white robes & quite clean showed us round. . . . Oh! I did wish you and I were Carthusian monks and had cells next to each other. . . . Oh! I did want you to see that monastery I loved it so much. The whole thing was like a bit of the Middle ages' (letter of 25 April 1898). Two years later on their trip to Locarno the family made the ascent to the pilgrimage church near there via the '20 queer little chapels of the stations of the Cross where you are meant to kneel but I sat.' When they reached their destination, lo and behold! 'there were several nice brown dirty Franciscan monks at the top and nice cloisters overlooking the lake & a heavenly view' (letter of 11 April 1900). So much at least, for one of the 'illusions' on which the youthful Evelyn had been bred—that cleanliness is next to Godliness! Not that she should have known any better for the monks and friars of her beloved mediaeval illuminations and painters are undoubtedly represented in a state of immaculate personal hygiene and, when shaved at all, clean-shaven.

It is when she is writing of paintings that she shows more of her deeper impressions and abiding preferences. Indeed, Hubert seems to have rather forced her hand on this issue, taking exception to some dismissive 'oh you wouldn't understand' type of remark about the picture in the Florence Accademia, for she writes on 25 April 1898: 'Of course I will tell you about them if you really care to know only I can't promise you will like them at first because it takes time to get the feeling of them into your mind. But you always used to mock at those sort of things so I didn't try to talk about them. This place has taught me more than I can tell you, it's a sort of gradual conscious growing into an understanding of things.' Giotto delighted her, too, when they stopped in Padua in 1903. Her letter of 16 April praises his work highly and continues: 'But the worst of Giotto is, he makes everyone else seem poor in comparison. I went through the Picture Gallery after lunch, & thought it horrid. Everything seemed gaudy & pretentious & wanting in emotion.' As she went back and back, she was enabled to have second thoughts, never tiring in particular of the beauties of Florence; she herself records her changing taste while furnishing only a little detail: 'Some pictures that I scracely used to notice now seem wonderful, & some that I once loved seem dreary. Botticelli's Spring now seems twenty times nicer than the Venus, & I used to think just the opposite. Isn't it queer?' (letter of 29 April 1904). Yet a certain consistency obtains. One is not surprised for example that the girl who, as a youthful art critic writing for The Midland Weekly News, singled out for special praise a *Girl's Head* by Greuze should fall heavily for the three Vermeers in the Rijksmuseum some eighteen years later (letter of 16 April 1912).

Of the on-going life of the people of Italy, social conditions, politics and the like, Evelyn says next to nothing in these letters. One scene did awaken the old compassion, though now with an added poignancy, the departure for Genoa, and presumably America, of a group of emigrants in 1899. The Underhill family made the trip from Bellagio to Police in a boat carrying a cargo of silk-worm cocoons. 'Coming back we had a much more tragic cargo; a party of emigrants going to Genoa to pick up the steamer there. All their sweethearts & mothers & wives came down to see them off, & wept & screamed, & some of the poor boys sang a farewell song, crying all the time; it was really dreadful. I think caring for a boy oneself makes one much sorrier to see other people parting from their boys, don't you?' Evelyn can hardly have failed to notice poverty in Italy but, for whatever reason, she fails to remark on it to Hubert. If anything makes her cross in the Italian scene, it is the prevalence of 'horrid Germans', 'loathly German women' who seem to get under her feet from time to time (letters of 14 April 1898, 30 March 1899, 4 April 1899).

It may seem to many who care about Evelyn Underhill's approach to more important matters, that these letters from Evelyn to Hubert are chiefly valuable in allowing us a glimpse of her tenderness, her concern, her love, the nature and quality of which we, who did not know her, could only guess at otherwise. Certainly everything about her early writings would oblige us to invent for her a capacity for passionate attachment. But in reading these her 'love-letters' as she herself calls them we may see the thing itself. Concern with Hubert's depressions, his tendency to shut himself away with his work, whether legal or craftwork, his general lack of confidence, figures largely. Evelyn, as her early pet name of 'Nursie' indicates, was for him an evidently much needed mother substitute with a general mandate to jolly him along, tell him he mattered and see he wrapped himself up carefully. On her first holiday she wrote back: 'I do hope you are enjoying yourself & having lovely weather like we are & getting very well & strong. Do please dearest dearest boy. You know you mean everything to your Nursie & it will be a very bitter sequel to her holiday if she comes home & finds her absence had prevented you from having a good time. I am sending you a little likeness of myself by the missis; please ask her for it. I know you would forget me without some reminder!!! That's right, sniff, I deserve it. Now I must pack. Good bye my own darling boy . . .' (letter of 18 April 1898). On another occasion in 1903, staying in Cernobbio on Lake Como she was thrown somewhat into the company of an unmarried man whom they knew, and confronted with the spectacle of honeymooning couples—it all made life very difficult; describing a ghostly scene in the garden, she writes, 'it felt so ghostly that I expected to meet a dead cardinal or a group of powdered ladies or something every minute—if not a fawn or some really elemental thing like that. If you had been there, you would have kissed me, I should have felt quite human & happy at once. I miss you most dreffully my darling retriever; much more than other years I think. Having another unattached man about reminds me of you I spose. I want to be held tight & ruffle up your nice little hair' (letter of 13 April 1903).

Such a love for such a man, whatever his talents or success, must contain a certain amount of fortitude. In a letter of 22 April 1907, when their wedding preparations were in full swing, she wrote from Orvieto 'I have a sort of idea you are feeling rather depressed & I do want you not to. I shall be home in a fortnight from the time you get this letter & we are going to be so happy together, with absolutely no clouds & differences between us.' It is practically certain that Hubert at this moment was especially bothered by the religious problem arising for him out of Evelyn's intention of being received into the Roman communion and was feeling to the full the difference in outlook between them which nothing could entirely gloss over. But Evelyn's reaction is resolute and strangely recalls a much earlier but similar reaction when some cloud must have darkened the family sky and evoked gloomy comments from her mother, 'We are a happy(!) family, we are, we are, we are' (letter of 10 February 1891).

The charm of the young Evelyn which is preserved for those who did not know her, in her letters, is evident and does not need to be insisted upon. She was, in the words of a remark about her recorded by Lucy Menzies, 'an enchanting friend'. But charm is not an especially estimable characteristic in itself; in Evelyn's case it matches up well with her wholeheartedly romantic outlook, her fondness for the picturesque and mediaeval, her love of the south, her impatience with many aspects of the stuffy middle-class stolidity of her parents' world. All this makes her a person of her time and attractive up to a point but it does not make her interesting. To be interesting for posterity a personage must, in the opinion of our own age, have a 'problem'.

We have already indicated in a rather rash and general way one aspect of Evelyn Underhill's 'problem'. Full treatment is not finally possible until some analysis has been furnished of the topics she chose to deal with in her novels and the way in which she dealt with them. In the meantime it is essential to try to piece together some picture of that side of her life which Hubert and her family did not see, which perhaps they could never have seen, even when the evidence was substantially before them in Evelyn's early books. The best point of departure is probably a passage from a letter to the depressed Hubert of just before the wedding in 1907. This letter was written from Bibbiena, probably in April, and begins by thanking him for one of his, received at Arezzo. It continues, 'I only hope you are telling me the truth and are really feeling purry and closer to one another [sic] in spite of the "depression". After all, as I have thought or I now think for many months, if it was to separate us you ought to have felt it coming on long ago and as the chief result has been to force us to talk openly to each other about all the real things which we sedulously kept from each other before, the final effect in spite of difference of opinion ought to be to make us much more real companions than in the past when we each had a water-tight bulk-head carefully fixed to prevent undue explorations.'

The ostensible point of this letter is to reconcile Hubert to the fact that his wife-to-be is proposing to become a Roman Catholic, a step Hubert strongly objected to chiefly on the grounds that Evelyn's confessor would virtually make a third in their marriage and constitute an alien power with certain rights of possession over her. The situation at this stage is still unresolved and Evelyn's letter goes on to point out that he may actually gain from being led by her to see 'the real beauties of Catholicism' and pay less attention to its 'superficial corruptions'. But leaving aside this aspect of the matter we do here have Evelyn's virtual admission of her 'double life' so far as Hubert is concerned, the nearest she comes in any extant personal document to revealing the efforts she herself made to re-integrate their relationship. Her grasping of this particular nettle is not to be taken lightly. If Evelyn Underhill at the age of thirty-one decided to get married to Hubert Stuart Moore, subordinating for this her cherished desire to be 'received', and in the full blood of enthusiasm for mysticism which produced her three 'mystical' novels, *Mysticism* itself, *The Mystic Way* and *Practical Mysticism*, all in the ten years 1904-14, we can be sure that she did so with her wits about her and some notion of inner self-consistency. It remains only to plot the terms of reference within which she took such a decision.

In order to do this we have first to consider her own description of her 'way' as she set it out in a letter of some years later (*Letters*, p. 125). 'For eight or nine years I really believed myself to be an atheist. Philosophy brought me round to an intelligent and irresponsible sort of theism which I enjoyed thoroughly but which did not last long. Gradually the net closed in on me and I was driven nearer and nearer to Christianity, half of me wishing it were true and half resisting violently.' To bring this all too brief and general account into some sort of relationship with the known facts is not easy. If we take 1906 as our *terminus ad quem* for the end of her doubts about the truth of Christianity it would seem that the beginning of the period of 'an intelligent and irresponsible sort of theism' might reasonably be dated from two, four or even five years earlier, 1902–05. The eight or nine years preceding this would be the years of apparent 'atheism' and would therefore begin approximately when we may conjecture she left school in 1891.

Leaving aside for the moment what Evelyn means by 'atheism' though bearing in mind that for the Evelyn of the early 1900s a certain kind of mindless Anglican practice was as bad as, if not worse than, 'atheism', her description of her development obliges us to look for an interest in 'philosophy' orienting her towards some sort of belief in an objective God or 'theism'. The evidence which we shall shortly consider both here and in the next chapter makes it certain that her theistic phase was going strongly in 1903–04 when her short stories and her first novel were published, and when in a letter of November 1904 she is telling Margaret Robinson that 'of course, on this side of the veil the perfect accomplishment of the quest is impossible'. The immediate preliminary question, then, is what kind of philosophical interests and influence caught her attention and, as we may surmise, launched her on both her literary and her spiritual courses.

At this point we enter one of the most intriguing and obscure aspects of Evelyn's life. Inevitably, since the personal documents

such as the letters to Hubert are, for reasons now obvious, largely
uncommunicative, we are reduced to making the most of what
we can deduce from the printed material and from various hints
and suggestions available in miscellaneous quarters. But before we
leave the 'love letters' let us make the most of them also. There
are one or two references, for example, to books. In a letter of
1 December 1898 from Hubert to Evelyn, we read 'I will call at
Mills for you and find out if they have got Maeterlinck's books'.
In another dating from 1900 (winter time) she writes to Hubert
that she has bought 'the new volumes of those Arthurian romance
books'.

Now the reference to Maeterlinck almost certainly indicates
Evelyn's interest in the two books of his published in English by
this date *The Treasures of the Humble* (1897) and *Wisdom and
Destiny* (1898). Both these books give ample evidence of a man
with, as his English translator put it, 'a mystic tinge to his mind'
content to pitch his reflections on life between rhapsody and sen-
tentious moralizing. Evelyn's request to Hubert can be seen as
the prelude to a characteristically vehement letter published in
The Academy for 31 March 1900 in which she rises in her wrath
against a certain Arthur R. Roper who had ventured some criticism of certain of Maeterlinck's plays in the March Contemporary
Review and which offers particularly valuable evidence of her already lively interest in things mystical. The central paragraph reads:

He [Mr Roper] entirely misses the note of Greek tragedy which
Maeterlinck strikes; the inevitableness of the action; the chorus
generally supplied by an old man or woman; the strange stillness of soul which is felt throughout his work. Finally he
attempts to assess Maeterlinck as a poet, dramatist and mystic,
while considering no more than the bare plot of 'Aglavaine et
Selysette', and without mentioning the essays, in which the
whole of Maeterlinck's artistic creed may be found.

The letter concludes, 'We still await a cool and judicious critic whom symbolism affrights not, and mystics do not annoy'. As for the 'Arthurian romances' they figure largely if indirectly as providing a theme in Evelyn's early writing. Evelyn's interest in such 'philosophy' is only a straw in the wind, but a significant one.

The only other important reference in these letters confirms that by 1904 Hubert and Evelyn knew Arthur and Purefoy Machen fairly well (Arthur had married for the second time the previous year) even if they themselves did not belong to the Machen 'set'. Writing on 28 March from Alassio Evelyn tells Hubert that she has been receiving lessons in bookbinding technique from 'my little friend the Bensonian who knows A.M. and all his set by the way'. This is a clear reference to Arthur Grimwood referred to earlier (24 March) as a person 'who was with Benson'. Later she writes, on 3 May 1904, on her way back to England via Paris, 'I've had a long letter from Winifred who has been staying at Stratford with the Machens. They seem to be having a good time, but she is rather dreading the time when they go on Benson's long tour, as it lasts 40 weeks! I'm afraid she will feel horribly desolate.' In the earlier letter of the 28th she asks, 'Did you arrange for those proofs to go back to A.M.'

There seems no reason to doubt that the 'A.M.' of these passages is Arthur Machen who at this moment was on the point of temporarily abandoning his attempts to make his way by writing and proposing to lend his talents to the well-known Benson troup of Shakespearean actors founded and managed by Frank, later Sir Frank, Benson. He made another long and exhausting tour with them in 1907. Evelyn's last novel, *The Column of Dust* in 1909, was dedicated to him and Purefoy as 'Friendship's Offering', and it seems probable that she came to know them through her friend Sylvia Townsend Warner, niece of Purefoy Machen. At this time they were living in London in Cosway Street, in what is described by the best available biography of Machen as 'a poor house in one of the worst quarters of London.'[1] Arthur Machen in 1904 was some forty-one years old.

Arthur Machen's influence on Evelyn Underhill is best considered after we have dealt with the question of the 'proofs' which Evelyn asked Hubert to transmit to him. These almost certainly were the proof copies of one or some or all of Evelyn's contributions to the monthly house paper of the Horlicks Company, The Horlicks Magazine and Home Journal for Australia, India and the Colonies, which in this year, 1904, published no fewer than five short stories by her, all of which appeared after the date of this letter to Hubert. Machen himself, besides other material at various times, published in this journal his 'mystical' 'Fragment of Life' which he seems to have begun in 1899 and again worked up and extended for inclusion in *The House of Souls*, published in 1906.

But for the moment Evelyn's short stories and Arthur Machen himself matter less than the unlikely editor of The Horlicks Magazine whose influence, directly or indirectly, on Evelyn's 'theistic' phase and indeed on her later career must first be considered. Arthur Edward Waite who sat in the editorial chair of The Horlicks Magazine from 1903–05 was at the time perhaps the most eminent, certainly the most prolific in a large field of students and devotees of occultist and mystical texts and rituals. His importance as an influence on the minds and sensibility of the early twentieth century has never been assessed. The first edition of Evelyn's *Mysticism* yields an impressive but by no means complete bibliography of his productions up to that date, including *The Occult Sciences* (1891), *Azoth or The Star in the East* (1893), *Lives of the Alchemical Philosophers* (1888), *The Book of Black Magic* (1898), *The Doctrine and Literature of the Calabah* (1902), *Studies in*

1. *Arthur Machen. A Short Account of his Life and Work.* By Aidan Reynolds and William Charlton with an Introduction by D. B. Wyndham Lewis. London, 1963.

Mysticism (1906), *The Hermetic Museum restored and enlarged.* His in fact is the only name to appear in the bibliographies of each of Parts II–V of *Mysticism* and there are, besides, numerous references to him in the text.

But the doctrine of Waite and Machen cannot be dealt with simply in passing. The reasons for supposing that both had a crucial and interesting influence on Evelyn's early outlook are, as will be seen, fairly strong. As we join her in their company we pass from the world of picturesquely garbed monks with slightly dirty faces into another world of, to borrow a later phrase of Evelyn's, 'practical mysticism'. In this world sacred symbols are no longer the objects of aesthetic appraisal on the part of life's tourists but imperious voices summoning to a mysterious destiny. It is into this world that we must accompany Evelyn if we wish to know more of her early noviciate in the ways of mysticism.

3
First Mystical Writings and Marriage

ALTHOUGH Charles Williams in his edition of the *Letters* and, more recently, Francis King, have given added circulation to the rumour that Evelyn Underhill joined the occultist brotherhood of the Golden Dawn, there has hitherto been very little evidence to support their assertions.[1] It is now, however, possible to state that incontrovertible evidence of Evelyn's membership is provided by two letters from her to Arthur Waite concerning Golden Dawn occasions in London in or around 1905. The first dated 14 November 1905 makes it clear that she was then on the point of undergoing examination for one of the lower grades in the brotherhood, the '3 = 8 degree' as she calls it, i.e. the grade of 'practicus' in the 'Outer Order'.[2] The second, also dating from November, possibly of the same year, contains a passing reference to the Machens and another to the same or a different hurdle in her testing as a G.D. neophyte. This letter reveals incidentally that she feels confident about the Hebrew element in the forthcoming ordeal 'but the astrology and fortune telling are quite beyond me!' These letters also reveal that her occultist pseudonym

1. *Ritual Magic in England (1887 to the Present Day)* by Francis King. London, Neville Spearman, 1970, p. 112.
2. An excellent succinct account of The Golden Dawn written by Mr Ellic Howe will be found in *Encyclopaedia of the Unexplained*, edited by Richard Cavendish, published by Routledge & Kegan Paul, London, 1974.

was 'Soror Quaerens Lucem' translatable as 'the sister who is seeking enlightenment'.

We do not know when Evelyn first entered the Hermetic Society of the Golden Dawn as it was officially styled—G.D. to its familiars—nor when she left it. It seems reasonable to surmise that she established relations with it and its leader through the good offices of Arthur Machen who had by 1905 known Arthur Waite for many years and had himself absorbed a good deal of Waite's influence. Given her lowly status in the hierarchy by November 1905 it also seems probable that she had not by that time been a member for more than a year or so, joining therefore after the virtual re-founding of the Waitean branch to which she belonged, in 1903. This implies that she was not a member of the same brotherhood nor practised the same rituals as for example the Irish poet, W. B. Yeats, whose association with the Order is largely responsible for its public notoriety at the present day; nor does it seem likely that her membership overlapped with that of Charles Williams whose occultist interests are reasonably well known but whose hermetic career remains, as to its details, shrouded in veils of appropriate mystery.

The nature of the group which Evelyn joined is not, however, entirely obscure. A good deal has been, and no doubt will continue to be, published about the Golden Dawn in its various manifestations, its membership, its creed, its ritual, its importance socially, culturally and philosophically. Seen in retrospect it looks very much the kind of society which a young woman taking an interest in the lively metaphysico-mystical scene at the time and detached from the official churches, might have felt drawn to. The Association did not in fact exclude church members; indeed it included several High Anglicans such as Arthur and, possibly, Purefoy Machen; but the emphasis was undoubtedly on what to outsiders appears to have been the acquisition of a certain 'gnosis' or private experiential contact with ultimate realities through the deliberate deployment of incantations and rituals, drawn from various sources, some genuinely ancient and associated with the historic rosicrucian movement, some ostensibly archaic but in fact of very recent concoction. Arthur Machen's biographers state that the members of this generation of the G.D. took it all in a fairly light-hearted spirit. On the other hand the possibility of notable 'happenings' cannot entirely have been precluded and the seriousness with which Evelyn approached all ritual to her dying day is almost certainly a direct consequence of this initiation.

How long Evelyn remained with the group must at present remain conjectural and depends on what one makes of her November 1907 article in The Fortnightly Review, 'A Defence of Magic', which might, from one point of view, be taken as a pro-Waitean tract against the out-and-out occultist magicians or, from another, as a not ungrateful valediction to all occult or hermetic ceremonial, however worthy in intention. The point will have to be taken up again. Whatever the precise facts, we have Evelyn's word for it that the 'irresponsible' theistic period 'did not last long'. It probably did not need to so far as she was concerned. In the perspective of later on it was only a staging post on the way, rather like one of those 'queer little chapels' on the path up to the pilgrimage church near Locarno. But to anyone looking for some line of organic or consistent development in Evelyn such a period is bound to hold a particular interest given that it is undoubtedly the moment when she first encountered and explored in a fellowship of like-minded seekers, the possibility of communication with the ultimate mystery. Those who prefer to think of her as entirely self-taught, if not actually inspired, until she met Friedrich von Hugel are of course free to do so. The fact remains that well before she came under the Baron's influence she had acquired a quite definite and personal point of view which only with difficulty and by degrees adapted itself to his rather different perspectives. The hypothesis of a formative 'noviciate' under auspices not only different but contrasting is at least worth exploring.

There is in fact nothing to be afraid of in Arthur Waite. His prose style and a certain pompous vanity are perhaps his most rebarbative features and one of the chief reasons why he is almost unknown outside the circles of the occult initiates and their sympathizers. His own memoirs reveal many aspects of his mind, his tastes, his ideals, though his statements must, Mr King assures us, be read with caution as to matters of fact. Later in life he confessed in flowing, even passionate, words to a monist faith of so deep a dye that, as he says, 'Smithfield and Tyburn would have entered into a transitory concordat in the old days, if they could have combined to draw and burn me.'[3] But that was written later, at a time when Arthur Machen too, who had known him for thirty-eight years without apparently being aware of these facts, came at last to realise that his friend and teacher was a 'pantheist'. Indeed, not the least of the paradoxes and enigmas surrounding Arthur Waite from first to last is his ability to hold together with his apparent heterodoxy and chosen extra-ecclesial status, his deep indebtedness and fundamental adherence to the faith of his baptism in the Roman communion. At the time Evelyn knew him, he could write in characteristically allusive phrases: 'The fact is that the Church has the Eucharist. . . . But not only is it certain that because of those elements we have to cleave as we can to the Church, but—speaking as a "doctor dubitantium"—I know that the Church mystic on the highest throne of its consciousness does not differ in anything otherwise than *per accidentia* —or alternatively, the prudence of expression—from formal Catholic doctrine. It can say with its heart of knowledge what the ordinary churchman says with his lips of faith; the symbol remains: it has not taken on another meaning: it has only unfolded itself,

3. *Shadows of Life and Thought*. A Retrospective Review in the Form of Memoirs. By Arthur Edward Waite. London, 1938; pp. 238ff.

like a flower, from within. .... Above all, the path of the mystic does not pass through heresies.'[4]

In this connection it may surprise many that the central importance given by Evelyn Underhill to the Blessed Sacrament as Divine Presence and abiding symbol of atonement should be derived from the teaching of Waite yet the fact seems indisputable if we compare the writings of both in so far as they touch the eucharist and the allied symbol of the Holy Grail. And not that alone. The central and transcendent significance of the fact of mystical experience as, in varying degrees, consummating that instinctive tendency and craving of human spirits to unite with the divine Reality, Evelyn almost certainly learned from Waite however much she may later criticize the emphasis in his message. In this respect Waite may be placed not simply at the beginning of Evelyn's course but also at the end. It will be sufficient to quote but one passage which will also serve the purpose of illustrating Waite's evaluation of the Grail legend. He writes:

The Grail at its highest is the simulacrum or effigy of the Divine mystery within the church. If she, as an institution, has failed so far—and as to the failure within limits there is no question—to accomplish the transmutation of humanity, the explanation is not merely that she has been at work upon gross and refractory elements—though this is true assuredly—but that in the great mystery of her development she has still to enter into the fruition of her higher consciousness. Hereof are the wounds of the Church and for this reason she has been in sorrow throughout the ages.[5]

Waite himself, having been brought up by the Passionist Fathers and passed through what he might have called the 'lower

4. *The Hidden Church of the Holy Grail. Its Legends and Symbolism.* London, Redman Ltd, 1909; p. 487.
5. *Ibid.,* p. 478.

grades' as an altar boy in the establishments of the Oblates of Mary Immaculate at Kilburn and the Oblates of St Charles Borromeo at Bayswater, had few if any dealings with institutional Christianity. But he acknowledged his debt; as he put it at 80 years old: 'I, being an "adept philosopher" and poet of Holy Rituals, proclaim once more with humble heart that I owe all to Rome, even the grace of having left it, as one who passes through the *Signum* in quest of *signatum est.* . . . I owe all my books to Rome. It gave me great pageants and suggestion of meaning behind them. It gave also iridescent clouds of doctrine which spoke of a voice within them. I have been listening for that voice in all the great literatures; I have been listening all my life. I am what I am because I have heard its echoes' (*Shadows*, p. 280). It is tempting to say of Waite that every vice is compensated for by an equivalent virtue. He might not have much use for Christian institutions himself but it is not difficult to imagine how he could have stimulated others to take them more seriously than he himself did. Arthur Machen, for example, returned to the practice of his religion and became a high and theologically orthodox Anglican in 1904. Waite's part in this is imponderable. Purefoy may have been more influential; yet Machen also returned to the 'mystical' *Fragment of Life* in this year. Evelyn, already having 'orgies of church ceremonies' at this time, would have approached them with, presumably, a clear eyed Waitean appreciation of their mystagogic significance. Her friends soon afterwards regarded her reception into the Church of Rome as certain. Waite would certainly not have approved such a step. On the other hand he could hardly have shirked all responsibility for it in Evelyn's case.

It is unnecessary to elaborate on Evelyn's experience in the Golden Dawn. The rituals as elaborated by Waite have been described elsewhere and contained nothing sinister or morally reprehensible. Aleister Crowley plays no part in this story. On the contrary, Waite not infrequently expressed his dislike and contempt for the like of such serious occultist mandarins as the kilted G. S. L. McGregor Mathers ('a comic Blackstone of occult law') and the more deserving Dr Wynn Westcott, described late in Waite's life as 'like a dull owl, hooting dolefully among cypresses over tombs of false adepts'. The great crime of Waite in the eyes of such people was that, having infiltrated their organization, apparently in perfect good faith, he then machinated a seizure of power and tilted the ritual in an orthodox or relatively orthodox Christian mystical direction. His 'revision' of the Golden Dawn ritual apparently abandoned 'Ritual Magic and all Astral workings' and re-wrote the texts 'to express' according to Mr King, 'a somewhat tortuous Christian mysticism.'

Evelyn Underhill's 1907 article, 'In Defence of Magic' already referred to, has the merit of showing starkly just how far the cultivation of Hermetic ceremonial and 'High Magic' might help the seeker to appease his thirst for the transcendant. It also bears indirect witness to the way which she considered had been her own. For, although this article is resumed and many passages from it fully incorporated into chapter 7 of *Mysticism*, entitled Mysticism and Magic, one misses in the very much longer chapter the clear apologetic tone of the article and also the perfectly explicit evocation as an exemplary figure of that master magician, the Spiritual master of Waite as of many others, Alphonse Louis Constant, *alias* Eliphas Lévi. The main point Evelyn makes on behalf of the cultivation of magical and occultist ceremonial is that in so far as it involves a mental, emotional or in general terms 'psychological' preparation of the adept for communion with the unseen object of his adoration, it is no better and no worse than all and any other sane ceremonial, under whatever auspices, which seeks the same end. She evokes the rites of the Roman Church as they were in her day, baptism in particular, also the Latin liturgy 'much of whose amazing—and truly magic

—power would evaporate were it translated into the vulgar tongue'. Magical rites properly understood and conducted, are therefore, perfectly normal techniques for removing superficial impediments to a higher kind of awareness, and concentrate the attention and will-power on the true if normally inaccessible object of man's quest. Such an adjustment is in effect a perfect vindication of the activities of Waite and his group.

There follows, however, a qualification which Evelyn must have considered important since she returns to it again some years later, in the pseudonymous *Spiral Way* of 1912. The trouble with magic, as, she maintains, Eliphas Lévi himself found out eventually, is that it awakens desires which it is unable to satisfy. Concentrating on the satisfaction of human curiosity and the craving to know strange things or, as we might say, the enlargement of experience, it leaves unrequited man's deepest yearning of all, which is love. And suddenly Evelyn observes 'It is the defect of all modern occultism that it is tainted by a certain intellectual arrogance. A divorce has been effected between knowledge and love, between the religion and the science of the magi: and, in the language of mysticism, till these be re-united the Divine Word cannot be born.' Is this to the address of Mr Waite? On balance it probably is, as are also the lines directed a little earlier to 'students of his [Lévi's] system, of whom the eminent occultist, Mr A. E. Waite, must be reckoned as chief'. Here Evelyn steps in to defend Lévi from the criticisms of Waite and the rest, which are motivated, she thinks, 'first, from the natural annoyance which is aroused in any school by the proceedings of a born "free lance"; next from an angry inability to comprehend Lévi's return to the Church of Rome; finally, from a misunderstanding of the degree of reality which he attributed to the symbolic framework on which he wove his deep speculations upon God and the soul' (art. cit., pp. 762ff).

Whether or not this cap fits Waite must be left to Waite

specialists, if and when there are any. What is interesting for the present argument is that in these pages Evelyn takes up and defends the course of a man such as Lévi who, as she saw him, began with 'a form of intellectual curiosity', was led on through magical practices to 'a mystic seeking of transcendental truth'; then passed on to a conscious and elaborate exploitation of artistic, conceptual and natural symbols; came to an understanding of compassion and the abiding value of suffering freely accepted; and finally brought the whole story to an evidently exemplary climax by becoming reconciled to the Roman Catholic Church to which he originally belonged. It is difficult not to read another story into this, the story of Evelyn's own career. Such a reading is, as we shall see, amply supported from her novels of the time if we care to take them in an autobiographical sense. The last word for the present should perhaps be with John Cordelier, the pseudonym under which Evelyn hid her authorship of two ostensibly 'devotional' works. In the *Spiral Way* (1912), which is a commentary of a quite unique kind on the mysteries of the rosary, when she comes to the fifth 'mystery' or meditation on Jesus' life, namely The Child amongst the Doctors, she interprets the disappearance of Jesus and his debates with the learned as an aberration typical of immaturity. Jesus *thought* he was 'about his Father's business' but in fact nothing could have been further from the truth; he had 'left the actualities of human experience for the abstractions and subtleties of the intellectual world.' Just so, says Evelyn, the 'crescent spirit' of the mystical neophyte seeks for 'something *known*, some secret imparted—a revelation given perhaps to the insistent neophyte, but guarded from the crowd by those who keep its shrine, an inward mysterious meaning evolved from a moribund tradition. . . . They dream of an initiation, some magical "Open Sesame" of the spiritual world, a ready-made solution that shall relieve them from the dreadful obligation of growing into truth. This solution, they think, . . . will rend the sanctuary veil. They know not that this veil shall only be parted when the soul dies upon the cross, "resisting interior temptation even to despair".' Yes, the seeking of 'an inward mysterious meaning from a moribund tradition', *that* cap certainly seems to fit.

The stories which finally arrived on the editorial desk of Arthur Waite in 1904 belong to a genre which was in its hey-day at the time of their appearance, the genre, that is to say, not just of the short story but of the *super-natural* short story, taking 'super-natural' in a wide sense to include also the preternatural, and the 'short story' to include anything short of a full-length novel. It is unnecessary to draw up a long list. It is to this taste or fashion that we owe the ghost stories of M. R. James or W. W. Jacobs and the uncanny tales of A. Conan Doyle, H. G. Wells and others, which were appearing at this time. More serious as 'literature' no doubt but recognisably in the same genre were *Owen Wingrave* and *The Turning of the Screw* by Henry James. Among associates of Evelyn Underhill two widely known practitioners of the art for their respective publics were Arthur Machen and Robert Hugh Benson. Benson, Machen, both the Jameses, and others, reflect a widespread interest at the time in the phenomenon of diabolical possession for which Huysmans and, behind him, Edgar Allan Poe and others, were ultimately responsible. But none of these leaves the deepest impression on Evelyn's stories. That honour falls either to the Oscar Wilde of *The Picture of Dorian Gray* or to the Emile Zola of *Thérèse Raquin*—possibly both.

Three stories adapt the portrait theme, found in Zola and Wilde, two blatantly, one moving away from and adapting it in a way which achieves its culmination in what is perhaps Evelyn's best and certainly her last and scarcest novel, *The Column of Dust* (1909). Of the remaining two stories, the first, *Our Lady of the Gate*, is an attempt to recreate in a mystico-symbolic world a story on the lines of the mediaeval *Miracles of Our Lady St Mary*, a selection of which Evelyn translated and published in 1905; and the second, *A Green Man*, a rhapsody to divine immanence in nature described through the symbolic language of the Latin mass, of a kind found also in Machen and repeated by Evelyn in her second novel *The Lost Word*. Of these two the former is the more notable in that it evokes the mystical experience as a vision of divine motherhood, thus offering us the first appearance of this important theme in Evelyn's early writing.

The stories in The Horlicks Magazine of 1904 which adapt the portrait theme are *The Death of a Saint* (pp. 173ff.), *The Ivory Tower* (pp. 207ff.), *The Mountain Image* (pp. 375ff.). In the first we are taken to the death-bed of a saintly priest, Father John. His two disciples, Alban and Cuthbert, sit by him. He is old but 'not very old'. He has 'keen dark eyes' which make 'the sweetness of his smile seem a paradox' and are 'signs of a fretting sword within'. Father John learns that he is dying and expresses an urgent desire to go through 'a door in the wall opposite his bed'. The disciples assume it is an oratory. Every morning Father John has been accustomed to go in there, sometimes 'depressed and nervous, almost morose', but always emerging 'after three hours of silence' serene and ready for the world'. Father John gets his way despite protests; but soon seems to be spending far too long in his 'oratory'. The disciples are worried and break in. They are staggered at what they find. They are in an artist's studio, but not that of a painter of visionary landscapes, madonnas or noble peasants. On the contrary, 'This was the workshop of a great painter; but his subjects were the grotesque, morbid, unspeakable secrets of the world'. Everywhere are strewed pictures in various stages of completion, depicting 'things' which are human, sexless and bestial. And all resemble Father John who lies dead before a particularly evil-looking self-portrait which he has apparently been attempting to obliterate. The room fills with an atmosphere of evil. One of the disciples is almost overwhelmed by it, but finally calm is restored. The wiser disciple, far from echoing his companion's 'Our saint was only an artist after all!', remembers with tears 'that Father John had always come from that room purged from the stain of earth and radiant with thanksgiving; with a heart . . . which had longed to help and comfort all the world. It seemed possible that had he been less of an artist, he might not have been quite so much of a saint'.

In Zola's *Thérèse Raquin* the murderous and adulterous artist paints a portrait through which, despite all his efforts, there constantly leers forth the hideous face of the body of the husband he has killed. In Wilde's tale, Dorian Gray is jealous of his portrait's beauty and expresses a wish that the normal relationship of portrait to sitter should be reversed, he remaining with his pristine beauty while the picture changes with the passage of time. His wish is granted. Dorian remains beautiful indeed but the picture records, pictorially, his increasing moral degradation until, attempting to destroy it, he destroys himself.

For most educated people of the era of Wilde and Evelyn Underhill art is the mirror of that in human kind which men themselves cannot express in other words. In that age still largely ignorant of the findings of the systematic exploration of psychological depths which was even then going forward, the deepest levels of consciousness were only approachable through the medium of symbols and human creativity. But, as Wilde puts it in his preface to *Dorian Gray*:

> All art is at once Surface and Symbol.
> Those who go beneath the Surface do so at their peril;
> Those who read the Symbol do so at their peril.

Art may be concealment. It can also be a medium of revelation of that truth which men carry locked up in their hearts. In Father John's creations 'were personified all the dark, obscene secrets of our common nature'. But in his case the artistic endeavour was also a labour of self-knowledge, of purgation. As in the age-old widsom of the children's fairy story, *Beauty and the Beast*, Father John's saintly maiden soul vanquished the bestial ugliness of the beast to whom she was yoked by embracing him every morning for three hours in the 'oratory' through the 'door in the wall'.

The Ivory Tower transposes the theme into the mode of 'the quest', in which a mythical journey is undertaken to a tower on a rock in which is reputed to live a very beautiful princess who awaits her lover, her rescuer. The seeker loves her before he knows her; he leaves 'the comfortable for the adorable, the known for the unknown'. He arrives at the tower in the midst of the western sea and finds a very old woman. *She* is the adorable princess and reproaches him for not having recognised her: 'Have I not had time to grow old whilst I waited for my lover? I have been here since the beginning of the world; yes, and before the world was, for I am older than God and more difficult of access and you are the first who has knocked at my door. None who are solitary can be young, and I am the most lonely thing in the world.' The seeker is disgruntled but knows he has found the Desired Princess when she kisses him. She shows him a mirror in which he sees that he too is now old. His childhood, she tells him, was over 'in the moment when you steered straight for the perilous rock but whenever you would have it again you need only refuse to look at me. He knows how to shut his eyes can always find the de-sired princess.' He replies: 'Oh, Truth, blind me for ever, for I had rather love than know.'

This story is more overtly mystical in tone. The solitary one who is beyond beauty but uses beauty as her bait suggests Plotinus who is again echoed in 'He who knows how to shut his eyes . . .' Plotinus writes:

Our country from which we came is There, our Father is There. . . . You must not get ready a carriage, either, or a boat.

Let all things go, and do not look. Shut your eyes and change to and evoke another way of seeing which everyone has but few use. (*Enneads*, 1.6.8.)

That a female symbol should be used for the One will surprise no-one who has read Dame Julian of Norwich. Augustine's exclamation 'pulchritido tam antiqua et tam nova ... sero te amavi ...' may also be relevant, or the words he puts into the mouth of Divine Wisdom which are frequently quoted by Evelyn, 'I am the food of the full-grown: grow, that you may feed on me. I shall not be changed into you but you shall be changed into me.' Here the Truth which is the object of the Seeker's quest transcends his personality and finally transforms the nature of his love from a desire to know into a desire to love.

In *The Mountain Image* we return squarely to Wilde's and Zola's notion that the symbol man creates may prove destructive of its maker. Evelyn here exploits an interest in the release of elemental forces in nature, or, in other words, in the subconscious life of man, which seems to have been characteristic of Arthur Machen years before this. The tale describes the efforts of a talented sculptor to carve a vast madonna on a mountainside. But his talent and his dream are commandeered by 'some antique and natural sorcery, against which the quiet religion of the valley gave him no defence—secrets of the evil rock that struggled with him, the awful face that looked to his for escape'. This powerful female figure, the 'mistress of the hill', becomes finally manifest in the rock. At night she visits him, a cynically triumphant smile on her lips. He is seized by 'that Hidden Panic Spirit which is in every artist's soul.' He burns to hold her, does so for an instant, enjoying the full sensual bliss of the experience, then is forced again madly to pursue her. She awaits him. Thinking that she beckons him and waits 'to lead him on to some hidden city beyond the ramparts of the sensual world' he plunges on towards her, driven by a dark spirit, and finally plunges to a grisly death, mocked by the hidden spirits of the mountainside.

The application of this fable to the quest for spiritual illumination seems obvious enough. The moral also, that such seeking can go badly wrong, is clear. More than any of the stories this one throws into relief the ambiguous nature of that passion which drives the man, or woman, who seeks to realise a transcendental dream. The irresistible urge to create and release the obsessive image stands in the story for the 'craving', as Evelyn so frequently describes it, of man for the Infinite. But is not such a desire mere hubris and excess? As a man's desire is, so will his reward be. Machen's stories using the notion of panic obsession seem merely 'creepy' by comparison, even if one concedes that they are better written. But it is a general rule that where Machen and Evelyn overlap, it is she and not he who gives the impression of deeply exploring the risks and perils of what she somewhere calls 'the supersensual life'. It is against the background of a story such as this, *The Mountain Image*, that one appreciates to the full her insistence in the article on magic that the craving for fulfilment or self-realization should be controlled by a *good* love. It is only in the novels that she works out fully the implications of such a love's existence for the dedicated mystical life.

What the readership of The Horlicks Magazine made of Evelyn's contributions it is probably now impossible to discover. High standards were expected of them. Waite himself was a not infrequent contributor under the *nom de plume* of 'The Old Student' and both the topics he chose and the manner of their treatment show that he deemed it beneath him to make any concessions to the nature of what was, after all, nothing more than a house periodical, distributed to the lowliest employees. Almost all items bear directly or indirectly on the transcendental quest and every number was studded with a number of pithy maxims, most, if not all, emanating from the fertile brain of 'The Old

Student' and virtually all 'mystical' in character. Having lasted nearly three years the periodical ceased publication in 1905 very much *not* thanks to any initiative on Waite's part. His final pithy maxim, printed just above the announcement that publication was to be discontinued, speaks volumes: 'To try moral suasion with some people is like recommending a physical exerciser to develop a conscience.' One wonders what the Horlicks board made of that!

Having emerged from under the wing of Waite, perhaps not very long before her marriage, Evelyn Underhill seemed to her friends to be on the point of 'going over' to Rome. Her vivacious friend, Ethel Ross Barker, later to establish a reputation as an archaeologist, wrote to her on 29 December 1906 'I'm inclined to bet heavily (1) that I never go over (2) that you go over one day, (3) that at all events you go over first. Voilà—what do you think?' Unfortunately we do not possess Evelyn's answer to this question but in the event no bet could have been less wisely laid since Ethel Ross Barker 'went over' in the August of the following year and Evelyn never did. Ethel's letters are copious and not uninformative; they would make a little psychological study in themselves of the state of mind of an Edwardian young lady of no small intelligence scenting, nibbling, biting and being hooked by the Roman church thanks, under God, to the combined efforts of various priests and a congenial convent or two. Ethel was perfectly aware that Soeur Eucharistie of the Southampton convent, where Evelyn also had stayed and where Ethel was finally received, was a collector of 'scalps'. The experience of 'submitting' was certainly far from delicious but, so far as the good nuns could, they made everything as pleasant as possible and, in so far as Ethel's letters have a common theme, it is that if only Evelyn would come to the convent with Hubert, the way to her eventual reception into the Roman Catholic Church would no longer be impeded since Hubert could not fail to be reassured.

Ethel's remarks reveal both the common ground and the differences between the two women. A great deal of the content of the letters concerns relatively trivial matters though much has an end in view—such as Soeur Eucharistie's message to Evelyn that 'those souls whom God calls to great perfection have always great trials'. Yet much is well put in Ethel's letters, above all her description of her attempts to reconstruct the 'natural' Soeur Eucharistie from 'the vaguest hints she lets drop.' 'It's rather like constructing an antidiluvian monster from a fossil of his back double tooth! ... I *think* she used to play.' But Ethel also thinks the Sister 'a perfect angel'. The description of the details of the reception ceremony on the other hand reveals a sort of tragi-comedy of a kind not calculated to reassure Evelyn. 'Father Dolman suddenly said: "Have you studied the New Theology?" and when I replied with a disgusted negative he smiled his relief and approbation, and said, in his funny foreign accent: "You must be a good child, and not trouble yourself with difficult matters"— I suppressed a smile and we parted.' The confession and submission over, Ethel was received into the convent community 'like some very black goat that had been showed inside the fold amongst the whitest of the lambs' (3 August 1907). In fact Ethel had thought seriously about the issue of intellectual submission. In a dense letter of 8 January 1907 she expounds her exposition to Evelyn beginning with the words 'we shouldn't make too big bogeys of the dogmas'. Her argument develops the idea that since the gap between all theological symbols and the reality they purport to describe is enormous, infinite, it is vain to quibble about the minute difference separating literal and liberal expositions of the dogmas of Christianity. Finally, 'in every department of existence we have to fling ourselves farther than we can see . . .'. She feels that Fr Tyrrell, if not Soeur Eucharistie, is behind her in her arguments. Fr George Tyrrell, the Jesuit writer and preacher with a gift for delivering a scholastic but intelligible account of the

Christian faith in terms many at the time, including Baron von Hugel, appreciated, was shortly in fact to be condemned by the Church Ethel was joining for, precisely, espousing the 'New Theology'.

Evelyn was being 'helped' in other ways by Ethel. With that endearing but often ill-founded belief that it is all a matter of 'finding the right priest' she suggests that Father Hugh Benson might be the right man to soothe Hubert's anxieties: 'Surely if *anyone* could reconcile him to confession, it would be Father Benson with his boyishness & his simplicity— & the fact that he is a decently educated English gentleman rather than a priest.' Indeed Ethel not only suggested, she acted, and in the same letter she says that Father Benson 'has been a brick over it.' (Letter of 8 April 1907). It is thanks to this letter that we know that Evelyn and Hubert, on the latter's initiative, are 'to read the gospels together'. Another letter expresses delight that they are also going together to High Mass in a Roman Catholic church. These developments no doubt followed on the opening of hearts which took place this month and has already been referred to.

Ethel's suggestion that Robert Hugh Benson might be the man for Hubert was duly acted upon but not until after the wedding that summer. Meanwhile this 'decently educated English gentleman', who was also the son of an Archbishop of Canterbury and who had been 'converted' to the Church of Rome not long before, had been appealed to for help by Evelyn herself. The decision to act appears to have followed a visit to the Southampton convent at the end of January 1907. In a letter to Mrs Meyrick Heath of 1911 describing this visit and its aftermath, she wrote: 'The day after I came away (Feast of the Purification) a good deal shaken but unconvinced, I was converted quite suddenly, once and for all by an overpowering vision which had no specifically Christian elements, but convinced me that the Catholic religion was true' (*Letters*, pp. 125–6). Evelyn was no stranger to the externals of Catholic worship and discipline. She had a knowledge of mystical literature well beyond that of the average lay Catholic. She was not therefore an ignorant stranger bowled over by the trappings of convent life and worship. Indeed the convent is described as something of an aesthetic 'desert' by Ethel Ross Barker. If she quite abruptly perceived the 'truth' of the Roman Catholic presentation of Christianity this must mean, not some moment of intellectual assent—the sequel makes it impossible to believe this—but a recognition that the Roman Church as an institution had in principle a valid claim on her allegiance. It was then, perhaps in this spirit that she wrote to Benson in or about the middle of March that year that, apparently back-tracking on her 'vision', she had got 'half-way from Agnosticism to Catholicism and could get no further'.

For almost the whole of this correspondence we have at present to rely on the quotations and paraphrases of Benson's biographer, Father C. C. Martindale, s.j.[6] Should all Evelyn's letters to Benson eventually turn up they will provide a fairly complete picture of her intellectual situation at this moment. It should only be added at this point that she may have felt the more emboldened to write to Benson in that she had not only heard him preach but must also have known him to be greatly interested in mystical experience. This year, 1907, was almost one might say the culmination of Benson's long-standing interest in mysticism, already apparent in earlier works such as *The Light Invisible* (1903). It is the year his *Mirrors of Shalot* was published and also his articles for the Dublin Review on spiritualism, possession and mysticism, and of his Westminster lectures, entitled simply *Mysticism*. Later that same year she recommends his *Papers of a Pariah* which had just come out and which she describes as 'rather a pleasant book which has several things in it which I thought extremely well put'

6. *The Life of Monsignor Robert Hugh Benson.* By C. C. Martindale, s.j., London, Longmans Green & Co., 1916; vol. 2, pp. 258ff.

(*Letters*, p. 67)—including no doubt two interesting short chapters on 'The Sense of the Supernatural' and 'The Mystical Sense'. Benson was in fact in this very year beginning to move away from mysticism viewed from the subjective and psychological angle. He no doubt sensed a certain hostility to such interests in his communion; however that may be, he later looked askance on his mystical phase and his Jesuit biographer, discussing this fact, chooses the moment, significantly, to evoke the spectre of modernism, that 'New Theology' over which her priest was shortly to quiz Ethel Ross Barker.

Evelyn's first letter to Benson opened squarely on the question of dogma which for her if not for Ethel evidently *was* something of a 'bogey'. 'Her difficulty was,' paraphrases Father Martindale, 'that Catholics declared that their dogmas were true historically as well as spiritually (thus, the Ascension must be as "true" as the Armada); this she could not believe and could not see to matter —In religion, mystical religion was alone intelligible.' The correspondence continues in a somewhat circular manner. Fr Benson's first reply looks almost evasive. 'God is a Spirit,' he says, *but* 'The Word was made Flesh'. He recommends humility and concentration on the purgative way; he suggests a visit to a convent. Evelyn replies that she will have nothing to do with a convent, 'the "atmosphere" of a convent was precisely what she dreaded, and in all her efforts, she was haunted by the dread of self-suggestion. The discussion therefore moves on to the question of the excellence or otherwise of laying oneself open to this 'self-suggestion'. It does not appear that Evelyn told Benson that this debate had retrospective as well as prospective interest for her.

At this point the exchange lapsed temporarily while Evelyn got married *without* becoming a Catholic. Benson said mass for them on the wedding day. Her friend, Ethel, took it for granted that Evelyn's reception was simply being delayed to allow more time for Hubert to absorb and accept the situation. Within six months

of her marriage, however, Evelyn returns to her correspondence
with Benson and her first letter in this new phase of their correspondence appears to be the only one in the entire exchange to
have escaped destruction through the accident of having been
copied with other miscellaneous items into a small book of retreat
notes kept by her in the twenties. This letter raises again rather
forcibly the issue of self-suggestion, the possibility, that is to say,
that the whole business of prayer and worship is some elaborate
self-deception. After all, she argues, certain of her friends, not
Christians, have raised themselves to what she would call high
states of prayer simply by deploying certain techniques devoid of
any religious connotation. One friend in particular, she does not
say who, has just written an entire novel in a state resembling
'quiet' in which apparently she just wrote as she was 'inspired'.
Had prayer, then asks Evelyn, really anything to do with religion?
We do not know exactly how Benson coped with this though Fr
Martindale describes in some detail lengthy sections of a letter on
the 'prayer of quiet' as Benson understood it. Whatever Benson
achieved he did not lay to rest Evelyn's anxieties on the subject of
self-delusion, as the sequel shows.

Finally in June that year, answering a letter in which Evelyn
admitted to feeling 'interior dereliction', Benson took up the
problem of the Institutional Church and said something to the
point. 'We are,' he wrote, 'made for two lives, the inner and the
outer. Materialism is the ultimate end of one, spiritualism (not
spiritism) of the other. The only reconciliation of the two, if
principles are carried out is Catholicism . . . (by which I mean not
just Sacramentalism or Symbolism, but corporate religious life,
that is, outer, supra-national . . . and all the rest). I can see nothing,
anywhere, that even intelligibly claims to perform this function
except the Catholic Church. Now it appears to me that you have
been trying to do without it, to develop an individual outer life
and to project an outer religious life *of your own.*' He goes on to

say that this is why she has come up against utter 'blankness'. For prayer, too, is 'half-crippled' unless it is 'planted in a soil external to itself, that is, in the organized religious life of the world, and this undoubtedly is Catholicism.'

Evelyn's reply points out that all *her* prayer has been nourished on Catholic writings in so far as an 'outsider' might do so. But she is in a quandary as to what *further* step she must take. Anglicanism being out of the question she nonetheless is loathe to sacrifice her 'intellectual liberty' for the sake of becoming a Catholic. The debate thus begins to return whence it began and Benson starts to argue in earnest: 'Honestly, I think your fear of losing intellectual liberty is a dream. . . . One does not lose one's intellectual liberty when one learns mathematics, though one certainly loses the liberty of doing sums the wrong way, or doing them by laborious methods!' Evelyn seems to have admitted the peril of isolation pointed out in this and the earlier letter, but to have denied the force of his analogy. In Father Martindale's paraphrase of her reply: 'No mathematical professor has the right to forbid a pupil doing problems his own way: no authority should dare forbid a mind to ask itself "where does this line of argument land me if honestly pursued," yet such is the Church's action, if she commands, for example, belief in the single authorship of Isaiah.' To this Benson once again returns an elliptical answer, the main burden of which is to point out to Evelyn the limitations inherent in any community life. The general intention of the Church is to protect the flock committed to her charge. She does not intend to suppress the truth, merely to prevent a 'precipitate' adherence to what may in the event only *seem* to have been true; the flock should not be disturbed. 'Personally I am a violent defender of the Cardinals against Galileo. . . . We are Christ's lambs after all.' As for Isaiah, it is only the 'brilliant young men' who will lose their liberty. Why protect them when many people would lose all credence in any Isaiah at all if their cherished ideas are shaken?' He concludes in words which recall those of Ethel's priest, *maxima debetur reverentia pueris*. Who would dream of treating a child by the policy of 'If it's true, he'd better know it'? and we Catholics are most of us children . . . and of such is the Kingdom of Heaven.' Evelyn's final letter is not reported in detail. She seems to have found the discussion was giving her more agony than she thought it was worth.

The papal decree, *Lamentabili*, condemning Modernism, was approved the day after Evelyn married on 4 July and published shortly afterwards. It was followed by the papal encyclical *Pascendi*. These documents bisect the correspondence with Benson and partly explain the turn it took. Evelyn attached a crucial importance to them when she wrote to Mrs Meyrick Heath in the same letter in which she describes her 'vision of the truth' of Catholicism, that they made it impossible for her to be received 'without suppressions and evasions to which I can't quite bring myself'. Her additional statement that she was both then and before a 'modernist' we shall consider after glancing at her works on mysticism of this period.

Stepping back for a moment from this abortive attempt of Evelyn to become a member in fact as well as in spirit of 'my ultimate home' as she believed the Roman Church still to be in 1911, one is struck by the apparent discrepancy between this apparent havering over intellectual scruples and her realization that the path of true enlightenment is not one of *knowledge* but of *love*. From one point of view her stand is oddly Waitean. Her letter to Mrs Heath continues: 'I no more like the tone and temper of contemporary Roman Catholicism than you do: it is really horrible; but with all her muddles, she has kept her mysteries intact' (*Letters*, p. 126). Rome, then, is in principle the custodian of the shrine of true knowledge for Evelyn but is quite unacceptable in practice. The trouble, therefore, was not so much that Benson had not really answered her first question about the general status of historical facts in Catholic dogma nor even her second concerning Rome's championship of palpably false 'facts' in particular cases; if Rome had preserved the 'mysteries' such details really mattered little. The trouble was that she could not lovingly hand her reason over blindfold to a custodian of the mysteries whose love of truth was not equal to her own. Intellectual scruples she might have, and things probably would have been a little difficult for Hubert, but in the end it seems worth suggesting that no amount of certitude about the validity of Roman claims, taken at large, could make up for the absence of love. There was indeed no clash of loves in her life in this respect: love of Hubert, and love of her 'intellectual liberty' *versus* love of Rome, For, if Christian moralists are right, a good love is not strictly dependent on the intellectual credentials of the potentially loveable object but on its actual or potential *moral* qualities. It must indeed have been difficult to love the Rome which hunted the modernists and could not be seen itself to love the truth. The only solution was to remain an 'outsider'.

4
Two Worlds or One? The Novels

THE starting point of Evelyn's novels is in the last analysis that 'first kiss of God' which for Coventry Patmore was the ground of all and any mysticism. Patmore defined mysticism in the sense of Cardinal Wiseman as 'the science of love' and his words on the first dawn of this love of God conveniently introduce the mystical dimension and subsequent predicament of all of Evelyn's main characteres. Allowing, he writes, for the infinite degrees of any such experimental knowledge of God, from the first sensible 'touch' of God's love 'which usually accompanied the first sincere intention of perfection for His sake', to the experience of the 'imitations of self-sacrifice of the saints,' such an experiment is generally final:

> The man who has made the experiment has seen God: and that is an event which he will never be able altogether to forget or deny, a positive fact which for reality and self-evidence, stands alone in his experience, and which no amount of negative evidence will be able, even for a moment, to obscure.[1]

We may come still closer to Evelyn's point of departure perhaps, if we follow Arthur Machen 'walking on air' down Rosebery Avenue at one p.m. in the November of 1899; or later, sitting in his room at 4, Verulam Buildings in Gray's Inn, when

1. *Religio Poetae and Other Essays.* By Coventry Patmore. London, 1913; p. 252.

he was 'shaken to his foundations' and, after a period of dejection, found himself in

> a peace of the Spirit that was quite ineffable, a knowledge that all hurts and doles and wounds were healed, that that which was broken was reunited. Everything, of body and of mind, was resolved into an infinite and an exquisite delight: into a joy so great that—let this be duly noted—it became almost intolerable in its ecstasy.[2]

For Machen this experience was an inextricable mingling of the two worlds of sense and spirit so that it became difficult to distinguish inward and outward. And the experience went with him for some time after—to his retrospective astonishment—'in dim Bloomsbury Square, in noisy chattering Gray's Inn Road, in a train on the Underground, amongst hustling crowds in common streets'. It was, he reflected afterwards, an introduction to 'a better world of which he saw the verges'.

Machen's 'experiment' as he called it, using Patmore's word, has important echoes in his work which in this respect runs on lines parallel to that of Evelyn Underhill. And Evelyn too, had an historic point of departure to which she could look. On 29 July 1908 she wrote to Margaret Robinson:

> Surely you have perceived for yourself the difference between created things as seen in the indescribable atmosphere which theologians call 'the love of God' and seen in the ordinary worldly light? I remember you told me once the first thing you 'found out' was a sense of intense refinement. The first thing I found out was exalted and indescribable beauty in the most squalid places. I still remember walking down the Notting Hill

---

2. *The Autobiography of Arthur Machen.* With an Introduction by Morchard Bishop. London, Richards Press, 1951; pp. 267–9.

main road and observing the landscape with joy and astonishment. Even the movement of traffic had something universal and sublime in it. Of course that does not last—but the after-flavour of it does, and now and then one catches it again. . . . One sees the world at those moments so completely as 'energized by the invisible' that there is no temptation to rest in mere enjoyment of the visible (*Letters*, p. 80).

Patmore, Machen, Evelyn Underhill insinuate the truth which G. K. Chesterton, for whom these matters were also of more than merely academic importance, expressed crudely when he said that 'a mystic is one who holds that two worlds are better than one'. But *are* two worlds really 'better' than one? What does 'better' mean in this context?—more conducive to happiness? better for getting on in life? for practising one's religion sincerely? for achieving something in the execution and appreciation of art? for living in love and charity with one's neighbour? for attaining union with God? It is with Evelyn Underhill's answers to these questions that we shall now be chiefly concerned as we survey her novels, though other aspects of her achievement in them will also have to be considered.

There are three novels, *The Grey World* (1904), *The Lost Word* (1907), *The Column of Dust* (1909). All are concerned with the problem of living in two worlds. The first and the last turn on a controlling metaphor which, as Machen would say, is 'real' but not 'actual', i.e. which introduces a genuine dimension of human life but is not intended in any sense to be taken literally. The second introduces the theme in what appears at first sight to be a more realistic manner but, in the end, rides as loosely to realistic convention as the other two. On the 1911 title-page of *Mysticism* Evelyn described herself as 'author of *The Grey World*, *The Column of Dust* etc,' a revealing choice, for the second novel is, while rewarding, particularly weak in construction. The progress towards the third and best of them is not even, therefore, and it is characteristic of Evelyn's effective self-criticism that after *The Lost Word* she was able to turn backwards, and adopt again her original idea and give it a totally new twist. Each book will be surveyed first in outline, then in greater detail bearing in mind especially the question which has already been raised in respect of the mystic's life being in some sense 'better' for its dual focus.

The story-line of *The Grey World* is soon told. The opening pages conjure up the picture of a slum child ill in a hospital. By accident—the untimely eating of a currant bun—he dies and is at once transferred to a Dante-inspired realm of wandering, groaning, moaning, restless, searching shades which people the 'grey world' just 'on the other side of ours' but still within touching distance of it. Not for long however; thanks to a benign arrangement of providence he is allowed to 're-incarnate' as a baby in the family of a very respectable middle-class tailor, Mr Hopkinson. Henceforward he is Willie Hopkinson, an ordinary middle-class lad. But not quite or entirely. Willie has been marked. He has relapses, throw-backs, sudden glimpses of that 'beyond' of which for a time he was part. Each time it happens he is 'shaken to his foundations' and his family are thrown into bewilderment. His school-days are briefly dealt with; he falls in with a group bent on spiritual enlightenment and makes a friend of one of them, Stephen Miller; he becomes an apprentice bookbinder and falls in love with Mildred, a fellow-apprentice; he also comes under the patronising influence of a middle-aged 'arty' woman, Mrs Elsa Levi; she helps him to discover Art and after a brooding moment in their relationship when things seem to be turning from the Platonic to the rudely carnal, he goes off to Italy to mature spiritually. On his return he finds an eremitical English woman in the depths of the countryside who is interested in arts and crafts, prayer and the mystics, and settles down at a safe distance from her to bind books and practise contemplation.

It is early borne in upon the reader of this story that it has no pretensions to elaborate plotting and characterisation. The initial idea which establishes the hero effortlessly on the other side of the veil as well as on this side of it, is exploited no further and indeed has to be quietly buried as Willie Hopkinson's experience deepens. Its function is to designate the hero strikingly as one of those 'mystic types', people of peculiarly sensitive psychological apparatus, who are able to see beneath the surface of ordinary life and who are especially susceptible to the specifically mystical invitation to love God. But Willie's growth in experience scarcely allows for any growth in character. He remains throughout more acted upon than acting, while he is subjected to a selective range of more or less vaguely 'mystical' experiences, which stop well short of ecstasy or indeed any sort of mystical 'prayer' as that word is usually understood. He is deposited on the last page in an admirable state, precisely, to *begin* a noviciate in mystical prayer.

Willie's states of mind are vividly described and the maximum of entertainment derived from them as well. As in her other novels, Evelyn displays a certain genius for high-lighting the collision between the harsh and ephemeral realities of this world and her chosen vehicle of more than ordinary insight. While Willie, for example, is strongly drawn to the tales of King Arthur and the Holy Grail, and finds books real and people not, his parental milieu strongly holds that poetry is 'dangerous stuff'. Of Willie's papa Evelyn writes: 'Modern science was his god, and Huxley the high-priest of his temple, but he had a way with heretics which savoured more of theology than of reason.' But Willie's encounter with poetry demonstrates to him that there are at least *some* other people who know that his 'transcendental perceptions' are not eyewash. Willie, after some ill-advised attempts to explain to his nearest and dearest what he knows of the fate awaiting them, learns to keep quiet:

he [had] learnt once for all the first rule of wisdom—never to emerge from the veil which you neighbour is accustomed to mistake for yourself.

Nor does his education help; at his school 'both cricket and Latin prose were serious things: but the soul was only mentioned on Sundays, and then in a purely official manner'. Education, indeed, tends to stultify his spiritual perceptiveness.

Willie's encounter with the occult society called the 'Searchers of the Soul' is not of great importance save as providing a satirical picture of such a body and introducing a confidant and fellow seeker, Stephen. To Stephen, Willie can describe his view of life and what it feels like to be aware of the grey world. The epic quality of his situation appears clearly in his description of himself as the lonely pioneer of a new world.

> I've thought sometimes . . . that perhaps I'm the first of a new regime. A trial-piece, you know; an experiment. It's about time something new was evolved from the race isn't it? And isolated specimens aren't usual in nature. Which is lucky; it's not nice to be one. That mixture of fatigue and foolishness which the first man who stood upright must have felt, when he limped and stumbled amongst the four-footed things, is just as what I feel now. That want of incentive for tree-climbing, weakness and lostness in forests made for creeping and leaping creatures, which he must have had—shame for his state mixed with secret knowledge of his new powers—all that is just a parable of my life, going with new perceptions amongst people who instinctively resent the light (p. 107).

Such a passage is a remarkable application of the evolutionary optimism of the time, which will also have to be noticed in connection with *Mysticism*. Here, among other things, Evelyn has given dramatic context to a thought of Inge's to the effect that the 'dim consciousness of the *beyond*' having led men to 'obstinate questionings of sense and outward things', we may call these if we will 'a sort of higher instinct, perhaps an anticipation of the evolutionary process' (*Christian Mysticism*, Introduction). This idea receives many an echo from Evelyn in her later Bergsonian phase.

There are many other passages in this book which would stand quotation. But perhaps nowhere does Evelyn's awareness of the comic potential of Willie's predicament show to better advantage than in the passage where he attempts to explain himself to his girl-friend, Mildred, a person 'of sharp, shallow intelligence' with whom, not surprisingly, he fails to persevere. This exchange rounds off a chapter:

> "I am lonely!" he said abruptly, "I want your friendship! We are in sympathy, I know—But there are things that I must tell you. I am not quite like other people."
>
> "Of course," answered Mildred, "I always saw that." She ceased on the expectant note, and Willie knew that his next words must be definite.
>
> "Yes," he said, "I am—"
>
> He stopped. It was absurd, but he did not know how to go on. He could not say, "I am an immortal spirit," and his condition as yet lacked other substantive. He thought a little, and then added: "I live in two worlds." The phrase came to Mildred as a spark in darkness. It startled but did not illuminate. She did not perceive that this was their moment of communion: she was a person who needed explanatory titles of her Book of Life. "How interesting!" she said (p. 158).

For much of the book Willie's perceptions inspire him chiefly with dread. He sees through far too much to be comfortable. He knows the minimum conditions required for his salvation and these appear to be the last consideration of those who purportedly love him. Thus, as his father burbles on about his future, Willie reflects: 'These careers that you speak of are all *maya*, illusion. The necessity is that my body shall be placed in surroundings which will help, and not stunt the soul, which is real'. Later he finds corroboration for his point of view in books and expresses his insight with a rather different nuance:

> Anything can be profoundly important so long as one is careful to look at nothing else. But once glance at the stars, once open the books of the mystics and the game is up—the panorama can never deceive us again (p. 183).

From this perspective there are 'prophets and truth-tellers' who should be listened to, and Willie sites Plotinus, Blake, Swedenborg, 'the Indian philosophers', Dante, and the poets, who 'have looked beyond the shadow of earth and seen another Reality'. Eventually, as Willie feels his way from his rather negative dread towards the Reality spoken of by the poets and seers, he comes upon the Churches, or rather the Church, and Art. Catholic ceremonial, the statues, the buildings, seem to promise a truly spiritual dimension; he is encouraged, as he enters such a church, by a regular worshipper who assures him that a Catholic church is a place where 'the other world passes through into this'. The Catholic worshipper continues:

> Catholic sanctuaries are charged with a kind of holy magic. They are so old, so venerable; their very walls are saturate with God. "Raise the stone, and there thou shalt find Me: Cleave the wood and there I am." But Protestants discourage ecstasy —Theirs is the religion of common-sense. They turn their enthusiasm towards work, not faith. You will find their churches empty except at the hours of service. . . . Even then you won't find any intimate sense of joy in the congregation. It seems natural to the Englishman to behave coldly and correct-ly to his God (p. 197).

The speaker concludes his 'word in season' with the observation
that 'the reformed religions knocked all the poetry out of
Christianity'.

As for Art, it is before a Florentine picture in the National
Gallery that Willie gains his deepest sense of reality as divine,
before a 'very lovely panel which is called "The Madonna adoring
the Infant Christ".' Evelyn's description of Willie's rapt absorp-
tion in this picture would have to be quoted in full to do it justice.
We shall almost certainly find no more accurate description of
the state of her own feelings as she paused before this particular
picture and others in Italy. Indeed it is impossible to ignore the
fact that Willie at this stage in his history is twenty-three years old,
the age Evelyn was when she first found Italy. Plotinus and Dante
are her chief authorities for most of Willie's experiences but his,
or rather her, reaction to this particular subject seems especially
her own. The nugget of Platonic philosophy which coalesces in
her description of this experience and her own interpretation of it
are summed up in two sentences which reveal Willie's understanding of the panel:

> He had a new vision of the world. He saw it as a shadow cast by
> the Divine Beauty—a loveliness of which material beauty was
> the Sacrement, the faint image thrown by God on the mirror of
> sense. In the Madonna he found the symbol of a reconciling
> principle looking lovingly upon humanity, which it cherished
> and fed (pp. 214ff.).

This 'symbol' in fact announces Evelyn's evocation of the pietà
in her remaining novels as a crucial hieroglyphic of reconciliation.
But pain, finally, is far from Willie's thoughts in *The Grey
World*. He does not really advance beyond a state of, for him,
satisfying metaphysical hygiene. Later less comfortable developments are faintly suggested in the words of the wise woman-
mystic of the concluding pages: 'Beauty after all is the visual side

of goodness: it is Christ immanent in the world: and its crucifixion still goes on' (p. 303).

Evelyn's second novel, *The Lost Word*, is a great deal more
ambitious; indeed, it is far too dense with mystical meanings and
happenings to be altogether digestible. Once again a young man,
Paul Vickery, is the hero. We are introduced to him as a boy and
accompany a rushed account of his adolescence up to and including his university days. Then we see him taken on as a private
architect to build a church on a friend's industrial estate, and
witness the enthusiasm and agony of artistic procreation on this
task while he simultaneously attempts to scale the heights of
mystical experience and falls deeply in love with an artistic girl,
Catherine. In the dénouement he settles for marriage and renounces the heights of mysticism to follow a 'lower road'. The
title of the novel derives from the notion familiar to masonry that
the task of the would-be adept is to find and exploit anew the
'lost word' of masonry, 'the lost Word of Power', by which the
temple of King Solomon had been built. Paul becomes conscious
of the mystical significance of this word and its importance to him
as the focus of his personal vocation and quest, when a masonic
rite of initiation in which he takes part in unsalubrious surroundings in Oxford, unexpectedly 'takes'. To begin with he does not
look back but struggles to achieve perfect realisation of his new
found goal at the twin levels of mystical self-realisation and artistic
creation of ideal beauty. In the event he fails at both levels.

The connection between this novel and *The Grey World* are
numerous, at least to start with. Paul has early intimations of his
vocation and his father, an Anglican dean, soon finds in him 'an
annoying turn for mysticism; a thing that reads prettily enough in
saintly biographies, but is rightly held to be out of place in an
Established Church'. Once again there is little sympathy between
the son and his father, described as 'a muscular clergyman who
drew a sharp distinction between Popish architecture and its

literary equivalents'. Yet Paul is very much a child of the close,
finding the cathedral 'the home of every mystery' and becoming
especially fond of a mutilated stone carving of an angel high up in
the roof away from the vulgar gaze. Paul, naturally, is destined
for Holy Orders and goes up to an Oxford where 'the ingenious
aberrations of modern theology had already effaced the imprint
of an intense and tractarian past'. Here he falls out with orthodox
Christianity and suffers a period of agnosticism qualified by his
college tutor as a typical instance of such 'little attacks of intellectual measles'. His attraction to the secret society of the Masons is
plausibly prepared for by the authorial comment: 'Your dreamer
may do without a creed, but he always wants a ritual . . .' The
external approach to the particular ritual thrown in Paul's way is
tawdry and off-putting, as was that of the occultist group in *The
Grey World*. Nor are the participants prepossessing here, either;
all are described as 'self-conscious' and the Jaeger socks of the
Tyler (doorkeeper) clash (if that is the word) with his sword. The
author again comments:

> The whole matter was a play, an archaic play robbed of the
> picturesqueness that it should have possessed by the absence of
> artistry and ritual sense in modern performers. Such things
> cannot, of course, appeal to a cultured public (p. 42).

Evelyn here, as elsewhere in her novels, shows herself a trifle
over anxious about what her readers may or should think. Her
irony is, to put it mildly, distracting at such a point, even if it
does help the biographer to see where her real sympathies lie.

For the ritual 'magic' works. Paul is transported by the masonic
words and gestures of initiation and he, and the reader, are treated
to a full-dress 'mystical experience', described over some eight
pages, during the course of which a 'new eager being' makes itself
felt in him and, using his eyes, convinces him of the unreality of
this insubstantial world and of the existence of a 'real and external

world whose faint reflection we are accustomed to call Nature and Actuality' (pp. 44–45). His vision has the effect of transposing his environment to his inward eye and he marvels:

> that where hideous houses stood, and hoardings clothed in the dingy vulgarity of provincial advertisements, where dirty pavements were flecked with paper, mud, orange-peel; there also, in another dimension more real than the sordid illusion our senses create, were radiant fields and magical forests very cool and dim: that angels, and the great and pure people who walk in the light, might jostle the undergraduates in the quads and the walls of the City of Sarras rise in and through the buildings of New College extension (p. 46).

One tends to follow Evelyn's descriptions of such experiences, of which this book offers several examples, with a certain fascinated horror. While there is much that is suggestive and intriguing the mannered and allusive style smacks of the 'purple passage' so that one puts the book down with the feeling that it is much harder to describe a mystical experience convincingly than some people think. Since Evelyn's time others have attempted similar descriptions more or less directly, Aldous Huxley and John Fowles for example, but generally with equally unhappy results. The indirect analogical mode of the historic mystics of East and West was, it seems, not chosen without reason. In the case of Evelyn's Paul Vickery, he is transported through a series of grandiose visions more or less connected with the rite he is undergoing and ends with a deep conviction of his call to set out on the quest for the lost word of mystic vision, the discovery of which seems to him inseparable from the actual exercise of the building craft.

We shall not follow Paul through the exciting business of building his church. Thanks to the introduction of this idea we are thrown into a well-coloured and characterised group of arts and crafts devotees, 'The Guild of Apprentices of Saint-Eloy', who include a more or less lapsed Anglican parson, another youngish man of apparently inexhaustible wisdom who is a Roman Catholic, Mark Gwent; a craftswoman bearing a strong resemblance physically and perhaps in other ways to Evelyn herself, named Emma Brewster; a 'garrulous little fool 'of an older woman, Letty, who is really a saint; and finally, the passionate Catherine who turns Paul from a Galahad into a Lancelot. Mark Gwent, the wise commentator, charts Paul's headlong career and tries very hard himself to save him from 'the corrupting influences of a merely human love'. In scenes of great passion Paul declares his love for Catherine, joyously declaring the 'dream' of achieving perfection through chaste adherence to the task in hand well-lost for his equivalent of love in a cottage. But Catherine renounces Paul for his own sake, in fact the plotting of the story arranges for her to do it twice, which somewhat mars the effect, especially as they do in fact marry. All things being possible in this rather strange world, Mark Gwent is unexpectedly married off to Emma Brewster.

The final chapters of the book are planned on an elaborate theological schema. While it is fairly clear that Paul is on the one hand a Christ who has failed to be crucified, it is made quite plain that his vocation is not thereby entirely renounced. Only now it has to be worked out at a 'lower' level. Instead of being given the 'Lost Word' of mystical knowledge he is given the 'Substituted Word' of 'sacrifice'. In a curious way this switching of horses in mid-career is made out to be a positive gain for him, so much so that one begins to wonder about the depth of Mark Gwent's reading of the way things should have gone for him. Paul Vickery, in abandoning the highest path, achieves a kind of maturity which, it is insinuated, he could not have achieved otherwise, an hypothesis amply justified by the passionate, egotistical and self-mascerating fervour he displays in the book's earlier chapters. Evelyn, describing how Paul at last sees the 'whole scheme of things' in the 'clear light of reality' puts his final situation as follows:

> He was snatched from the false dualism of matter and spirit to the mystical union of the shadow and the idea. No longer with the single eye of the determined visionary, but rather with the sane outlook of an immortal spirit that has learned, not despised, the lesson of the flesh, he perceived the life of the body also to be holy, needful, consecrate. It was no squalid illusion, no foul miasma from which one must escape, but a firm and friendly highway which led by difficult places to the mystic City of the Quest (pp. 312–13).

And yet Paul remains under the sign of the maimed angel, and the church whose construction is carried forward *pari passu* with his apparent advance in the spiritual quest is not completed by him but achieves an inglorious banalisation at the hands of his sponsor, the industrialist.

Where Paul's career leaves us in some doubts about the intentions of the novelist that of Catherine is handled with greater clarity if not with much more elegance. Indeed she almost comes to usurp the centre of the stage and it is she who is represented as in some sense redeeming Paul by her unselfish attempt first to avoid his marrying her at all, secondly to see that his suffering through the loss of his high vocation is ultimately redemptive for both of them. The theological mystery involved in this second strand in her reasoning is brought home to her before an image of the mother holding her crucified Son, or pietà, in the cathedral of St Nazaire at Carcassonne, where she and Paul have called on their honeymoon. As she gazes on the image during mass Catherine receives a strong sense that she can be herself a mediator for Paul and give him a new start on his road to the 'Better Country'. Evidently Catherine here *is* the image she contemplates. If Paul has not been crucified his anguish at being shut off from his visionary world inflicts wounds as grave. She is his nurse, suffering for him even as he suffers on account of his love for her. Thus, for this pair at least, love is in very truth a great equaliser. While a certain doubt remains about a Paul who has renounced a clear invitation to the 'pursuit of perfection and beauty' there is no ambiguity about the reply each would have to make to the question put originally to Catherine: 'Are you so finely built that you must be your own redeemer?' Each progresses from a relative egoism to maturity through realising that redemption is, *for them*, only to be attained through the other.

It is not easy to handle a romance in such a way as to lay bare the mystery of atoning love each lover can and perhaps should be, to the other. It is doubly difficult when your hero is someone as complicated as Paul Vickery is in *The Lost Word*. In her final novel *The Column of Dust* Evelyn satisfies herself with a single passably split-minded protagonist and charts her, and only her, career from immaturity to maturity, from romantic mystical questing to self-fulfilment and self-transcendence through self-forgetting. Her heroine, Constance Tyrrel, dabbling in the solemn art of conjuring spirits, finds herself possessed by one such who has been rather angling for just this kind of opportunity to survey the sublunary scheme through sublunary eyes. Constance's consciousness comes in fact to be shared by a denizen of Plotinus' world of intelligible spirit, the world of 'nous', in which a brilliant intellectual and aesthetic sensibility may be combined, on Evelyn's reading of the Alexandrian philosopher, both with an ignorance of the higher reaches of mystical union with the One, and a certain itching desire to know how the metaphysically lower orders manage things. Constance becomes reconciled to her fate and takes this Plotinian 'watcher' on a tour of her life. But soon this life begins to take an unusual turn. Going on holiday from her prosaic activities as second-hand and antiquarian bookseller she comes, it seems by accident, upon the shrine of the Holy Grail, hidden in a chapel deep in Cumberland hill-country. She is accompanied on this occasion, as she has been for much of her life apparently, by a mysterious girl child, named Vera, of more than ordinary detestableness. The guardian of the Grail is a wild young ex-priest called Martin, who also turns out to be a repository of mystic wisdom on the lines of Mark Gwent in the earlier novel. Back in London Constance's affairs become more complex. She strikes up an innocent relationship with a married man, Andrew, and through him with his wife, Muriel, a superficial woman of artistic pretensions whose like has also been met with. A crisis begins in Constance's life when her developing relations with Andrew seem to oblige her to make clean breast of the fact that Vera is her illegitimate daughter. Becoming ill herself, she is suddenly faced with the prospect of tending her sick daughter Vera. Almost simultaneously Martin, apparently also far from well, bursts in on her, bringing the Holy Grail with him, and decrees that she is to be its next guardian. She accepts and also fully shoulders her responsibility for Vera whom she nurses to life, surrendering her own existence squarely for the sake of the revolting little girl's. She is rewarded by mystical union with the one, bearing with her the Watcher, now released by her death from his temporary encapsulation in human consciousness and free to return to his abode a sadder and a wiser spirit.

The Column of Dust contains some of the best pages Evelyn ever wrote. The handling of the initial chapters is especially remarkable when, after evoking the mental world of Plotinian intelligences and the characteristics of the one about to be 'incarnated' in Constance Tyrrel, we are abruptly transported into the latter's private seance in the back room of her shop, and see the 'door' being opened from her side. The upshot is a perfect example of what can be done by exploiting M. R. James (the James of 'Whistle O' my Lad' and 'I'll Come to You' in particular) for the purposes of constructing metaphysical fables. It is a success which prompts the reflection that *all* Evelyn Underhill's novels open well, whatever the bad patches which afflict them as they develop.

In this case, once 'possessed', Constance begins to suffer the advantages and disadvantages of carrying about with her an illuminated consciousness with which she is not always entirely in accord but by which she is constantly being instructed. Sometimes, the experience of the Watcher within her is described as taking place in her consciousness as though *she* were experiencing in the *same* way. Sometimes their reactions are contrasted and a dialogue ensues. It is only after a certain interval that the disaccords begin, as it were, to reverberate upon the Watcher and he in his turn begins to learn from her.

The first effect of this sharing of minds is to change radically Constance's way of looking at things, though the realisation of *why* this has happened is only very gradually borne in upon her. Originally Evelyn writes of her heroine that 'she believed nothing, and was therefore the more ready to believe anything; having all the transcendental curiosity of the true materialist' (p. 11). But after her occultist experiment she encounters 'a rift in the solid stuff out of which she had built her universe' and the text continues:

> She had seen, abruptly, the insecurity of those defences which protect our illusions and ward off the horrors of truth. She had found a little hole in the wall of appearances; and peeping through, had caught a glimpse of that seething pot of spiritual forces whence, now and then, a bubble rises to the surface of things . . . (p. 32).

In fact, under the impact of the Watcher's visitation, her standards of 'reality' are largely reversed. The visible and palpable becomes in some sense less real for her than the invisible and intangible. It is from this standpoint that she finds herself saying of the 'Grand

Grimoire'—her 'conjuring' manual: 'this is modern science and
the things that modern science hasn't yet got to' (p. 45).

But Constance's sense-life must go on, however much it may
vex the transcendentalist within. Seeing how his 'vehicle's' own
life, as well as that of her fellows, is apparently obsessed by rushing
hither and thither on a thousand and one trivial pretexts, he is
forced to exclaim: 'This activity is a loathsome illusion it has no
relation to the real.' And even, he feels, if people can't keep quiet
·in their lives, at least they might have the sense to long for death.
But this, Constance explains, is 'against the rules'. One consequence of her double life is that Constance, as Willie Hopkinson,
becomes subject to attacks of fear and dread. Her sense of the
vanity, futility and evanescence of human existence is such that
she even comes to doubt her own existence: 'She thought,
"Suppose that I were not real? Suppose that I, too, were a dream?"
She turned from that vision in horror and fear' (p. 68). But the
Watcher also has moments of dread. As he accompanies his carnal
envelope on the London Underground their common eyes light
on an evangelical poster: 'Be not deceived: God is not mocked.'
The Watcher is at once reminded of Reality and taken back to his
former days of eternal seeking of 'the Idea'. The nightmarish
possibility strikes him that he may be for ever cut off from
transcendental Beauty and enmeshed in the hideous dream of
common human experience: 'Oh, cruel, treacherous and blinding
dream!' (p. 105).

Various opportunities are taken in the story to exhibit to the
Watcher the human penchant for cultivating illusion, apparently
for its own sake. In the two most conspicuous examples, a stage
play and the pageantry of a state visit, the Watcher and his pupil
undergo contrasting experiences. At the play Constance, in
Andrew's company, is carried away by the 'triumphant sentimentalism' of the production ('The Breton Bride') and feels the
burden of everyday reality lifted from her. She suddenly becomes

deeply conscious of herself as she really is in her loneliness and
need for Andrew. At which the Watcher, having first felt contempt for the whole performance as a 'lurid and untruthful simu-
lation of an existence that was itself untrue' (p. 108), is brought to
realise that these strange people among whom he is living need
'artifice' in order to become 'natural'. After the show, standing
with a Constance left alone and sad under the mocking eternity
of the night sky, the Watcher knows the warmth of compassion.
On the second occasion, the state pageant, Constance's enhanced
vision, her 'new-found adoration of beauty', leads her to revel in
the splendour and display but at the same time she is led by an
equally strong clear-eyed disenchantment to dismiss the whole
thing as 'a picturesque sham' (p. 181). Here the Watcher steps in
to correct her dismissive rationalism and to point out that all the
panoply enhances a genuinely important 'ideal truth' viz. 'the
mighty ideal of government' which finally makes sense, to him at
least, only as 'a projection of omnipotent Will' (p. 183).

Initially the Watcher and Constance are never so close as when
contemplating nature. In a chapter placed under an epigraph from
Gerald Manley Hopkins:

> Nature is never spent
> There lives the dearest freshness deep down things;
> And though the last lights from the black West went,
> Oh, morning, at the brown brink Eastward, springs!

she explores a north western England transfigured by her new
vision:

> There was a hay-rick in the neighbouring field, its patient shape
> responsive to the play of slanting light. In the hedge by which
> they walked, the sharp and eager fingers of a hawthorn were
> stretched out against the greenish sky. Its clear crisp edges were
> instinct with vitality, and with beauty, which is the spiritual

aspect of intensest life. These leaves—and behind them, the teeming earth with all its children—cried out for recognition to this Sister of theirs, this impassioned amateur of experience. Constance was glad with a vicarious vanity to think her mother so beautiful: proud that she, who was one of the family, might show to her visitor one of the lovelist moments of the dear earth (p. 121).

The experience is transferred to the Watcher himself when he sees the wild flowers of the countryside in 'their essential reality, their unsullied radiance: matter for the exploration of many aeons tossed into the pageant of one sunny afternoon' (p. 129). But this is also a matter for humiliation of the Watcher whose own eyes are washed by such a 'luxuriant out pouring of beauty' enabling him to catch 'as it were, a sidelong glimpse of God'. He is humiliated in a different way, however, on another occasion, at an earlier stage when Constance had been quite bowled over by a dazzling vision of a 'shining tree', a tree as it is really is. The denouement of this incident announces later developments for the contemplative moment is broken by a seller of violets with a hideous infant. The Watcher, ecstatic like Constance, is revolted and has a violent desire to take evasive action. Constance, more than aware of his point of view, yet also feels a deeper sense of compassion and 'reverence for life'. After a struggle the Watcher is cast down but not yet defeated.

The final climax of Constance's disagreement with the Watcher is also the climax of the novel. It is the moment when she is forced to choose between the ecstatic categories of mystical consciousness and the relatively trivial and demeaning demands of a human love totally devoid of emotional rewards and consolations. The struggle grows in intensity as Christmas approaches and the Watcher is driven by his 'malignant love' for Constance to declare war on her for her own sake. The basic issue is: 'Why bother about Vera?' For if the illegitimate Vera, who is the visible remainder of a period when Constance revolted against the class and privilege of her inheritance to establish a stake of some sort in real life as she *then* imagined it, were out of the way, her mother could, the Watcher argues, regain peace of mind and pursue the vision beautiful without let or hindrance. Vera, whose radically vitiated nature is never in doubt from the first moment we meet her, will never, in the Watcher's terminology 'transmit the Idea' (p. 270), she is a 'selfish, cruel creature', 'a little heap of appetite and habits' an 'incompleted thing' (pp. 289–91). Even the saintly Martin's exhortations are somewhat ambiguous at this critical moment. For Martin, in delivering the cup of the Grail to her, had said:

> Yield yourself to love—don't shirk it—that is all! You are on the very verge of waking, you know. You have fear and amazement; and that is the initiating touch, the peep through the bars (p. 234).

And his words urging her to find a place for the Grail in her life contained more of romance and ecstasy than of pain and sacrifice.

It is in a church upon which she has accidentally stumbled in a dense London fog that Constance finally perceives that she is being asked for her life in exchange for Vera's. It is thus that the Grail transforms her into its own likeness and a living vehicle of atonement, that she becomes, in her turn 'that antique symbol of incarnate divinity: a weary self-less mother wholly concentrated on the well-being of her child' (p. 276). Her acceptance of this destiny takes place to the accompaniment of the recitation of the litany for the dead, for she has wandered into a church belonging to a religious order devoted to such prayers. One petition strikes her particularly: 'That thou wouldst be pleased to admit them to the contemplation of Thy adorable Beauty, we beseech Thee to hear us.' This she understands fully at the very end of her life.

'One must share in that Beauty, contribute to it, as the one condition of true sight' (p. 295). But even before this, when she was still in the throes of her battle at the bed-side of Vera, she had been briefly reminded that beauty has many manifestations. As she enters a nearby fish-shop she feels a 'sudden agony of love' and senses deeply her solidarity with its prosaic humanity: 'Its dust and hers were of the same company. In loving it she loved her own people, her nearest kin.' Constance lays down her life for her fellow-dust and thus fulfils the conditions laid upon her by the symbol of the Grail, visible sign of 'the folly, the quixotry, the humanity of the Cross' (p. 276). She also becomes redemptive and mediatorial for the Watcher who finally contemplates in her a reflected ray of the divine Beauty, as Dante did in Beatrice. This Plotinian gazer is thus 'redeemed by that humanity into whose august secrets he had tried to look' and 'initiated into heaven' (p. 304).

Do Evelyn's novels, taken together, suggest therefore that, for the mystic, two worlds are 'better' than one? In the first place, certainly, for Evelyn mystical experience seems inseparable from some kind of enhancement of consciousness, some expansion of perceptual and indeed, aesthetic horizons. To be mystically initiated is to see things as they are, in their meanness and insignificance when viewed in opposition to the divine, in their luminosity and grandeur when seen bathed in divine radiance. But at this stage the mind is also subject to fear and insecurity: it may get enmeshed in deceptive loves, is relatively immature and its powers undeveloped. The first novel hardly takes us beyond this point. But further stages have to be attained and they demand suffering. Mysticism involves *life*, not merely vision; it is not simply a matter of cultivating a latent potentiality of the soul in cosy isolation from all other cares. In this sense it is not 'better' to live in two worlds. It is pain, tension and finally the loss of one's private claimful ego-centred life for the sake of 'the other'. The first 'kiss of God', thanks to which the world first appears to be bathed in eternity, seems on Evelyn's view to convey little or no inkling of the sacrifice involved in the later stages of the practice of 'the science of love'. Her two later novels are built up on the idea that total self-surrender even to the apparent sacrifice of the vision itself, is necessary if the fullest possible integration of human life is to be achieved. Once the sacrifice has been made the mystic has worked out in himself mystically the life-story of Jesus and is re-united with the vision, no longer as mere spectator but as part of it. If this dimension of self-loss and resurrection is worked out in *The Lost Word* in such a way as to cast some doubt on its general inevitability, there is no room for doubt in *The Column of Dust*. Constance Tyrrel's physical death only reinforces dramatically the mystical death to which she has already by the end surrendered herself. Chesterton's dictum therefore needs qualifying if it is to be applied to the 'mystics' of Evelyn's novels. Two lives *are* better than one but only on the condition that a process of painful re-integration intervenes eventually to re-establish unity at a higher level.

Such a brief account of the contents and themes of the books could both make them sound better than they are and ignore many incidental delights. Evelyn may have suffered from the lack of searching criticism of literary style and presentation normally available in sixth form and univeristy. Most of her books in the pre-war period suffer from a tendency to 'over-write', to affect an archaic-seeming special mystical language which may for some be an insuperable obstacle to perfect enjoyment. She at times also indulges to excess her preference for dialogue over reported speech or description, as, for example, when the distraught Constance Tyrrel finds herself beset by a second inward voice which engages in argument with the Watcher, to her, and the reader's, deep discomfort. Some defects of plot arrangement have already been indicated.

In general Evelyn tends to load her stories with symbolism, some of which is obvious, some less so. Thus in the middle of the highly charged interview between the preying Elsa Levi and Willie Hopkinson the latter breaks the spell she is weaving round him simply by turning his face to the sunlight as it streams through her drawing-room window. Even in the short story of *The Mountain Image* the sky and the clouds represented the eternal, and are evoked in the same sense in the novels. Constance Tyrrel's discovery of the Holy Grail is entirely due to the fact that the hired pony and trap run away with her on the fells and this event thus 'stand in' for the deep, unconscious impulse which drives her in pursuit of her destiny. In the last analysis all the characters in these books, major as well as minor, derive their interest primarily from the theological meanings and values which attach to them and it is this avowedly symbolic or fabulous character of her fictional writing which leaves one free to appreciate her often ingenious handling of so much incidental symbolic material. The minor characters also add an extra dimension of humour at which Evelyn excels. Even *The Column of Dust* is at times highly entertaining, mostly at the expense of one female character's pseudo-mystical cackle but sometimes also through the theme of the discrepancies which can arise between appearance and reality, to which the discussion of book-bindings lends itself.

All Evelyn's mature fiction was written in the six years between 1903–1909 and it is scarcely surprising that it should have a rather distinctive flavour. It well represents her four major discoveries of that and the immediately preceding period: philosophy, i.e. Neoplatonism, theism or mysticism, the Roman Catholic Church, human love. The first two of those headings can only be touched on summarily here insofar as they need to be linked with what we already know of her personal contacts at this time. Our consideration of the remaining two will help to complete the portrait of Evelyn Underhill as she begins to embark on *Mysticism*.

If we wish to find any literary theory or doctrine behind the strongly symbolical drift of Evelyn's fiction it is probably unnecessary to look further than the literary creed expounded by her friend Arthur Machen on more than one occasion but chiefly in his *Hieroglyphics* of 1902, which represents an expansion of his article 'The Paradox of Literature' in the periodical *Literature* for 27 August 1898. As summarised in the words of his biographer, Machen's view was that:

> there are certain truths about the universe as a whole and its constitution as distinct from the particular things in it that come before our observation, which cannot be grasped by human reason, or expressed in precise words: but they can be apprehended, by some people at least, in a semi-mystical experience, which he calls ecstasy, and a work of art is great insofar as this experience is caught and expressed in it. Because, however, the truths concerned transcend a language attuned to the description of material objects, the expression can only be through hieroglyphics, and it is of such hieroglyphics that literature consists (op. cit., p. 67).

The application of these words to Evelyn's writing does not need to be laboured. They help to explain her carefree espousal of certain blatantly improbable, indeed miraculous and all but absurd situations simply for the sake of their metaphorical or symbolical value or, as Machen would have put it, for their value as 'hieroglyphs' of some ineffable aspect of the human condition. In an age which doted on 'the psychic' she was open to misunderstanding and, as her reviews show, was misunderstood by those who wished to see in her books a fresh witness to transmigration of souls, supersensory perception and allied 'phenomena', whereas nothing could have been further from her intention.

On the other hand she was unwilling to have *The Column of Dust* read as an 'allegory'. In an unpublished letter to Margaret

Robinson she wrote: 'No! it's not an allegory, never thought of such a thing. It's my idea of a realistic novel!' Realistic certainly, but in a very special sense quite other than that attributed to the word by Machen when castigating such 'realistic' writers as Jane Austen, Thackeray and various contemporary 'realists' in a more conventional sense of the word, for whom he had no use whatsoever. In what appears to be her only published statement of her literary point of view, an article of 1908 defending May Sinclair's novel *The Helpmate* from the Grundy-ite aspersions cast on it by Lady Robert Cecil, Evelyn wrote:

> The true business of the novelist is to shew eternal things in and through temporal things. This, and only this, gives permanent value to his work.

In the case of May Sinclair it was not 'realism' which had been violated in Eleanor Cecil's eyes, but convention, she having ventured to illustrate how a man might achieve salvation and indeed return the better to his marriage through an unconventional sexual relationship. For Evelyn May Sinclair's novel is governed by the fact of 'the sanctity and necessity of mortality, together with the fact that for those souls which are immersed in human life the spiritual is best attained by a faithful acceptance of material things.' So expressed May Sinclair's objectives would seem to have been very close to those of Evelyn herself although Evelyn never aspired to May Sinclair's particular excellence which Lady Cecil sneeringly referred to as the 'deft manipulation of psychology, fact and sentiment'. In Evelyn's case the quest for psychological realism, even in a sense she and May Sinclair might have accepted, is entirely subordinate to larger metaphysical considerations which she shared with Arthur Machen rather than with her friend and sister woman novelist.

Thus both Machen and Evelyn Underhill incorporate the Holy

Grail into their 'fiction'. Machen's interest in this topic was stimulated by Arthur Waite and he did a little research on the subject, publishing his findings in a series of Academy articles published in 1907. The theme occurs dominantly in his novel *The Secret Glory*, published in 1922 though written some fifteen years earlier, and in his long short story, *The Great Return*, published in 1915. For Machen the Holy Grail is perhaps *the* hieroglyph, *the* crystallisation in one sacred emblem of all man's transcendental yearning, *the* gateway to vision and lasting appeasement of his discontents. But it is not, for him, the centre of specifically atonement-linked meanings as it is for Evelyn Underhill, and it is worth at this point taking up again her letter to Margaret Robinson in which she dwells on this aspect of her last novel, the aspect of sacrifice which Miss Robinson had particular difficulty in accepting into her scheme of things. This letter which, amazingly, the editor of her *Collected Letters* did not publish, states succinctly a position from which she never retreated and which is fundamental to her fiction, as to her later work: 'Don't marvel at your own temerity in criticising', she writes to Margaret Robinson,

Why should you? Of course, this thing wasn't written *for* you—I never write for anyone at all, except in letters of direction! But I take leave to think the doctrine contained in it is one you'll have to assimilate sooner or later & which won't do you any harm. It's not *mine* you know. You will find it all in Eckhardt, the Imitation & lots of other places— They all knew, as Richard of St Victor said, that the Fire of Love *burns*. We have not fufilled our destiny when we have sat down at a safe distance from it, purring like overfed cats, 'suffering is the ancient law of love'— & its highest pleasure into the bargain, oddly enough. Even Father Figgis says 'If you wish to be comfortable don't be a Christian'. A sponge cake and milk religion is neither true to this world nor to the next.

As for the Christ being too august a word for our little hardships—I think it is truer that it is *so* august as to give our little
hardships a tincture of Royalty once we try them up into it.
I don't think a Pattern which was 'meek & lowly' is likely to
fail of application to very humble and ordinary things. For
most of us don't get a chance *but* the humble & ordinary:
& He came that we might *all* have life more abundantly,
according to our measure. There that's all!

The novels are predominantly theological and mystical but
we can reasonably suppose that they are also very much about
Evelyn's life and her practical decisions. Enough unflattering
references to the Anglican Church have probably already been
cited to illustrate what she considered typical Anglican attitudes,
and the '*even* Father Figgis' just quoted (he was a noted Anglican
writer and preacher of the time) speaks volumes, notwithstanding
the fact that she had admitted to quite admiring him in a slightly
earlier letter. It is enough to add that one of the very few really
nastily unchristian acts described in any of her books occurs when
Constance Tyrrel's supposed friend, Muriel, spurns her after her
avowal of Vera's identity. Muriel, in so doing, is described as
recollecting 'the parental code', i.e. the moral standards of her
father, 'an archdeacon of the established church' (pp. 250–51).
Anglican clergymen only seem tolerable to the Evelyn Underhill
of the novels if they have abandoned their cloth and become
'outsiders'. Conversely, although we have no exemplary Catholic
priests in her fiction it is evident that the Catholic atmosphere is
the one she prefers both literally and figuratively to breathe. One
of the climactic scenes in *The Lost Word* takes place in the chapel
of Our Lady of Sorrows in what is evidently Westminster
Cathedral, the choice of chapel being clearly related once again
to the pietà theme. Constance reaches her decision to sacrifice
herself in the church of a Roman Catholic religious order; even

Willie Hopkinson has his moments of illumination in Catholic churches.

It is probably idle to speculate whether any of Evelyn's characters are based on her acquaintances. Once it became known that she had written a novel she was naturally taxed with being 'on the watch' as it were. She described what it feels like to become an 'author':

> a sort of dirty floppy ugly Mrs Levi [a character in *The Grey World*] asked me if I was taking notes in Alassio for another novel!! I replied that I *never* drew my characters from life. . . . Sylvia the wretch has advertised me as an 'author' and uncanny persons say 'how interesting' in a hushed voice, & then ask me to advise them about a publisher for books they have not yet written, & how many hundreds they might expect to make by it (letter of 28 March 1904).

But if Evelyn didn't unload her notes on particular individuals into her novels, she could hardly leave *herself* out and we return once again for what they reveal of *her*.

It seems impossible to doubt that her own 'way' is to some extent charted in these books. This way would have been through an awareness of a metaphysical dimension of the universe, a sense of a 'beyond' both transcending and transfiguring the world of space and time; then an awareness that this other world was that of ancient metaphysicians such as Plotinus and modern ones, such as Maeterlinck, the world also of ideal reality as imagined in the legends of mediaeval chivalry. After this we know that she entered on a definite commitment to engage in the quest via occultist initiation. Finally, perhaps through a growing knowledge of mediaeval mysticism and church art and symbolism, she grew aware of the cross of Christ as symbol of atonement and of the Church as guardian of the mysteries which continuously present that atonement to mankind. And once all this had taken root in her mind we must imagine her most probably trying to conceive how it could relate to life in Great Britain in the first decade of the twentieth century and proposing in her novels through various symbols and metaphors the kind of experience which might follow in a London full, on the one hand, with 'mystical place-spirit' (*The Grey World*, p. 175) and, on the other, with signs of 'loathsome illusion' (*The Column of Dust*, p. 65).

It also makes sense to imagine her deciding her *own* problems within the terms of reference plotted in the novels, which brings us again to the figure of the pietà. *The Grey World* lacks a mediatorial figure. In *The Lost Word* the mediator looks as though he is going to be Paul, the mystic hero, but at the last minute turns out to be Catherine the maternal redeeming sweetheart bearing the damaged Paul upon her knees. In *The Column of Dust* the mediatorial idea is grasped from the beginning and from the start it is Constance, aptly so named, who is to offer her life in sacrifice for the ugly reality which she has perpetually shied away from but has been destined to embrace. Vera, whose name also needs to be related to its Latin cognate *veritas* truth, is the human fact, human life, the flesh which has to be loved always and at whatever cost. In *The Path of Eternal Wisdom* (1911) published under the pseudonym 'John Cordelier' Evelyn returned to this symbol as she meditated on the traditional fourth 'station' or stage of Christ's passion, Jesus' meeting with his mother on the way to Calvary. She writes of Mary's anguish and says:

> Here, too, perhaps we may see under the veils something of the share taken by God, the infinitely loving Who is, says Julian of Norwich, not only our Father but our Mother—in the necessary passion of his striving sons . . . God's love, then, which is Height, Might, and Sweetness brooding above us, sorrows for our pain. (pp. 56–7.)

And again, reflecting on the thirteenth station, Jesus Taken Down from the Cross, she writes:

It has been said by a great preacher that 'Jesus dead in the arms of Mary is the central fact of the world's tragedy . . . (for) this is the meeting place of matter and spirit, the world of nature and grace, the higher synthesis of earth and heaven, of man and God.' (pp. 129–30.)

Certainly Evelyn could hardly have seized on a truth more central to Christianity. Since the Creator dirtied his hands in picking up the clay with which to make man, Godhead, Beauty had forever been coming into this world to embrace what is ungodly and un-beautiful, to share its life in order to transform it. The human burden is, therefore, in Evelyn's view, perpetually to renew such redemptive action in space and time.

Thus from 1903 to 1909 we are able to document a single theme in Evelyn Underhill's work, the theme of mysticism and incarnation. In the short stories mystical experience means the quest of the mysterious truth. The priest struggles to embrace it in his oratory, the voyager hands himself over to it blindfold, the carver meddles unwarily and is struck down; the element of pain is present, especially in the case of the priest, but it is not sacrificial. Nor is there any reference to sacrificial pain as such in *The Grey World*. But in the last two novels, those of 1907 and 1909, the quest is no longer self-justificatory and the theme of sacrifice enters. For, according to the standpoint of these novels, the quest of mystical experience for its own sake is illusory. The deepest meaning of life is not ecstasy alone but ecstasy prepared for by sacrifice. It is difficult not to read some of Evelyn's own history into such a paradigm of the human situation. Called as she no doubt believed to a life of union she was also committed by her love of her fiancé to incarnation. With her vivid sense of the gulf fixed between the two worlds of spirit and sense, a gulf so heightened in her novels as to leave no doubt about its reality in her experience, she found in the figure of a redeeming mother

both a hieroglyph of divine maternal love and an apparent reconciliation of these two worlds of spiritual and mundane experience.
What higher vocation could there be than to tread in the foot-
steps of redeeming love so conceived? and become oneself 'a
meeting-place of matter and spirit, the worlds of nature and
grace, the higher synthesis of earth and heaven, of man and God'?
If her reasoning implicitly and explicitly followed something like
this pattern, as her books suggest, the decision to accept incarnation was, we may assume, the greatest of her life, whatever
particular form it may have taken. Her teaching on mysticism
as well as her day-to-day life as Mrs Stuart Moore in the large
house in Campden Hill Square were the continuing reflection of
this choice.

Evelyn's novels were well received on the whole by contemporaries though none so well as the first and none so badly as the
last. The reviews of The Grey World were all pasted, probably by
Evelyn herself, into a hard-bound notebook which survives, and
bear witness to the great impression made by her originality on
Edwardian critics. The New York Evening Post (25 October
1904) in a perceptive half-column headed 'Mysticism and Daily
Life' well summed up the style and content of her first book:
'Written in a style at once "literary" and simple of unusual charm
and sureness, the story is an interpretation of the realistic details
of the daily life of some such mysticism as Blake and Maeterlinck
express in poetry.' But the last word on The Column of Dust was
uttered by Punch's literary critic who, before briefly impugning
Evelyn's 'sincerity', states that 'after reading Miss Underhill's
latest supernatural novel' he is inclined to quote the famous
criticism upon Jaberwocky: 'It fills me with ideas only I don't
know what they are.'[3] Margaret Robinson's difficulties have
already been referred to. She seems to have had the impression

3. This review of Punch, 10 November 1909, is referred to in a letter of
   1 December 1909, Letters, p. 107.

from this book that Evelyn, whom she had not met personally, was a 'pious and pain-enduring individual'. Evelyn's reply is a useful corrective to a too solemn view of her work:

> Do get these ideas out of your head! No, everybody does *not* "find my works painful!" Some find them dull and some eccentric—and others read their own prepossessions into them!! They don't tear themselves to ribbons over them anyhow— and neither do I. I just write what comes into my head and leave the rest to luck.

But the abiding impression of Evelyn's novels has been unfavourable. R. H. Benson seems to have been the only contemporary to pay her the compliment of imitation in rather distantly invoking a symbolical pietà at both the beginning and the end of his novel, *Initiation* (1914). He also sets the death of his (inevitable) Catholic baronet in the winter and evokes the Grail as the 'Cup of Sacrifice' on the penultimate page of book. Charles Williams damns all Evelyn's novels with faint praise and, if he pauses over *The Column of Dust*, it is only to find that:

> though the moral of the . . . book is not less than noble, its literary effect is less than exciting. She had not, on the whole, an imaginative style. . . . (*Letters*, p. 10).

Against which judgement Mrs Belloc Lowndes had some strong words to say in *The Merry Wives of Westminster*, but she brought no supporting analysis to the works she wished to champion. Mrs Belloc Lowndes had met Evelyn through Mrs Crackenthorpe, who as we know from another source (letter to Hubert 6 May 1905) published a ballad of Evelyn's in her periodical The Outlook.[4] In fact their first meeting must have taken place at about the same date as the publication of this poem, when Evelyn had just written *The Grey World*. Mrs. Belloc Lowndes found that

4. The Outlook, vol. 15, no. 378, April 29 1905, p. 614: 'The Backward Glance'.

Evelyn was 'exceedingly modest and (she) ... never spoke of herself or of her writing'; she also made an impression with her 'puckish sense of humour'. Had Mrs Belloc Lowndes had her way, Evelyn would have continued her novel writing 'instead of writing the volume which in time placed her among the leading modern exponents of Mysticism'.

It is idle to speculate what sort of fame Evelyn might have achieved as a novelist had she indeed persevered on this road. She would certainly have received short shrift from the world which admired the rising school of 'realistic' writings of Arnold Bennett and others. In any case, even before handing her *Column of Dust* to the printers she was already working on *Mysticism* and she did not look back once her last novel had been published. Perhaps she had said all that she had to say in that medium. Certainly the final impression left by the novels is that of a problem worked out. They give us above all a remarkable insight into what we may assume was the personal option of Evelyn herself. They show in dramatic form just how and why for her one type of response to the mystical vocation at least was ruled out of court. As St Augustine relates of himself in his *Confessions* she had come to see as a temptation what he calls 'fuga in solitudinem'—the flight into solitude—or as Plotinus described it the flight of the alone to the Alone. And, like St Augustine also, she associated the rejection of solitude with the loving, positive acceptance of this world, supremely exemplified for Christians in the vocation of Jesus. Her way had henceforward to be by way of *inclusion* not *exclusion*. 'Pure' mysticism, bereft of redemptive values, would continue to be a source of temptation and instability for many years and even the apparently 'final' solution of *The Column of Dust* is not without its ambiguities in this respect, as we shall see. One has a curious sense that the strongest possible affirmation of redemptive and incarnational values to be found in the novels expresses an even deeper conviction than that to be given such ample publicity in the books on mysticism which followed them. At any rate these earlier works cannot be ignored when considering Evelyn's winding path to a whole-hearted acceptance of Christ and Christianity.

5
Mysticism (1911)

EVELYN'S largest, and, perhaps, her most lasting book was written at 50, Campden Hill Square, which she and her husband occupied on their marriage in July 1907 and in which they remained until the outbreak of the second world war. The house had been left to Hubert by his father and provided enough space for him to have a workshop in the basement while Evelyn adapted a first-floor room as a study. The drawingroom and diningroom opened into each other on the ground floor and we learn that the predominant colours in these rooms were provided by grey wallpapers and purple linen curtains. The care of the house as of the cooking would have been in the hands of servants whose number and identity remain obscure. Lucy Menzies goes so far as to say that Evelyn Underhill 'probably never boiled a potato in her life' and it is fitting to remember that her great industry and its fruits reflect a leisure common to women of her class and status even if seldom so profitably employed. At this stage in her life Evelyn Underhill did not have to write or, indeed, to do anything in particular. She might without reproach have remained a purely domestic figure administering her household, carrying out her social obligations and pursuing a life of prayer and a little self-gratifying research; it was her choice to work and she did not do things by halves. Looking after her husband and running the house, entertaining and being entertained, reading, research and writing, worship, prayer and meditation, visiting in poor neighbourhoods, holidays away from home, care of her parents, all had to be fitted together. It was a fundamental axiom of Evelyn

that all of life was sacred. That, after all, was what incarnation
was all about.

Hubert left the house early and returned at about six in the
evening. He was a barrister-at-law of the Inner Temple and
followed his open air interests even in his law books, editing
Coulson and Forbes' *On the Laws of Water*, and collaborating in
two standard works, *Salmon and Freshwater Fisheries* and *The
Rules of The Road at Sea*. He was also joint author of *The History
and Law of Fisheries*. He became in 1912, and remained until his
death, secretary of the Selden Society, founded to promote the
knowledge and the study of English Law. Besides his interest in
crafts which we have already seen, he enjoyed walking in the
countryside and exploring churches with his wife. They used for
their excursions first a motor-cycle **and** side-car, then a Baby
Austin, known as Augustine, finally a bigger Austin called
Monica. Hubert drove and Evelyn read the maps. It seems that
Hubert was always ready to help Evelyn's less practical friends
with their mechanical problems and was generally tolerant of
the rather different world in which she moved. The anxious
enquirer who approaches a connection of the family, seeking
information about Mrs Stuart Moore, finds his perspective
refreshlingly adjusted when he receives the reply 'Oh I didn't
really know her at all but he was a very good sort'! It has to be
borne in mind, also, that the Stuart Moores did have a social
round and Evelyn, so far as we know, made no efforts to cut this
down or skimp the external engagements to which her rôle as a
barrister's wife committed her, and to which her own fame added
in due course. In the last weeks of March 1909 for instance she
explains to a correspondent that she has not had 'a large margin
of leisure' having been to five parties that week and given two of
her own. Such a programme does not suggest any shrinking away
from society.

On the other hand Evelyn and Hubert Moore seem not to have

been members of any particular 'circle', literary or otherwise, in
Edwardian London. Women are not 'clubbable' as men are and
tend perhaps less to wear their commitment to literature as a sort
of uniform among like-minded companions. Or possibly there
just are, or were, fewer opportunities for women to establish
contact with other women of similar interests. The phenomenon
of Women Writers' Dinners, one of which Evelyn describes in a
letter of 16 June 1908 (*Letters*, p. 77) is merely the exception which
proves the rule. In a traditional framework the wife's circle of
acquaintances must inevitably follow the husband's. In the case
of Evelyn Underhill, her friends included several men and women
who were, or were to become, known as writers or scholars
such as Maurice Hewlett, Arthur Machen, Alice Herbert, Ethel
Ross Baker, May Sinclair, not to mention Arthur Waite and
Friedrich von Hugel. She was admired by Victoria Hunt and
Mrs Belloc Lowndes and, as we have seen, was introduced into
the wide literary circle of Mrs Crackenthorpe, through which
she could in theory at least, have rubbed shoulders with all or
most of the great literary figures at that time in London, from
Jerome K. Jerome to Henry James and W. B. Yeats. But nothing
suggests that she was ever more than an occasional eavesdropper
on this illustrious and eventful world.

The routine of Evelyn's life at home was well established. Lucy
Menzies says that she disposed of purely household matters by
ten in the morning, kept from ten to one o'clock for her 'literary
work' and wrote letters in the evening 'on her knee by the fire'.
In February 1912 she wrote to her friend Mrs Meyrick Heath, 'I
write all morning and read in the evening; at least as long as I
can but I generally collapse with dimness of mind about nine
o'clock!' Another glimpse of her life is provided in an earlier
letter to the same correspondent (15 April 1911, *Letters*, p. 128):
'Gardening takes up most of my play hours in London and I do
a little Health Society and Poor Law visiting, and seem to go out

to tea a terrible lot and have lunch with my mother every day.'
Lucy Menzies says that the visiting took place regularly twice a
week. Later, Evelyn writes rather more fully about it, as we shall
see. By this time she had given up binding books and tells Mrs
Heath that she can weave and has on board (the letter was written
from her father's yacht *Nepenthe*) a lace maker's cushion. As to
prayer and meditation, since we have no other indication we must
assume that she set aside a period in the morning when in principle she attempted a set meditation. This at least is the advice
she gives to others (*Letters*, pp. 71ff., 127; letters of 16 January
1908, 25 July 1911). She also went to mass regularly in Roman
Catholic churches, usually at the neighbouring church of the
Carmelites in Kensington Church Street or (for High Mass) at
Westminster Cathedral, sometimes, perhaps, accompanied by
Hubert. She seems in this respect to have behaved to all intents
and purposes as one of the Catholic faith, keeping the festivals and
fasts of the Church together with the Calendar of Saints, using
established devotions including the Way of the Cross and the
rosary, genuflecting before the tabernacle. She, like von Hugel,
had a special penchant for Benediction, the nuns of the Assumption in Kensington Square being especially recommended for
this service, and found the Corpus Christi ceremonies at the
Sacred Heart Convent, Roehampton, especially congenial (letters
of April, June 1908, *Letters*, pp. 75, 77). We also learn from a
letter of Ethel Ross Baker that she accumulated in these years a
collection of pious amulets or 'holy medals'.

She also continued to accompany her mother abroad at Easter
time, leaving her husband behind. This spring holiday was a
regular event from 1908 to 1913 and not once does it seem that
Hubert accompanied the Underhill family. Perhaps it was a
case of old habits die hard or, possibly, he simply could not leave
his work when Mrs Underhill insisted on travelling; in any case
there are signs in Evelyn's letters to him that neither very much

liked this procedure and husband and wife generally took a
holiday together after her return. In 1908 Evelyn and her mother
were in South France and Italy, in 1909 they toured in Belgium
and Luxembourg, in 1910 they spent an eventful month or two
in Italy, mostly in Rome; 1911 seems to have been devoted
chiefly to France, especially Paris, and in 1912 they went to
Holland. Finally in 1913, she returned to Italy and Umbria.

The letters from abroad to Hubert continue the lively flow of
description of people, places, objects and situations of the earlier
letters; judgements are if anything more liberally bestowed and
the wit is even less sparing than previously. Evelyn might display
an interest in pious practices and devotional objects but she was
not in the coloquial sense 'pious' and her view of the pietistic
English Roman Catholic milieu of their boarding house in Rome
in 1910 is caustic: 'I am learning a lot about the lower walks of
piety as I sit at a very goody table! The discussion during Holy
Week as to what one might or might not eat equalled Huysman's
story of the lady who thought cream a penitential diet if only it
had been whipped! One lady on being invited to eat macaroons
containing a very little cheese and being told that the Romans
always ate it on Good Friday replied very bitterly "I daresay.
But many of them are going to a place where I do not wish to
be"!' But the letters of this particular holiday are dominated on
the one hand by her mother's sickness from a mild form of para-
typhoid followed by her own, and on the other by her efforts
to gain entry to a papal audience. Through the good offices of
J. A. Herbert and Father R. H. Benson the necessary ticket for
the latter was finally obtained. Evelyn might find St Peter's
'hideous' but she made no bones about being impressed by the
Pope. Several times she refers in letters to the impression made
on her by Pius X. To Hubert she wrote: 'The papal guard came
in and then the Pope in his white things and ascended the throne
so quietly and simply that he was there before one had noticed

him. He has a beautiful voice and gives one an intense impression
of great holiness, kindness and simplicity.' After Mrs Meyrick
Heath had made a visit to Rome two years later, she again wrote:
'Isn't the Pope impressive? I never saw the last one—but the
simplicity and radiant devotion of this simply left me grovelling.
However unsuitable he may be politically and intellectually, I
am convinced that inside he is a great Christian and would be an
ideal Pope if a Pope's job were purely spiritual (as it ought to be)'
(*Letters*, pp. 113–14, 137).

Her mother's illness in Rome that year was a great trial;
although Mrs Underhill was properly nursed and cared for, the
strain told on Evelyn and she was confined to bed for several days
with what was diagnosed as 'bronchitis'. She was still in poor
shape when they returned. In one of the last letters from Italy to
Hubert she puts in a plea that they should take their holiday in the
country somewhere on their own and not on the parental yacht,
Wulfruna. They duly spent a week or two in May that year at
the Savernake Forest Hotel, near Marlborough, in Wiltshire.

Evelyn's writing and research suffered no respite as a result of
her marriage. On the contrary her efforts seem to have redoubled.
Despite her claim on 16 June 1908: 'nowadays I seldom write
rhymes', she did still produce verse from time to time, and had in
fact published some lines on the feast of Corpus Christi in the
month preceding this letter. To her great vexation they were
printed a week *before* the feast itself, and seemed to her to lose
thereby much of their point. In the same letter she writes of producing a little book of 'those sort of verses' for all the feasts and
seasons of the Church's Year. In the event she seems only
to have published verse in any quantity some three years later
when she became a regular contributor to the Nation and other
periodicals. She also tried her hand at art history and published
in the April number of The Burlington Magazine of 1910 an
essay entitled 'The Fountain of Life; a Iconographical Study'.

But the work that came more and more to occupy Evelyn Underhill's time after her marriage in July 1907, especially once *The Column of Dust* had gone to press in March 1909 (*Letters*, p. 94), was the research for and writing of *Mysticism*. Even then *Mysticism* itself was never alone on her agenda since she began work on it before finishing *The Column of Dust*, and was composing her meditation on the Way of the Cross and thinking of her edition of the *Cloud of Unknowing* well before it was completed. The Burlington Magazine article of 1910 was tossed off *en passant*, while articles which were published in the Quest in July and November 1910[1] as well as articles on Ruysbroeck in the Seeker in 1911, were more directly related to the main work in hand but suffered considerable alteration between book and periodical.

Evelyn Underhill's *Mysticism* is a very large subject. Since despite its great and lasting success it has not yet been analysed in depth and at length by professional theologians and has, even more surprisingly, been neglected by students of literature, almost everything remains to be said about it from an historical and philosophical point of view. In these conditions all that can be undertaken here is to sketch the manner and the stages of its construction, to characterise in a general way its contents and style, to give some account of its historical and theological background and finally in a later chapter to report some contemporary opinions on the work and indicate its subsequent history. Since, unlike so many of Evelyn's books, it is still readily accessible in its final edition, following a revision of 1930, reference will be made to this, although as we shall see, it differs in important respects from the work which issued from Methuen's publishing house on 2 March 1911.

First, as to the stages of the book's growth and the objectives

1. 'A Note on Mysticism', 'Another Note on Mysticism', vol. I, pp. 742–52, vol. II, pp. 135–47.

of the author, we have a certain amount of information in the valuable correspondence between Evelyn and her principle collaborator, Margaret Robinson, about whose work for Evelyn it is also necessary to say something. Those familiar with *Mysticism* and with Evelyn's *Letters* as edited by Charles Williams, should not have had too much difficulty in identifying the 'M.R.' with whom Evelyn discusses the progress of the work in the latter, with Margaret Robinson whose help is duly acknowledged in the Preface of the former. Charles Williams's selective editing does, it is true, help to disguise the exact nature and above all the sheer amount of the work done by Miss Robinson, and on this as other points, one sense a certain anxiety on the Editor's part to prevent the correspondence giving a 'wrong impression.'

Margaret Robinson who lived in Liverpool where she appears to have been, for a time at least, a school teacher, had first written to Evelyn after reading *The Grey World*. Evelyn's guarded reply, from which we have already quoted, is dated 29 November 1904. The initial exchange was brief and the correspondence only resumed in May 1907 (*Letters*, p. 63). By May the following year a certain amount of personal information had been exchanged though Margaret Robinson's main object was to draw Evelyn on the subject of her ideas and, finally, to adopt her as spiritual director. That she was at least some years older than Evelyn is indicated in a letter of 9 May 1908 (unpublished section) in which Evelyn laughingly writes 'you frighten me very much by the artful suggestion that you are years older than I! Can it be *you* who is 75? I am 32, which is quite a mature age—so perhaps things are not as bad as they look.' Margaret was an Anglican but clearly not very familiar with the Catholic approach to worship and only gradually familiarising herself with Catholic mystical and ascetical writing. A large part of Evelyn's letters to her is taken up with recommending and discussing suitable books for her to read.

Margaret Robinson typed Evelyn's manuscript of the National Review article in defence of May Sinclair towards the end of 1907. She did a great deal more typing for Evelyn in 1908, not sparing the whole of the Whit Sunday of that year. But it is not until the letter written on 22 October 1908 that Evelyn asks for her collaboration over *Mysticism*. The request at once outlines the scope of the help desired: '[This letter] is really to ask whether you feel like being *extremely* angelic and helping me at your leisure with the job I have on hand just now? I am writing—or trying to write—a "serious" book on Mysticism and of course want to make use of the German mystics and some of them have never been translated whilst others have been done from such a controversial point of view that one dares not trust the translators. I am particularly hung up over Meister Eckhardt and Mechtild of Magdeburg, but there may be others. Now if I sent you the books, *would* you read them leisurely through, check any passages I sent you and extract and translate for me any bits you thought specially good bearing on points of which I would send you a list?' (*Letters*, pp. 85–6). Margaret Robinson almost immediately accepted and returned a sample of what she could do, for Evelyn writes on 4 November, 'My dear friend, You really are a lamb—obviously from the scraps you quote in your letter you are going to find me just the "right things!".' She promises to send Margaret 'a more manageable Eckhardt', discusses ordering St Mechtild from Dr Williams's library (which together with the London Library she chiefly used) and ends 'It may comfort you to know that I shouldn't be able to do this book at *all* without you. There is no one else I could trust to do my hunting in this way!'

Charles Williams did not, unfortunately, publish the letter Evelyn must have written shortly after 4 November to enumerate the 'points' on which she wanted Margaret to be guided in her 'hunting', and in her translation. Evelyn's aims are set out in it with remarkable explicitness and we quote the whole of the relevant section. The original text appears to be a copy, possibly in Margaret Robinson's hand. It is not in Evelyn's. 'I send you Eckhardt,' she writes. 'Wd you please put your remarks in the enclosed note book, & on one side only of the paper: and give the *chapter*—not necessarily page—each bit you happen to quote comes from. I want

1 To know what Eckhardt's "main line" is: i.e. is it "contemplation" passing on to ecstasy, as a means of divine union? or is it more philosophical? How does he compare with Ruysbroeck, who is supposed to be his master? [sic]
2 Does he recommend "introversion"? If so, I want translations of short passages describing the process, and dealing with the mystical result.
3 Does he preach the doctrine of Divine Darkness? If so, please quote.
4 Are there traces of pantheism?
5 Does he go in for Visions & Visual images?
6 Any traces of the beginning of the Sacred Heart devotion? His predecessor, S. Mechtild, has it—a fact which no one seems to have perceived yet.

Would you either translate or send a note of anything that strikes you as specially fine? I want most passages in metaphysical rather than definitely Christian language: i.e. references by name to Our Lord, the Blessed Virgin etc. or bits flavoured with scraps of Scripture aren't much good: but those in which the same things are called the Eternal, the All, the Divine Love, etc. etc. will be useful. The book is not going to be explicitly theological as I want to make a synthesis of the doctrine of Christian & non-Christian mystics—so no "over-beliefs" are admissible.'

This letter is interesting in several ways. For one thing it betrays

how very ignorant of Eckhardt Evelyn was at the time of writing
Mysticism, an ignorance which is soon overtaken by a fervent
admiration and frequent quotation; 'how gorgeous he is!' she
exclaims two or three weeks later. For another it reveals how
Evelyn was able to cope with the immense number of works
from which she assembled material for her book. Those who
always doubted whether she could possibly have read all those
books by herself will here receive ample confirmation of their
suspicions. Indeed, she to some extent exonerates her helper also,
for a postscript to this same letter, after referring to the edition
of Eckhardt she is sending 'because it looks funny' and seems to
be written in 'medieval German or some other unreadable
tongue', adds 'There's no need to read it *all*, you know—just
skip through!' Finally the general orientation of the final paragraph is likely to offer some explanation as to why Evelyn notice-
ably fights shy almost throughout her book of specifically Christian,
theological and scriptual language. For some this is still the book's
greatest recommendation. For others it has always seemed evidence that its author had placed herself well outside the pale of
accepted Christian belief. For the moment it may suffice to say
that Evelyn's type of Christian belief cannot really be assessed
without also considering her quite explicitly 'Christian' *Mystic
Way*, a book which is in every way the complement in this respect
of *Mysticism*, and which appeared very shortly after it.

Evelyn was delighted with Margaret Robinson's contribution.
On 24 November she writes: 'I don't know what to say to you.
I'm so grateful for the Eckhardt notes. They are just lovely:
exactly the sort of thing wanted & just the right English. To have
one's needs so perfectly understood is like having a second & more
efficient self to work for one.' (Unpublished section in letter on
p. 87 of *Letters*.) Of her collaborator's translation work she again
wrote on 9 March 1910: 'You seem to have a special genius for
translation: personally the moment I begin it, all the right words

fly out of my head, & the result is horrible. I don't know what I *should* do without you!' Indeed, Margaret Robinson's zeal knew no bounds and one letter from Evelyn interjects: 'No, I don't want Mechtild in verse. . . .' Besides Eckhardt and St Mechtild, Margaret Robinson also seems to have translated passages from the relatively little known fifteenth-century mystic Gerlac Petersen, in spite of the fact that his work was available in Latin which Evelyn usually coped with by herself. And the work was paid for. It is not clear upon what basis exactly, but Evelyn did send Margaret some remuneration, overwhelming in the end her attempt to refuse or evade this. It was, as Evelyn herself described it, 'a business arrangement', if not merely that.

Mysticism divides into two unequal parts. The first and shorter part, entitled *The Mystic Fact*, comprises seven chapters in which Evelyn attempts to define the phenomenon of mystical experience and situate it in relation to other cognate areas of human experience. The second, entitled *The Mystic Way*, comprising some two-thirds of the book's length and ten chapters, sets out the historic evidence for the experience as expressed in the written records of East and West. So far as the periods of composition are concerned everything suggests that both the two parts and the seventeen chapters are with one or two exceptions in the order in which they were written, due allowance being made for the continuous process of reading, selecting and compiling quotable material, which certainly ante-dates the request of November 1908, and even probably, Evelyn's first express notion of writing a book on the subject so long dear to her heart. Thus we learn from a letter dated 17 February 1909, that the 'first three chapters' have been typed by one of Hubert's clerks (Evelyn is rather apologetic about this). One chapter is being sent to Margaret for typing with this same letter since 'a rather good theologian' is going to look at it for her, and 'the other three chapters have been revised, lengthened and partly re-written'. The chapter singled out for the attention of the 'rather good theologian' is almost certainly that referred to in November of the preceding year: 'I'm going to insert a short chapter on mystical theology between 3 & 4. Can't get on with it which is a bore' (unpublished letter). In the event chapter V, Mysticism and Theology, of Part I of *Mysticism*, was not much shorter than the other chapters of the book even if it was less satisfactory than most. The theologian in question may be conjectured to have been the well-known Anglican writer and Dean of St Paul's, W. R. Inge, whose own lectures on Christian Mysticism had appeared in 1899. We shall return later to his opinion of Evelyn's book.

There are occasional references to the work on *Mysticism* in Evelyn's published letters but none is greatly revealing. She had decided on the Colophon, or concluding quotation, from St Bernard's *De Consideratione*, Book V, by January 1909 (*Letters*, p. 89) and we must assume that it was at her request that this should for ever appear in editions of her book in Gothic letter. By 20 March that year she had sent off chapter V of Part II, of which she wrote: 'I am glad the vision chapter strikes you as "imposing". Really it is rather a fraud being easier to get up than the more elusive parts of the subject. The only difficulties were in arranging it neatly and speaking what one believed to be the truth without hurting the feelings of the pious.' By August in the same year she had reached chapter IX, The Dark Night of the Soul, having just completed its predecessor Ecstasy and Rapture. By this time she was getting into deep waters and felt strongly the inadequacy of her own experience to guide her. In a passage which is eloquent for a great deal else in the book for which she evidently *did* feel she had the warrant of her own experience, she writes: 'I am glad Ecstasy is not entirely illegible. I have done it very badly I think: it was altogether too much for me—just piecing things together and guessing in the dark. But I have been working very poorly lately and now can hardly work at all, which is a dreadful waste of time when one is shut up in the house. The book gets more and more difficult. I am past all the stages at which scraps of experience could guide one, and can only rely on sympathetic imagination, which is not always safe. Now I am doing the Dark Night of the Soul for which the chief authorities seem to be that gushing Madame Guyon who spent seven years in it, and Suso whose taste for consolations and annoyance when they were withdrawn will be rather congenial to you!!!' (*Letters*, pp. 106–107). The illness in Rome of the following spring (1910) enforced a respite from the manuscript but by 12 June she could write: 'I am on my last chapter now, glory be! and only the ghastly processes of revision and appendix-making will remain' (*Letters*, p. 119). A letter to Hubert makes it clear that she had in fact already, while abroad, done some work on the historical appendix in which she set out 'an historical sketch of European mysticism from the beginning of the Christian era to the death of Blake'.

One point of some interest remains concerning the title of *Mysticism*. It emerges from a triangular correspondence between Evelyn, Mr Pinker of James B. Pinker and Son, her literary agents, and the publisher, Methuen, that the title Evelyn originally chose for the book was 'The Quest of the Absolute' (letter to Mr Pinker from Methuen and Co. 10 June 1909). By 1 July 1909 doubts as to its suitability had been expressed by the publishers and by 10 February Evelyn had offered them four others from which they chose 'An Introduction to Mysticism, A Study in the Nature and Development of Man's Spiritual Consciousness'. Yet when the book finally appeared the short title had been abbreviated to *Mysticism*, the sub-title altered by one word 'of' for 'in'. and the original title relegated to a somewhat indeterminate status as a heading preceding Chapter I and as running title thereafter. It is understandable that Evelyn should not have wished to abandon a claim in the title to 'introduce' mysticism but the effect of this final change in the short title of the book is to present it interestingly in stark contrast to, rather than in competition with, Dean Inge's *Christian Mysticism*, already referred to and also published by Methuen and Co.

Mysticism which finally appeared in 2 March 1911 has been received in a number of ways. It has on the one hand, although less commonly, been made use of as a theoretical treatment and guide-book to the subject of mystical experience. It has also and pre-dominantly been used as a useful quarry for mystical texts and second-hand quotation, with and without acknowledgement. The trouble with either of these approaches to such a work is that they risk overlooking both its strength and its weakness. In the second case, manifestly, if one only turns to *Mysticism* to find out who the mystics were and what sort of things they wrote about themselves and their experiences, one is implicitly discount-ing the text of the author who spun all the quotations together. the first, one is implicitly adopting an attitude of docility to the text which it certainly seems to claim but which can only be justified after some effort has been made to sort out its specific peculiarities as a document both deeply personal in nature and abundantly conditioned by the age which gave it birth.

In fact Evelyn Underhill's greatest book is distinguished by the very qualities which make it inappropriate as a straightforward textbook or *vade-mecum* to anything connected with mysticism. This is why it will probably continue to be read after numerous so-called objective or scientific treatments of its subject have long been replaced and mouldered into oblivion. The spirit of *Mysticism* may be summed up by saying that it is romantic and engaged rather than dispassionate and objective, empirical rather than theoretical, actual rather than historical. If we make a brief examination of the book with these characteristics in mind they may help us to a clearer idea of both the real scope and the limitations of Evelyn's achievement.

Evelyn Underhill's *Mysticism* is romantic in most of the available senses of that word. It is romantic in the popular literary sense because it exalts the spiritual life as a full-blooded love affair between men and women of profound passions and their God. From this point of view the spiritual life is seen predominantly as an 'adventure', an exploration, an act of daring and almost reckless boldness accompanied by high risks and ineffable rewards. It is romantic in a more technical literary sense in that it exalts the mystics of the Christian middle ages, especially those of Western Europe, at the expense of all others. It is romantic also, in that it is a deeply personal and confessional work which makes no secret of its author's belief that this experience is the pearl of life and that she would draw all men to prize and admire it, even if she could not help them to share it. These characteristics are so conspicuous throughout the work that demonstration is superfluous. They set its tone and announce quite naturally what the choices of the author will be at a more philosophical level.

Her empirical approach to her subject is also a logical consequence of such 'romanticism'. She has little use for, or interest in, theoretical explanations and little use for the dry as dust approach to religious experience generally; herself no academic, it is likely that she repels those whose primary interest is ideas or the analysis of phenomena. One might simply describe this as a consequence of her committed romantic approach but it is clearly more than that. We have seen already how in her short stories and elsewhere she exalts love over knowledge as the high road to satisfaction of the mystical aspiration. It is fully in line with this depreciation of purely intellectual enlightenment that she should also deprecate formal classification and analysis. From this point of view nothing in *Mysticism* is more revealing than the airy way in which she dismisses what she calls 'William James's celebrated "four marks" of the mystic state'. James in his pioneering study *The Varieties of Religious Experience* (1901) to which all writers on

mysticism inevitably return again and again, had specified
Ineffability, Noetic Quality, Transcience, and Passivity as four
marks or characteristics of what he called 'mystical states of
consciousness'. Perhaps it was unwise of James to have admitted
as he introduced his 'marks' that his own constitution shut him
off 'amost entirely' from the enjoyment of mystical states, and
that his treatment would, therefore, be as external and as objective as he could make it. However that may be, if we compare
his tentative carefully justified descriptive categories with Evelyn's
'four other rules or notes' which distinguish mystical consciousness we catch at once the difference between their respective
viewpoints. It will help us to grasp her point of view if we pause
over them for a moment.

The four characteristics of the mystic consciousness Evelyn
substitutes for James's are described as follows: (1) Mysticism is
practical, not theoretical. (2) Mysticism is an entirely Spiritual
Activity. (3) The business and method of mysticism is Love.
(4) Mysticism entails a definite Psychological Experience. Since
we are considering these points under the general heading of
Evelyn's stress on the empirical and practical rather than the
theroretical, it will be convenient to glance briefly at the first and
fourth of them before passing on to the others. As to the first
point, then, it is clear that Evelyn discounts as non-mystical all
merely other-worldly philosophy or theology, however ele-
vated or symbolical, ruling out of the fold in particular all
Platonic philosophers as such. Some Platonic philosophers might
also be true mystics, she says, but in so far as they are theorists
and thinkers only they are but 'stepping stones to higher things . . .
no more mystics than the milestones on the Dover Road are
travellers to Calais'. All this is perfectly in accord with her definition of mysticism as an 'act' i.e. as ordered to praxis or actual
achievement, but it appears seriously to distort, for example, her
view of the English Platonists of the seventeenth century such as

Benjamin Whichcote, Cudworth and, above all, John Smith, so
much loved and quoted by Dean Inge. She refers a few pages
before the lines we have quoted to 'the tepid speculations of the
Cambridge Platonists', and we know from a letter that she had
difficulty in appreciating the then recently rediscovered meditations of that ardent seventeenth-century eulogist of divine beauty,
Thomas Traherne (*Letters*, p. 122). For practical purposes we
may consider that her position here is adopted in opposition to
Inge besides being for her a necessary corollary of other aspects
of mystical experience considered as the art of pursuing a beloved
object purely for its own sake, or, in other words, as an act of love.
Speculation, however shot through with mystical lights, does not
qualify. The raw 'feeling state' is all and its only tolerable covering
is poetry.

On the other hand Evelyn's decision to regard the mystical
consciousness as 'a definite Psychological Experience' can in no
sense be said to distinguish her from William James, or even from
Inge. It was indeed what everyone would have expected her to
assume and something so obvious to James that he nowhere
bothers to state it categorically. If Evelyn did bother it was once
again because of particular preoccupations of her own, preoccupations which one may describe as partly apologetic, partly
procedural for the unfolding of her general thesis.

The background to Evelyn's insistence on the psychological
approach to mysticism is not far to seek. Psychology was the
glamorous 'science' of the pre-war period. Although biology
might steal the limelight as a general framework for the evolutionary optimism of the age, psychology offered the key to open
the secrets of specific human advances in intelligence, creativity,
genius, sensibility and demonic power. By the first decade of the
century specific applications of psychological findings were
beginning to be made even in theology. It is for example with an
air of guarded excitement that the learned and respected Oxford

theologian, William Sanday, reports his investigations and conclusions in respect of the application of psychology to Christology in his *Christologies Ancient and Modern*, published exactly one year before *Mysticism* and representing lectures given some time before that. His efforts were applauded and defended by Evelyn in a brief piece in The Hibbert Journal of April 1911, pp. 644–46. But years before the psychology of 'subliminal depths' had become interesting to academic theologians the famous Catholic poet Francis Thompson had written about the new interest which many were taking in the subjective or psychological aspects of religious experience, thanks largely to the impetus from France. Thompson, whose orthodoxy is beyond question, distinguished in any treatment of mysticism a permanent unvarying element and another which is subjective, variable. He wrote: 'The way to God is through Himself and is conditioned by His Own nature. It is alike for no two men. And it is the study of its adaptation to the personality which is so psychologically interesting in the writings of individual mystics.' But Thompson, writing in 1900, does no more than echo the widely read Jesuit writer and later 'modernist' Father George Tyrrell who three years earlier had introduced Henri Joly's *The Psychology of the Saints* with a neat summary of the reversal of fortunes in hagiography generally which interest in psychology had brought about. According to Tyrrell this reversal had exposed as superstitious the very men who a century earlier had scoffed at the abnormal experiences of the saints as pure fiction. They were now (in May 1898) seen for what they really were, 'instances of well-known psychological manifestations'. If some went further, Tyrrell wrote, and tended to explain '*all* the phenomena in question' by purely physiological or psychological laws this was simply for lack of what he calls 'a sounder criticism' which should 'fix the limits of what may be so explained, and shall assign to Nature the things that are Nature's and to God the things that are God's'. Such was the task

Henri Joly had set himself on Tyrrell's view, to counter the reductionist psychologists such as Henri Delacroix with whom Evelyn Underhill also takes issue from her rather different standpoint. By the time Evelyn came to write *Mysticism* therefore the psychological and subjective approach to mystical experience was no novelty but still held all the excitement of a territory as yet only tentatively opened up and explored. It was also one which when properly handled seemed especially promising to many apologists for religious belief among whom Evelyn must after her fashion be numbered.

Evelyn's further proposition that mysticism is 'an entirely spiritual activity' and that 'the business and method of mysticism is love' serve to reinforce points she considered of overwhelming importance at this time, viz. that mysticism is not, like magic, a technique which subserves utilitarian or self-regarding ends but demands complete surrender to a *ne plus ultra*, eclipsing all creaturely expectations and demands; and, the same point transposed to the intellectual plain,—mysticism is in no sense a technique designed to open up hitherto unexplored worlds to the scientist, psychologist or dilettante of experience, but inseparable from a personal commitment of which the motive power is love not intellectual curiosity.

It will be seen that Evelyn's four marks so little resemble an analysis that they might almost be said to be a device for emphasising the single point she wishes to make, namely that mystical experience involves man in a unique spiritual adventure to which the nearest human analogy is the experience of falling in love. It may not surprise anyone therefore that we should also describe her approach as 'actual' rather than historical. Indeed it is thoroughly in keeping with this view of mysticism as an act of love that she should treat all apparently mystical experiences as in principle equally relevant, without too much regard for differences in historical period, cultural and geographical milieu, or theological creed. The important thing is the experience itself and its fundamental categories are mental and emotional; classification must therefore be according to kinds of feeling, or 'feeling-states' as she calls them, in the wake of James; the other factors affect the mode according to which the experience finds its way into words, sometimes its depth and intensity, but none can abolish or detract from the unique common denominator of all mystical experience: men and women in love with God.

This is one aspect of the 'subjectivism' which many, including von Hugel and Evelyn herself when she came to review her own book for its twelfth edition, saw as the chief flaw in *Mysticism*: on the one hand a rejection of any objective attempt at handling the data of mystical experience according to the terms and criteria of the philosophical psychology of the time as represented by James; on the other, an impatience with such aids to objective discrimination as she might have found in the traditional categories of mystical theology, elaborated especially by counter-reformation Catholic saints such as St John of the Cross and St Teresa, and considerably developed since. Von Hugel whose *Mystical Element* pays at least as much attention as *Mysticism* to mystical experience as such nevertheless retains a far greater awareness of classic theological distinctions than does Evelyn's book. We have seen already one of the reasons for this disregard for traditional theological terminology which she felt might compromise her work in the eyes of sincere non-Christian seekers. But there was another reason also which was that, quite simply, she had discovered another philosophy or other philosophies, which seemed to harmonise with her vision of the world opened up by mystical experience far better than the more staid intellectual elucidations of either psychology alone or academic theology.

It is difficult to convey to those accustomed to the philosophical atmosphere of the later twentieth-century world, especially in

Great Britain, the temper of thought in the first decade of the twentieth century in which *Mysticism* was written. In our own day English-speaking philosophers must it seems begin, and stay, at the beginning, locked in debates about grammar or the sensations induced by hot bath water or what it means to speak knowledgeably of a remote Asian peninsular they have never seen, or to pronounce that 'the King of France is bald'. Thus we may find it all but impossible to imagine a time when men of academic standing and philosophical training or aspirations argued familiarly with one another about the Absolute, Mind, Truth, Reality, Being and Becoming. It was a time, the last in our history up to date, when philosophers and theologians did, in Britain at least, in some sense 'speak the same language'. P. T. Forsyth, theologian and preacher, who reacted against this state of affairs from the side of theology, could take it for granted in 1916 that the contemporary philosophers' 'doctrine of the absolute' corresponded to 'the theological doctrine of the holy' (*The Justification of God*, p. 68). As the prevailing philosophy was Hegelian in inspiration and stressed the immanence of the Absolute or, in religious terms, of the Divine and Ultimate Reality, so also contemporary theologians stressed the immanence of their Divine Being or Ultimate Reality. Some such as William Newton Clarke might reflect on immanence in a judicious and interesting way which brings theology and mystical aspiration into the kind of fruitful relationship which makes for the enrichment of orthodoxy. Others, such as R. J. Campbell in his *New Theology* of 1907, so exalted immanence as to all but identify both the phenomenal world and human consciousness with the Absolute or Divine, of which these were but superficial manifestations. The orthodox at such a time had their hands full in holding the immanentists at bay. Charles Gore for example took on Campbell; the youthful R. A. Knox sharpened his polemical skill on the much respected R. C. Moberly's famous book *Atonement and Personality*;

and von Hugel, at least from the publication of his *Mystical Element*, looked the foe steadily and critically in the eye wherever he found him, in Pringle-Patterson, in Rudolf Eucken and even in Evelyn Underhill, as we shall see.

Two contemporary philosophical writers in particular, one German, one French, dominated Evelyn Underhill's thinking at the time she wrote *Mysticism*. They were Rudolf Eucken and Henri Bergson. In her second chapter, Mysticism and Vitalism, Evelyn gives her reader a fair idea of what she owed to their inspiration. Their impact is duly acknowledged with apologies in a footnote to the twelfth edition, but nothing she could do would remove their traces from her book. By 1911 both were attracting a great deal of attention; they were indeed highly fashionable. The prolific Eucken seems to have had a considerable English following which clamoured for translations of his voluminous works as they appeared. Bergson, whose output at the time was relatively slight, and consisted chiefly of rather technical lectures on psychology and his most famous book *L'évolution créatrice* (1907), was certainly the more glamorous philosophical personality and his impact on the London and the Evelyn Underhill of those days is vividly described in a letter to Mrs Meyrick Heath (*Letters*, p. 146). Having said that in a particularly busy week she had been 'simply *living*' for Bergson's lectures, she goes on 'I don't feel in the mood for theology and am not going to argue with you about Sacraments. I am still drunk with Bergson, who sharpened one's mind and swept one off one's feet both at once. Those lectures have been a real, great experience: direct contact with the personality of a profound intuitive thinker of the first rank! London isn't quite so silly as it seems. It provided him with a deep attention which one could almost *feel*.' The letter containing these details concludes by recording the shock she felt on discovering that Bergson's 'Conclusions on the nature of spirit' — 'Conclusions', she observes, 'which sounded like a metaphysical version of the Communion of Saints'—were 'exactly the same as' what one of her spiritual followers (described as 'my mystic') had actually seen. It was apparently in the middle of these four university of London lectures, in the mid-autumn of 1911, that she had to cope with 'a sudden demand for an article on him— ordered Thursday and printed Saturday!'—just at the same time as a note arrived from Methuen asking her to revise *Mysticism* for a third edition (*Letters*, pp. 146–47. This letter is incorrectly dated 1913 by the editor.).

Neither Eucken nor Bergson displayed any interest in mysticism yet both seemed to many of their disciples to advance a spiritual explanation of the universe which entailed the possibility, indeed the necessity, of special experience of a mystical-intuitive type. Both insisted that, as a matter of fact, progress in man must take the form of an ever-increasing improvement of his intellectual, artistic, creative, life-enhancing capacities. In the case of Eucken this entailed man's progressive introduction into a spiritual dimension or noos-sphere in which his deepest aspirations would find expression and satisfaction. For Eucken religion indeed assumed great importance as a signpost or guardian of this deepest aspect of human destiny which nevertheless he was able to describe without undue recourse to traditional theological frames of reference, despite abundant use of that traditional German mystical vocabulary ever to be found in a state of suspension in German idealism. But if Eucken tended to exalt his readers through a language of metaphysical optimism which opened vistas of ineffable significance behind all their wisest and deepest thoughts, Bergson, as became a Frenchman, showed more interest in the practicalities of the method. To Bergson we owe the popularity in Evelyn's generation of the ever fertile idea of the *élan vital*, or 'holy thrust' as she evokes it in one of her poems, that unsleeping dynamo which throbs in all life from the lowest to the highest, like a 'sainte inquiétude' which leads biological creation through achievement after achievement until finally it attains in man the power of conscious self-orientation and true creativity. For Bergson the queen of sciences is biology, but biology tends inevitably to psychology, to the study of human consciousness, to value; but it was only at a much later stage of his career that Bergson drew any very explicit religious consequences from his philosophy.

Admirers of Teilhard de Chardin will have no difficulty in appreciating the intellectual milieu of *Mysticism*. This is not to say that Evelyn Underhill took from her philosophical *ambiance* exactly what the Jesuit poet found there. She describes the fashionable creed of the time as 'vitalism' and the term adequately sums up the prevailing worship of life in all its exuberance, variety and apparently limitless possibility, which pervaded every aspect of pre-1914 culture and society. On Evelyn's view the philosophical discoveries of contemporaries such as Eucken and Bergson confirmed the deepest intuitions of the mystics. The Bergsonian emphasis, for example, on the very imperfect correlation between subjective perceptions which register a static, strictly delimited, universe, and the ever-fluid, ever-dynamic nature of a reality which knows no once-and-for-all definitions nor any single moment when it is not in passage *from* one state *to* another, seemed a perfect confirmation of the mystics' assertion that the world is fundamentally *maya* or illusion, a perpetually evolving flux which the mind breaks up for convenience into a series of scenes and believes to endure. Such 'science' is for Evelyn a springboard: the lesson is to avoid identifying with the flux as such, and to find the really real which both overarches the process and constitutes its centre. To this the only possible access is through 'intuition', i.e. through an illuminated consciousness thanks to which the mind is raised to the level of that which it would know and knows it as both imminent in the flux and transcendent to it.

It cannot be said that Evelyn gives an entirely coherent account of the metaphysical universe as she sketches it in colours borrowed from Bergson and Eucken. One ambiguity in particular deserves attention since it dogs virtually all Evelyn's attempts at this period to articulate her mystical vision of the nature of things. This concerns the status of the flux. On the one hand there is the purely psychological angle, best illustrated as Bergson had already done with the aid of the newly invented cinematograph projector. The world is perpetually *en marche* even though we apprehend it statically, just as the apparently stable pictures on the cinema screen are composed in fact by a constant flow or succession of 'frames' even when a single scene or action occupies the screen for some time. Just in so far, says Evelyn, as our world is thus in reality perpetually ebbing out it is illusory, ephemeral, unreal. But on the other hand, Evelyn adds, there is also a sense in which God or the Absolute is immanent in what she calls 'the dynamic side of things'. Because the divine is also there and very much there, man, too, is called upon to immerse himself in that flux. 'The mystic', she writes, 'knows his task to be the attainment of Being, union with the One, the "return to the Father's heart"; for the parable of the Prodigal Son is to him the history of the universe. This union is to be attained, first by co-operation in that Life which bears him up in which he is immersed. He must become conscious of this 'great life of the All' merge himself in it, if he would find his way back whence he came. *Vae Soli.*' Apart from the fact that this is almost certainly one of the passages in which, as Inge complained, Evelyn totally misunderstands Plotinus, the interesting thing about it is that she is here contrasting this approved 'Bergsonian' mystical outlook with 'the nihilism of Eastern Contemplatives' who are taken to task precisely for *failing* to see 'a reality in the dynamic side of things'. The seeker of the real must then, it would seem, both look beyond the flux *and* 'immerse himself' in it to find the object of his quest. Such paradoxes which smack of sophism to philosophers are likely to prove more rewarding when translated into the language of human feelings and emotions. It is here rather than in the area of philosophical speculations that Evelyn's main contribution lies. If there are rare occasions when Evelyn can write of normal human sense-inscribed experience in excoriating derogatory rhetoric which suggests an unwavering subscription to the most extreme doctrines of world hatred to be found in both East and West, this sort of language does not represent her last word; it is in fact at a tangent to the main line of her thought in *Mysticism* and its impact is considerably qualified as soon as we take to heart some of her more explicit judgements of value on the place of feeling and temperament in the mystical life.

When Evelyn stated in the second of her four marks of mysticism that it was 'an entirely spiritual activity' nothing could have been further from her thought than to proclaim that mysticism entailed 'angelism' or the attempted annihilation of all sentiment and emotional experience. She was, as we have seen, simply claiming that mysticism could not, like magic, be reduced to a technique for obtaining abnormal results. If we seek to discover, on the other hand, the clearest statement of what she believed mystical endeavour positively to entail it may well be best to look outside *Mysticism* itself to sharper and more precise statements contained in her paper delivered to The Religious Thought Society in October 1912, entitled 'The Place of Will, Intellect, and Feeling in Prayer'. In this address she describes concisely what she means by will, intellect and feeling and the rôle each must play in any approach in prayer to God, from the most humble to the most exalted and ecstatic. To intellect she allots the foot of the mountain, to feeling and will the ascent itself. As prayer begins, she says, an 'intellectual adjustment' takes place in the mind which surrenders itself to spiritual things while it also banishes 'other objects of thought'. But at this stage 'nothing happens'. For something to 'happen', for someone to enter a state of prayer, there must be 'contact'. Evelyn goes on to quote an unnamed religious psychologist to the effect that there must therefore take place a 'synthesis of love and will' which she paraphrases as 'a fusion of feeling and volition'. The paradigm of the faculties' deployment in prayer is thus summed up in a sentence: 'Reason comes to the foot of the mountain; it is the industrious will urged by the passionate heart which climbs the slope.'

So far there is nothing very remarkable in Evelyn's account even if the 'fusion' of love, i.e. feeling, with will, sounds vague. It is what follows which distinguishes her treatment of the subject. Her title had distinguished three faculties for prayer in the order will, intellect, feeling. The order in which she deals with each in her text is intellect, will, feeling. Feeling is last because feeling is the highest and the best, the most that prayer can aspire to. Feeling, not feelings. What she calls 'ecstatic spiritual feelings' are not of course necessary for prayer. Discussing 'will' she makes the customary distinction, made by all spiritual writers, between a 'determined fixing of the will' which involves self-donation and resolution, and the 'fair weather breeze' of passing moods and satisfactions. As she told the Religious Thought Society with a flourish of nautical metaphor: 'the most spiritual of emotions is only a fair weather breeze. Let the ship take advantage of it by all means, but not rely on it. She must be prepared to beat to windward if she would reach her goal.' But having said this, having brought in grace as an 'inflow of divine vitality' which solicits our 'voluntary appropriation' of it, she has still not dealt with feeling in the sense in which it stands on an equal footing with intellect and emotion. As she comes to feeling in *this* sense the reader is quite prepared for her question, indeed has already asked himself, 'What place have we left for the operation of feeling in prayer?'

Beginning from her perfectly innocuous suggestion that feeling 'inflames' the will, it takes Evelyn but two sentences and a quotation to establish 'impassioned desire' as her Jacob's ladder between earth and heaven: '[But] I think we can say generally that the business of feeling is to inflame the will, to give it intention, gladness, and vividness, to convert it from a dull determination into an eager impassioned desire. It links up thought with action, effects in psychological language, the movement of the prayerful self from a mere state of cognition to (misprinted 'and' in the article) a state of conation, converts the soul from attention to the Transcendent to first-hand adventure *within* it, "All thy life now behove altogether to stand in desire", says the author of the *Cloud of Unknowing*.' (The Interpreter, pp. 250–51.) Such living within the transcendent is achieved, she believes, by what she calls an 'intercourse of emotion and feeling' in which man experiences above all the 'fundamental emotions' of *Humility*, as he approaches all that he so manifestly falls short of, and *Love*, which issues from adoration as 'the highest exercise of the spirit of man'. The final relationship of the three components of her description is summed up as follows:

> Thought has done all that it may when it has set the scene, prepared the ground, adjusted the mind in the right direction. Will is wanted only whilst there are oppositions to be transcended, difficult things to be done. It represents the soul's effort to struggle to be where it ought to be. But there are levels of attainment in which the will does not seem to exist any more as a separate thing. It is caught in the mighty rhythms of the Divine Will, merged in it and surrendered to it. Instead of its small personal activity, it forms a part of a great action of the Whole. In the higher degrees of prayer in fact, Will is transmuted into Love. We are reminded of the old story of the Phoenix: the active busy will seems to be burned up and utterly destroyed; but living Love, strong and immortal, springs from the ashes and the flame (The Interpreter, pp. 242–53).

The phoenix is a valuable emblem of Evelyn's scheme of mystical growth according to *Mysticism*. If the article sums up the
fundamental pattern of this, the figure of the phoenix who arises
a renewed being from the ashes of his former existence, resumes
both book and article. Again and again in *Mysticism*, Evelyn
returns to the point that mystical life entails 'a definite and peculiar
development of the whole self, conscious and unconscious . . . a
remaking of the whole character on high levels in the interests of
the transcendental life' (*Mysticism*, p. 90). Often she speaks of
breaking down old habits and of re-establishing the personality
around 'new centres of consciousness'; or she may refer to 'that
transformation of personality which is the essence of the mystic
life;' but she never leaves us in any doubt that it is the *whole* self
which is being broken down or consumed or purified, and re-
made, the self, that is to say, whose nature and quality is determined by the nature and quality of its *love*. Throughout *Mysticism*
Evelyn is aware, indeed her whole treatment is guided by the
supposition that falling in love with God usually absorbs the
whole human personality into a process of organic, cataclysmic,
development of which the traditional three stages, purgative,
illuminative and unitive, give a rough and ready outline. The
article in The Interpreter is especially valuable in relaying this
message with perfect explicitness. Having asked the question
whether in the mystical life men and women need those 'possibilities of self-expression' which serve them in all mundane contacts
her answer is unambiguous: 'Christians, I think, are bound to
answer this question in the affirmative. According to Christianity,
it is the whole Self [sic] which is called to turn towards Divine
Reality—to enter the Kingdom—not some supposed "spiritual"
part thereof. "Thou hast made us for Thyself", said Augustine;
not, as the Orphic initiate would have said, "Thou hast made one
crumb out of our complex nature for Thyself, and the rest may
go on the rubbish heap". It is the *whole man* [her emphasis] of

intellect, of feeling, and of will, which finds its only true objective in the Christian God.'

It is unnecessary perhaps to draw attention to the importance of the phrase 'according to Christianity' in this passage. Incarnation for Evelyn, as we have seen in examining her novels and stories, involves that *nothing* shall be lost. And it is not only the Orphic initiates whom she accuses of neglecting half human reality in the name of 'spirituality'. With less than entire justice but in full agreement with others of her time such as Inge, she associates the Eastern religions and the neoplatonists with the negative outlook. It is a theme to which she returns with renewed vigour in *The Mystic Way* of 1912. She might, had she had time or felt inclined, have included many Christian writers in her scope and pointed out their short-comings in this respect; some of those she does quote, Augustine himself for one, could not then have been recommended without qualification for the divide at this point in the history of mystical doctrines goes very deep indeed, distinguishing and opposing not only schools of thought but individuals against themselves. Nevertheless, the prevailing impression we take away from *Mysticism* is that the mystics are on Evelyn's side and preach the sanctity and inevitability of emotion, that which pierces and purifies equally with that which ravishes and transfigures; here, she implies, mystics of the rarest abstraction such as Eckhardt, as well as those of the 'cosier' sort such as Mme Guyon, are all united at least in presenting the object of their quest and the way to it 'through a temperament, through vivid feelings which enter as an essential ingredient into all they through vivid feelings experience and describe'. It follows that no one who has read *Mysticism* attentively, and broadly accepted the account of mystical experience which it contains, can continue tamely to accept the easy account of 'purely spiritual' or 'supernatural' stages and objectives which are so piously bandied about in the ascetical manuals and all writers who take after them. Such books will do anything but pause to consider for example what St John of the Cross means by that common little word he so often uses 'sentir', a word which, while it certainly means in Spanish 'to perceive', can and must also mean 'to feel'.

We have not laboured greatly Evelyn Underhill's definition of mysticism. Such definitions, while interesting, lend themselves to scholastic quibbling. Many other aspects of her book have also had to be passed over. As a source of biographical information for example it tells us much less than the novels and letters, although prolonging the views there expressed into the realm of discussion or, as some might say, projecting them on the plane of history. Careful readers of *Mysticism* will not fail to notice certain 'we' passges in the course of the narrative, which, far from being an elaborate device for 'including' the reader bear every sign of being autobiographical indications designed (if designed at all) to assure us the writer knows first hand what she is talking about. Passing to another stylistic aspect of the book it would be agreeable to find some equally disarming explanation for her use of the figure of prosopopeia or address by personification in *Mysticism*, where long passages of direct address to the reader are sometimes put in quotation marks and into the mouth of 'the mystics'. Such obvious artificiality strikes us as unbearably mannered today; the best that can be said of it is that it highlights Evelyn's pressing sense of mission, her desire not simply to *tell* her readers about mysticism but to summon them to 'taste and see that the Lord is sweet'.

Our conclusion therefore concerning *Mysticism* is that it, too, is very much a book written 'through a temperament', the temperament of a time and of an individual. The effervescence of the cultivated classes of the Edwardian age, their aestheticism and taste for opulence enlivened by freshness, vigour and life-enhancing emotion, the contemporary psychology, philosophy and science with their emphasis on the immanence and dynamism

of whatever aspect of the 'Life Force' chiefly concerned them,
the sense of an on-going inexorable progress of the human race
towards a greater fulfilment of human potentialities; all these
find their way into *Mysticism*. And there, too, is Evelyn's personal
creed: that mysticism entails the insertion of *all* human dynamism
into the one source of life's fullness, because the mystical life is
not just a way of life some people fancy but is truly the destiny
of the race, the crown and summit of all evolutionary process
whatsoever. Temperamentally she was incapable of seeing such
fulfilment except in terms of a love richly embodied and fully
incarnate, the pursuit of an object of 'wild adoration and supreme
desire'[2] in whom such desire itself assumed divine proportions.
Her God, as she herself, has no time to distinguish between love
as eros—desire, and love as agape—charity, but moves in haste
to complete his ever uncompleted task; as her inelegant but heart-
felt lines to *Dynamic Love* bear witness:

> Not to me
> The Unmoved Mover of philosophy
> And absolute still Sum of all that is,
> The God whom I adore: not this!
> Nay, rather a great moving wave of bliss,
> A surging torrent of dynamic love
> In passionate swift career,
> That down the sheer
> And fathomless abyss
> Of Being ever Pours, his ecstasy to prove.[3]

2. p. 464 (Third Edition. The phrase is modified in the twelfth edition, p. 389).
3. First published in The Quest, January 1914. Collected in *Theophanies*, pp. 3ff.

6
The Mystical Revival

THE years following the publication of *Mysticism* and preceding
the outbreak of the first World War in late 1914 were some of the
busiest and most productive of Evelyn's career. A third and
revised edition of the book appeared in January 1912 and it had
reached its fifth edition by February 1914. It was, in fact, an outstanding success and avidly bought by a public apparently thirsty
to absorb hundreds of pages dense with descriptions of the joys
of the illuminated consciousness, the pains of the soul in the
agonies of purgation, and its ecstasy when finally released to
appease all desire at the fountain of life. The success of *Mysticism*
was as we have seen but a straw in the wind, a wind which was
nevertheless, at the time, beginning to blow with hurricane
strength, so that even to such a sober critic as Dean Inge it seemed
for a moment as though the whole world was going over to
mysticism. It is scarcely surprising if Evelyn felt emboldened to
follow up her first real success with two further original works
related to mysticism, one short, devotional and pseudonymous,
The Spiral Way (1912), and one long, discursive and scholarly,
The Mystic Way (March 1913), besides contributing to the
movement with a continuous flow of small scale literary productions. And her application to writing seems in no way to have
diminished her social activity which, if anything, increased in
these years as she became better known and even more widely
admired. With Rabindranath Tagore in particular she established
a brief but warm and productive friendship. With Friedrich von
Hugel she entered into a more lasting relationship, later to become

of great personal importance to her, but which began on the occasion of the first appearance of *Mysticism*.

Before considering von Hugel's reactions to the book, however, it may be as well to glance briefly at those of some others then qualified to express their opinion. It would be intriguing to know, for example, the considered judgement of Arthur Waite upon this achievement of his ex-neophyte. He does refer somewhat laconically to it shortly afterwards as a 'useful compilation' in a book which may well show a certain rebounding influence of Evelyn's upon him, witness, for example, his statement, emphatically supported in the surrounding context, to the effect that 'to attain the very end of mysticism there is one thing only needed and this is love'.[1] Certainly the future author of *Western Mysticism*, Cuthbert Butler, later Abbot of Downside, appears to have been unstinting in his praise and took the trouble to write and tell her so.[2] Another future Abbot of Downside, at that time still a Benedictine at Erdington Abbey, Birmingham, later a correspondent of Evelyn, also gave her book high praise at the same time that he partly divined the intention behind it. He wrote shortly after its publication:

Evelyn Underhill's is the most readable—and I think the most enlightening book on mysticism, I have read. Of course it has some omissions from the Catholic point of view. But I think the authoress wanted to be read by non-Christians and semi-Christians. For example, she avoids saying that the 'transforming union' in the greatest saints is but a part of their exile and [she says] that they all—Buddhists and Mahometans inclusively look forward to heaven as the consummation.[3]

1. *The Way of Divine Union*, London, 1915; p. 309.
2. *Letters*, p. 130, letter of E.U. of 16 November 1911.
3. *The Spiritual Letters of Abbot Chapman*. London, 1938; p. 244; letter dated 11 November 1911.

Interesting as the judgement of one who had already established himself in the field and who, it seems, had a major share in recommending Evelyn's book to the publisher is the reaction of Dean Inge. The Dean seems in fact to have been a good deal more enthusiastic about *Mysticism* in public than he was in private. Evelyn herself refers to his public view somewhat ungratefully in a letter to Hubert from Versailles, dated 11 April 1911, in which she describes how a Lutheran pastor who had lived in London, felt it should be 'given to our literary world', i.e. translated into German, and had finally become convinced by Inge's approving review. 'The old wretch,' adds Evelyn, referring to the Dean, 'seems a useful advertising medium doesn't he?' Evelyn almost certainly had by this time some inkling of 'the old wretch's' qualifications of her achievement which he had cause to set out for Methuen in early 1909, presumably in response to a request on the publisher's part to comment upon it for them. His opinion is ably summed up in a letter from the firm to Mr Pinker, Evelyn's literary agent: it was later to be repeated with interesting additions in his review of *The Mystic Way* in the Times Literary Supplement, to be dealt with later. Inge told Methuen that the book was well worth accepting, that is was 'attractively written and made all the more interesting by the evident enthusiasm of the author'. He felt that Evelyn had read deeply in the literature of mysticism and that critics would regard it as 'an important contribution to the study of criticism [sic: for 'mysticism'?]. His qualifications were that it was stronger on the side of psychology than of philosophy; that, though up-to-date in many respects, it referred neither to Edward Caird nor to Bigg nor to 'Dr Inge's own books' (a later hand—Evelyn's perhaps?—here adds an exclamation mark in the margin of the copy which was certainly in her possession). Inge also found that she had 'a prejudice against Platonism' assorting ill in his opinion with her 'Convinced "Absolutism" '; that she completely misunderstood Plotinus and, finally, that she was

'strongly influenced by the French school of "Vitalism" represented best by Bergson, and used for apologetic purposes by the
"Modernists" ', but quite failed to see that 'this philosophy is
incompatible with such a belief in an Absolute God as she, (with
all true mystics) holds firmly'.[4]

Others, and they were many, might more or less warmly
approve of Evelyn's book but only one is on record as having
offered to make it still better, and that was Baron Friedrich von
Hugel. The Baron, at this time some fifty-nine years old, the
leading Roman Catholic philosopher of the age resident in
England, revered inside but even more outside his own communion, had established his reputation in the area of mystical
theology with his *Mystical Element in Religion*, first issued in
December 1908. This voluminous two-volume work, the fruit
of a decade of hard labour undertaken while the Baron simultaneously wrestled with the direst theological problems and personalities of the period, had landed on Evelyn's desk within a few
days of its publication.[5] Any serious study of the relations between
the two will have eventually to examine the impact of von
Hugel's work on the later stages particularly of *Mysticism*, but in
the meantime it will suffice perhaps to transcribe the Baron's own
hitherto unpublished expression of his congratulations to his
new colleague, together with the offer of help already referred to.

The letter, dated 30 October 1911, is sent from the Baron's
home at 13 Vicarage Gate, Kensington, and runs:

Dear Mrs Stuart Moore,
    Let me congratulate you on the persistent, well-deserved
success of your 'Mysticism', and say how little I have been
forgetting any promise concerning my *complete* careful reading
of the whole work.

4. Unpublished letter, Methuen to J. B. Pinker Esq., 26 May 1909.
5. Unpublished letter to Margaret Robinson, 10 December 1908.

That very difficult revision of Prof. Eucken['s] long work engrossed every half-hour of working time and strength till Sept. 8th—almost all my poor holiday. And after barely 10 days of respite I had to plunge into my 'Eternal Life' article which will now engross me, with white nights to dodge as best I can, till, doubtless, the end of November. And then there will be another Paper to complete, and some rest will have to come to the jaded brain and nerves. But pray let me in all simplicity propose the following alternative plans to you.

(1) Either you rest content, as far as my little help is concerned, with those corrections proposed for the first 4 chapters,—yet with this extension,—that you would carefully go thro' all the passages concerning (a) the supposed identity of the deepest of man's soul and God, and (b) the supposed non-necessity of institutional, historical etc. religion for many or for some, and you would strictly weigh and reconsider them all.

Or (2) you would get your publisher to defer the reprinting till the beginning of February, in which case *I willingly undertake to give January to a careful study of your entire book.* But it must be clearly understood that I cannot touch it (again) till Jan., and that I thus study it then, because you are going to consider, in view of this 3rd edition the results of such reading[.] I do not, myself, feel that your waiting these three months, in matters of such extreme importance, would be too much especially since you cannot know that this 3rd Ed. may not be the last of the book for a good many years, at least. Yet, this is, of course entirely a matter for your own judgment. It would not make me drop the reading of the book, but I would, then, probably read it less strenuously. Wishing you every success, I am yours sincerely

Fr von Hugel

The context of this letter is provided by a letter of Evelyn to

J. A. Herbett, another Roman Catholic, whose help is acknowledged in the Introduction to *Mysticism* and who collaborated in
Evelyn's edition of *The Cloud of Unknowing*. On 16 September
earlier that year Evelyn had written to him in characteristically
enthusiastic words of her meeting with von Hugel: 'I forget
whether I told you', she wrote,

> that I have become the friend (or rather, disciple and adorer)
> of von Hugel. He is the most wonderful personality I have ever
> known—so saintly, so truthful, sane and tolerant. I feel very
> safe and happy sitting in his shadow and he has been most
> awfully kind to me (*Letters*, p. 129).

Was the meeting with von Hugel arranged by the same friend
who, some months earlier, had approached him for advice about
a friend of hers, a young 'speculative lady', i.e. Evelyn herself,
who felt drawn to the Roman Church? It seems perfectly likely.
On that occasion the Baron had discouraged the exertion of any
pressure enunciating his 'general rule in such cases' which was 'to
do what I can to feed in such souls the true and deep, in their
degree, Catholic instincts and practices that I find in them, either
already active or near to birth, and, whilst warning them (if
they show a velléité to come to Rome) as to the grave practical
difficulties for *them* on the side of any vigorous and sincere intellectual life, that are now to be found in the Catholic Church, to
let them feel that, nevertheless, in the Roman Catholic Church
resides a depth and tenderness and heroism of Christian sanctity
greater and richer than, as a matter of fact, is to be found elsewhere.'[6]
   Given the great tact and diffidence of which his 'general rule'
gives evidence, for von Hugel to offer to read Evelyn's book

6. Baron Friedrich von Hugel: *Selected Letters*, 1896–1924. Edited by Bernard
   Holland. London (Dent & Sons) 1928, p. 187.

'strenuously' we must assume there to have been a fair amount of mutual confidence between them; and, indeed, it is clear from the Baron's wording that he has *already* suggested some 'corrections' for the first four chapters of the work. As to the alternatives which he offered Evelyn, the publication date of the third edition speaks for itself. The revised edition appeared in January 1912. For whatever reasons Evelyn did not accept the Baron's offer of a thorough revision for this edition although one cannot exclude the possibility that his suggestions were incorporated in still later editions. But this is not to say that she ignored his advice altogether. If we compare the first and third editions of *Mysticism* some corrections do come to light, few in number and relatively minor though they appear. As we should expect a number of passages which seem to insinuate an identity or process of identification of the individual soul with the Divine, dwelling within it, have been altered. Chapter Five in particular, Mysticism and Theology, yields some four points at which alterations have been made. Thus 'this divine essence, or substance, which the introversive mystic finds dwelling, as Ruysbroeck says, at the apex of man's spirit' becomes in 1912 'this "divine" essence, or substance, etc.'. On the same page, in 'He (the mystic) is face to face with the "wonder of wonders"—that most real of all experiences, the fusion of human and divine' the word 'fusion' is replaced by 'union' in the later edition (*Mysticism* 1911, p. 120; 1912, p. 120). Some pages later (p. 131) the sentence 'the individual soul is merged in the life of the All' becomes in later editions 'the individual soul touches the life of the All.' Only one alteration of this type seems to have been overlooked in preparing the third edition; whereas the phrase 'conterminous with God' is eliminated on page 65 of this edition it survived on page 38, whether by oversight or for some other reason, until the edition of 1930, when it finally vanished.

It is difficult, on the other hand, to find a passage altered in the interests of institutional religion. The trouble here or with the more abstruse theological points is to know why some sentences or phrases should have been changed while others were left untouched. Possibly this occurred also to Evelyn whose corrections in the second part of the book are perfunctory by any standards. The only alteration which could conceivably have to do with von Hugel's second point occurs on page 366 where Evelyn in the third edition takes a softer line on ' "Prayer" as understood of the multitude'. Where she originally stated that this 'is wholly incapable of suggesting the nature of those supersensual activities which the mystics mean to express in their use of this term' she later changes the core of the sentence to 'does not really suggest'. It seems that Evelyn at this stage of her life, though she might 'adore' von Hugel, was too much under the spell of her original inspiration to undertake the thorough overhaul of her book which the Baron insinuated it needed. For the Baron was not only 'saintly . . . truthful, sane and tolerant' but also, despite his alleged 'modernism', deeply committed to Catholic orthodoxy on the particular issues which he raised in his letter to Evelyn. It was only much later, after his death, that she herself faced the task of seriously revising her work.

Evelyn's own position vis-à-vis Christianity at this time is rather reminiscent of that of the hermits who peopled the Egyptian deserts in the third and fourth centuries, men and women who on the one hand felt themselves to be utterly committed in their profession of Christianity but who on the other avoided involvement in the institutional church like the plague. Of the intensity Evelyn equated with the profession of Christianity we can glean something from a letter to Mrs Meyrick Heath of February 1912. She was attending a series of lectures delivered by a Miss R. which apparently related together physiology, psychology and Christian theology. Evelyn's comments are illuminating:

(But) when she approaches metaphysics or theology the thin ice begins! It is all very well but this teaching does leave out something which seems to me an essential of Christianity as I understand it. It aims at making a healthy all-round efficient even-tempered creature, a perfect machine for doing God's Will: but not a 'God-intoxicated Spirit', a *lover* of the Eternal Beauty. Miss R. said on Wednesday . . . that modern Christians would never think of meditating on the sufferings or crucifixion of Christ but would give all their attention to making the world the sort of place where 'such an episode' would be impossible. Rather a tepid, remote impersonal kind of religion, don't you think? And wholly wanting in the great qualities of wildness and romance (*Letters*, pp. 133–34).

It would be hard to find a more forthright exposition of the individualistic stance in religion and one is not surprised to learn of an interview with von Hugel possibly less than a year later during which, Evelyn says, she received 'a firm but gentle lecture on my own Quakerish leanings'. 'Quakerish' in von Hugel's terminology meant something akin to 'unitarian' as he used the word. Both words designated for him an independence of inherited creeds and religious institutions which he considered both untrue to human experience and contrary to the intentions of Christ. It has to be added in defence of the Friends that the term in no sense implied a lack of developed community sense and mutual charity, possessed by both Quakers and the Evelyn of these years. But von Hugel had his own word both for the state and state of mind of people in Evelyn's ecclesiastical position. He designated such people as D's—i.e. people 'detached' from any communion, and he tended to be wary of their influence.

Perhaps it was the sense of being detached, of being an 'outsider' if a deeply committed one, vis-à-vis the institutional church, which drew Evelyn to Storrington for Easter in 1912. There 'in

the corner of the Anglican churchyard', i.e. not amongst his
fellow Catholics, was buried the best known English modernist
—though he was in fact an Irishman—Father George Tyrrell
who had died excommunicate in the nearby priory some three
years earlier, assisted in his last moments by, among others, von
Hugel and the Abbé Brémond. Evelyn in 1912 duly attended the
Easter ceremonies performed by 'four doddery old monks and
one brisk one' and found them not unimpressive thanks largely to
the fine solo performance of the 'brisk one'. But her comment to
Mrs Meyrick Heath adds the now familiar dimension of discontent. First she praises the ecclesiastical experience then she qualifies
it:

> It sounds weird but really it was most impressive. . . . But as
> on many previous Easters, I found nature a great deal more
> spiritually suggestive than ecclesiasticism! *Everything* seems
> then to surge in on you with new life, doesn't it? It is too much
> to be pushed down at the moment into any rites and symbols
> however august, isn't it? It's only after the glory and the mad-
> ness have worn off a bit that one can bear them (*Letters*, p.
> 134. Letter dated Low Sunday).

It is not altogether surprising to find her *determined* (her emphasis)
to get to Camaldoli during their autumn holiday in Italy in
October 1913: 'We had a wonderful day in the Casentino,' she
wrote. 'I was *determined* to get to Camaldoli because there are still
hermits there . . .'

If Evelyn fought shy of institutional Christianity it was not that
she had become positively unsociable or neurotic about it. In
May 1912 she consented to join the committee of the Religious
Thought Society under the direction of Dean Inge, his astringent
headship being, she thought, 'a guarantee that it will not vapour
off in the direction of sentimentalism'. The Society's aims, according to Evelyn, were 'to get hold of the modern mind and deepen

its spiritual life'. 'Of course,' she adds in a later letter, 'a lot of purposeless talk will go on and a lot of rope be given to the pious babblers, but that's unavoidable.' But she did also feel that many people, especially 'young sceptics' and many intelligent Christians were 'blissfully ignorant of their own theology'. There was also, she thought, 'a lot of religious loneliness about' and such a society might attract 'seekers' and help them through association with others like themselves (*Letters*, pp. 139–40). It is not difficult to see how Evelyn could indeed wholeheartedly support the objects of such a society for she had, we may assume, taken to heart and well learned over the years her lesson read to Margaret Robinson in a letter of 28 August 1908:

> The Communion of Saints and all that is implied by that does not occupy a sufficiently prominent place in your creed, I think. . . . This is a trap specially set for those who are attracted by the personal and mystical aspect of religion and find their greatest satisfaction in unitive prayer. . . . The kingdom of heaven is not a solitude à deux (*Letters*, p. 81).

It is typical of her in the same letter to point out that she has had to learn this lesson the hard way by having someone else—she does not say who—point it out to *her*:

> I remember some years ago being told that I was all wrong because I had not learned to recognise Christ in my fellow-creatures. I disliked the remark intensely at the time—but it was true.

It was by all accounts very easy to reverence Christ in a fellow creature and indeed to rejoice in the communion of saints when one met so illustrious a 'seeker' as the man who claimed a large part of Evelyn's attention in these years 1912–15, Rabindranath Tagore. The story of Tagore's brief but intense vogue in those 'mystical' years before the Great War, his impact on Britain and the United States and the consequence of it all for himself, have been described elsewhere. Patronised by Sir William Rothenstein and A. C. Bradley he became in British drawingrooms, in Mary Lago's words, 'the wisdom of the East personified', accepting as she also puts it 'the West's demand that he symbolise something missing from its own culture'.[7] Such enthusiasm indeed did he inspire generally that he was awarded the Nobel Prize for literature in 1913 and knighted by King George V in 1915. Evelyn came across him through Sir William Rothenstein, thanks to whom we may reasonably assume she came to review Tagore's collection of prose poems (as they became in English) entitled *Gitanjali* (The Nation, 16 November 1912). A letter to Rothenstein, dated 23 November 1912 begins:

Thank you so very much for your kind note. I am *delighted* that my reviewing Mr Tagore's poems did not displease you, so that you even think he may like it.

The letter goes on to say that the review was

deliberately made as detached as possible, partly because it seems to me that the personal note was much overdone in the Introduction [by W. B. Yeats] & partly because he is too big to sentimentalise over.

She adds that she regards the book itself as a priceless possession and she is always turning to it.

A review that Evelyn considered 'as detached as possible' might well be mistaken by someone else for a 'rave' review. Readers of the Nation were not unfamiliar with Tagore's poems, a number of which had been appearing in its columns over the preceding months, but if they had acquired any taste for him at all they

7. *Imperfect Encounter*. Letters of William Rothenstein and Rabindranath Tagore, 1911–1941. Edited, with an Introduction and Notes by Mary M. Lago. Cambridge, Mass., Harvard University Press, 1972; pp. 19–20.

must perforce have leapt to buy *Gitanjali* after reading what the author of *Mysticism* had to say about it. After introducing her remarks by saying that the poetry of mysticism is both the 'crown of literature' and seldom met with 'in its perfection'; having stipulated that it demands 'a disciplined craftsmanship, an untamed ardour, a fearless and vivid intuition of truth' requiring in its poet the qualities of artist, lover and seer, Evelyn goes on to find that Tagore meets all requirements. It is perhaps unnecessary to rehearse her paean of praise in its entirety. Tagore is counted with the Sufi poet Jelalu d'Din Rumi, with Jacopone da Todi, and St John of the Cross. His thought meets that of St Augustine, Eckhardt, Mechtild of Magdeburg and Julian of Norwich. More significantly, perhaps, for Evelyn could hardly have bestowed higher priase on an Eastern mystic, his verse is wholly 'positive'. 'Coming,' as she writes:

> out of the midst of life, it accepts life in its wholeness as a revelation of the Divine mind. This is not the 'Via Negativa' of the Neoplatonists, but a positive mysticism, which presses forward to a 'more abundant life' (The Nation, 16 November 1912, p. 321).

It was perhaps inevitable also that she should find that Tagore's vision matched perfectly the Bergsonian vision of the universe she was so given to celebrating in these years:

> The flux of life, the living, changeful, onward-pressing universe of modern vitalistic thought is the stuff from which this seer has woven his vision of the truth.

Rabindranath Tagore *did* like Evelyn's review and in a letter to Rothenstein dated 16 December 1912 asked him to thank her for it: 'I appreciate it very much for she has written it with true understanding' (Lago, p. 82). Just a year later, in The Nation for 13 December 1913, Evelyn also reviewed at length *Sadhana: The*

Realization of Life and *The Crescent Moon, Child Poems*. From the former, among other things, she singled out Tagore's statement of his attitude to the Upanishads which, he wrote, had always been to him 'things of the spirit, and therefore endowed with boundless vital growth'. 'I have used them,' he went on:

> both in my own life and in my preaching, as being instinct with individual meaning for me, as for others, and awaiting for their confirmation my own special testimony which must have its values because of its individuality.

Evelyn's gloss upon this reads like a personal statement of her own faith. 'Observe here', she exclaims:

> the instinctive mystic appeal to experience as verifying formulae, as against the dogmatic appeal to formulae as verifying experience. Realization, actualization is the inspiring principle from first to last (The Nation, 13 December 1913, p. 499).

In her letter to Tagore of 29 November that year which tells him of the recent arrival of these books for review she wrote that reading *Sadhana* straight through (she had originally heard the material as lectures) she had found it impressed her enormously and had given her 'a more just & solid idea of the spiritual genius of India than I have ever come near before. I think the chapter on Realization in Action [referred to in the review] especially beautiful & important'. The letter ends with a direct and enthusiastic expression of her personal indebtedness to Tagore:

> I want so much to tell you—but it is not possible—what your kindness and friendship has meant to me this summer, & will always mean to me now. This is the first time I have had the privilege of being with one who is a Master in the things I care so much about but know so little of as yet: & I understand now something of what your writers mean when they insist on the necessity and value of the personal teacher & the fact that he gives something which the learner cannot get in

any other way. It has been like hearing the language of which I barely know the alphabet, spoken perfectly.

By the time this letter was written Evelyn's collaboration with Tagore was already well under way. It is clear from it that she had recently sent him her newly published collection of verses, *Immanence*, but already by 18 May she had shown him some of her verses and received his approbation of them. This same letter of May invites him to 'dine with us quietly' on Wednesday 28 May. At some stage, probably during the summer (the relevant letter is undated), she assembled Tagore and Dean Inge together under her roof. A letter of 12 July tells him how '*very* beautiful' she thought his play *The Post Office* had been. The same letter reveals that she is engaged on reading the manuscript of an English translation of the autobiography of Tagore's father, to which she suggests various improvements. This work, the translation of which seems to have been due to one of Tagore's brothers and other collaborators, was published by Macmillan & Co. in 1914. It carries a thirty-six page introduction by Evelyn in which she elaborately fits the spiritual autobiography of Tagore's father (he died on 17 January 1905) into not only the religious framework of India, for the benefit of English readers, but also into the traditional pattern of mystical development of Western mystical saints and sages, nearly all of whom she manages to evoke at least by name in the course of her exposition.

But the chief work in which Evelyn and Tagore collaborated was not the autobiography of Maharishi Devendranath Tagore but the translation of a number of mystical lyrics by them attributed to the fifteenth-century Bengali poet, Kabir. The little book which resulted from their labours entitled *One Hundred Poems of Kabir* and first published in early 1915 under the auspices of the India Society,[8] has constantly been reprinted since with

8. Now published by Macmillan (India): latest edition 1973.

Evelyn's eighteen pages of Introduction. So far as one can tell it is impossible at present to allot exact shares of responsibility for the version now so popular. Tagore had to hand not only a Bengali translation of such Hindi texts as were available at the time, but also a manuscript English translation prepared by two fellow-countrymen whose role is fully acknowledged in the Introduction. Evelyn's own part can only remain conjectural. She was certainly ignorant of Eastern languages and appears to have made no effort to acquire any of them; but she did undoubtedly have her impact on the final wording as a letter of 16 November 1913 referring to 'the various changes I made in the translation' makes clear. By this time the India Society, of which the leading light was A. H. Fox Strangways, a friend and correspondent of Sir William Rothenstein, was pressing to get the book into print. In the event publication was long delayed due to misunder-standings and difficulties as to who should have the final say in its disposal to a publisher. Evelyn felt herself empowered by Tagore in his absence to offer the manuscript to Macmillan's, a move fiercely resisted by Fox Strangways. On 20 March 1914 Rothenstein wrote to Tagore:

> He [Fox Strangways] is at present engaged in his last battle on behalf of the India Society—with the Stuart Moores. I think the calm way this lady [Evelyn Underhill] has tried to carry off the right of the society in your name has a little shocked most of us. In your last letter you gave me a very different feeling.[9]

Despite Rothenstein's umbrage, the editor of his correspondence with Tagore believes that the lady in the case *did* act on the latter's instructions. The question of who should be paid what in the already complicated equation seems to have been relatively easy to dispose of.

9. Lago, pp. 159–160: see especially p. 160, note 2.

The collaboration with Tagore certainly gave Evelyn great pleasure. It is almost immaterial that the poems they gave to the world are almost certainly not by Kabir and gave an impression of his doctrine totally at variance with reality. Evelyn for her part was simply 'writing up' material supplied to her by Tagore who was himself certainly a deeply sensitive contemplative man of letters—albeit possessed by a demon of restlessness like his father, but not interested in scholarship as such. Evelyn's view of the doctrine of Kabir reflected Tagore's own. But the points she singled out for special comment were not unnaturally those where the poet seemed to share a common mystical experience with his counterparts in the West or to add lustre to positions adopted by Evelyn herself. She could indeed cite no fewer than nine of the lyrics to reinforce her statement: 'Everywhere Kabir discerns the "Unstruck Music of the Infinite"—the celestial melody which the angel played to St Francis, that ghostly symphony which filled the soul of Rolle with ecstatic joy' (p. 14). How much of Evelyn this Kabir seemed to her to possess may be illustrated by her statement of the way in which he seemed to elude the third of the three great dangers which threaten mystical religions. 'Lastly', she wrote:

> the warmly human and direct apprehension of God or the Supreme Object of love, the Soul's comrade, teacher and bridegroom, which is so passionately and frequently expressed in Kabir's poems balances and controls those abstract tendencies which are inherent in the metaphysical side of his vision of Reality: and prevents it from degenerating into that sterile worship of intellectual formulae which became the curse of the Vedantist school (pp. 11–12).

Insofar as these lyrics did indeed represent the warmly devotional or bhakti approach to religion Evelyn was not here, perhaps, so far off the mark. But it is sad that the real Kabir as known to modern scholarship could not possibly have recognised himself in her account of him as one who extolled 'the life of home, the value and reality of diurnal existence, with its opportunities for love and renunciation'. Perhaps that really was too much to demand of any Indian mystic![10]

Evelyn also wrote an article on Kabir which develops slightly points made in her Introduction to the poems. It appeared in the Contemporary Review for February 1914 with the title *Kabir, the Weaver Mystic*. The only important addition to the material of the Introduction concerns the doctrine of the poems and Christianity, the affinity between the two being much more emphatically brought out in the article. For Evelyn the strongly devotional monotheism of the poems, together with their sense of Divine Fatherhood and 'perpetual insistence on the virtues of meekness and love' argued some influence on the part of Christianity. It was natural for her to attempt such a rapprochement for she did sincerely believe that of all the ways to the beloved Reality the Christian one, rightly apprehended, was best. How and why this should be so she did her best to demonstrate in the book which was the other great preoccupation of these years, *The Mystic Way*. This work is in fact all the more telling for having been written during a period of major influence from two such eminent 'outsiders' as Kabir and Tagore. Machen, who had no patience with self-important and self-imported Swamis who disembarked on English shores to distribute mystical crumbs and loftily to inform us that we had reached the lower slopes of the mystical mountain, scoffed bitterly at the national tendency to proclaim 'ex oriente lux'.[11] Evelyn on the contrary rejoiced and, seeing the challenge, did what she could to meet it. The encounter

10. See Charlotte Vaudeville, *Kabir*, Oxford (Clarendon Press) 1974, vol. 1, p. 18 especially footnote 5.
11. An established phenomenon even at the turn of the century if Machen is to be believed. See *The Autobiography of Arthur Machen*, pp. 277-8.

with Tagore, with whom she does not seem to have continued to correspond (they both died in 1941), may indeed have been an incitement to do so.

Evelyn's remarks about the aims of the Religious Thought Society show that she was deeply concerned at this time over the ignorance typical of many Christians about the mystical dimension of their faith. After telling Mrs Heath that she had for some months held out against joining the committee of Inge's society for fear of its being a 'mere excuse for religious talk', she goes on:

> However I do see that whilst Theosophists, Higher Thoughtists and every other kind of heretic are having organized campaigns and 'group meetings' and the rest and getting hold of those who think themselves intelligent by the score, it is idle for Christians to sit tight and talk about the merits of 'wholesome Church Discipline' etc. We must meet them on their own ground and show what the treasures of Christian philosophy are. Not one in a thousand believers or unbelievers knows anything about them. I look on it as a sort of educative and missionary work really worth doing if it can be done in the right sort of way (*Letters*, pp. 138–39. Letter of 15 May 1912).

This passage, it is true, says nothing about mysticism but if we turn to the book in which she had already said a few months earlier, in February, that she was 'immersed', it is quite clear that the treasures of Christian mysticism is what she *meant*.

This book was *The Mystic Way*, first published in March 1913. Its sub-title, *A Psychological Study in Christian Origins*, gives some idea of the angle from which both mysticism and Christianity are approached in its pages. What it does not prepare the reader for is the complete 'take-over' of the New Testament and early Church history by mysticism and their thorough reinterpretation almost exclusively as a record of mystical experience. As such a re-interpretation it is indeed a *tour de force* and deserves to stand as a classic exposition of a point of view which it must be assumed will recur constantly in different forms in the course of Christian history. At the time it was published other thoughtful people were trying to explain the philosophical 'treasures' of Christianity in similar terms, for example Rudolf Steiner in his *Christianity a Mystical Fact and The Mysteries*, first published in 1910, or Annie Besant in her numerous theosophico-mystical writings. But Evelyn's is perhaps the most thoroughgoing, even plausible, of such attempts and both for its own sake and as an illustration of her long held convictions on the subject, her book deserves some consideration. After all, even some six years later, in 1919, when all the brouhaha about her heretical opinions had died down and she was on the point of becoming a communicant of the Church of England, she could write to Horace Hutchinson, who had just tried his hand at a similar exposition:

> Of course I thoroughly agree with you that Christianity was from the first essentially a mystical religion; to me, the doctrine of the New Testament is duly intelligible from that standpoint (*Letters*, p. 148. Letter dated 7 January 1919).

The Mystic Way does not so much take over where *Mysticism* had left off as throw into even sharper relief the philosophical positions adopted in the earlier book and show how Christianity, in so far as it is the story of a given corporate and individual religious experience, is their logical fulfilment and their crown. At the philosophical level it is Bergson, run now a poor second by Eucken, who dominates the view. His language of Becoming, Intuition, Action, Life, Evolution, supplies Evelyn with that amplitude of metaphysical resonance which every mystically oriented interpreter of sacred scripture has needed to have at hand. For the detail of particular incidents and experiences it is the language of depth psychology which she brings to bear, displaying in the process that almost pugnacious willingness to take at face value the abnormal and the miraculous element in Holy Writ which, as we have seen, inspired the 'Catholic reaction' of Fathers Joly and Tyrrell as they scented an ally for the defence of literal inspiration in the wierder corners of clinical documentation. Finally Evelyn's treatment in this book displays even more graphically her tendency—one which she elsewhere explicitly linked to the 'mystical temperament'—to sublimate recalcitrant time-conditioned history in the interests of the ever actual criteria of comparative psychology. It was indeed this last tendency which so shocked her friends, as we shall see.

In retrospect it seems strange that the religious dimensions of the idealist and immanentist vogue in philosophy were not more eagerly grasped by Christian religious apologists. After all, Thomas Aquinas in the thirteenth century had warmly embraced Aristotle even before the pagan mud had been decently washed from him. In pre-war Germany no doubt things were different but in Britain it could even seem ungracious and ultra-suspicious to scent Hegel behind Moberley's 'There is nothing in the Church that is not Holy Spirit,' or to read the doctrine of that same arch-prophet into the favour enjoyed among English theologians by certain theories of the atonement which frankly abandoned the immutability of God in favour of a suffering Absolute along lines we have already seen adumbrated by Evelyn. Other aspects of the immanentist vogue in connection with the excesses of R. J. Campbell have already been glanced at. Evelyn is therefore a fairly rare example of a theological thinker who unashamedly seized upon the alloy of a contemporary philosophical doctrine and attempted to transmute it into the pure gold of a mystical symbol. Even her only partial success makes many of the theologians of her and the preceding age seem rather dull dogs.

The world, she wrote, is 'one great stream of Becoming'; it is characterised by 'thrust and effort', a struggle between matter and spirit, in which struggle becomes act and act itself emerges as, quoting Bergson, 'an internal push, which has carried life by more and more complex forms to higher and higher destinies'. Thus Life seeks to reach out beyond itself, is full of 'cravings and intuitions' which the physical environment cannot satisfy but which egg it on to achieve consciousness of its destiny in a transcendent beyond.

An Immanent Thought in ceaseless development is then discerned by us as the Reality manifested in all existence: as artistic inspiration which, like the little inspiration of men, moulds matter and yet is conditioned by it. Piercing its way to the surface of things, engaged as it seems to us, in a struggle for expression, it yet transcends that which it inhabits. It is Becoming yet Being, a Growth, yet a Consummation: the very substance of Eternity supporting and making actual the process of Time. In such hours of lucidity we see in fact, the faint outline of the great paradox of Deity, as it has been perceived by the great mystics of every age' (p. 5).

This passage and the ideas surrounding it are the foundations upon which Evelyn builds her doctrine of the person and work of Christ. Jesus, in his person, in his heroic struggles, in his visions and achievements, in his darkness and agony, is the very archetype and exemplar of what it means to be Being swept up in Becoming, Eternity posted in Time, Spirit entombed in Matter, God incarnate in Flesh. And Jesus *is* the exemplar for we are all to a greater or lesser degree called to follow in his steps. The Life which Jesus handed to his disciples at the last supper was, and is, that which assimilates to itself all lesser lives, and is responsible alike for the tentative development of the amoeba and the groans too deep for utterance of the lovers of God.

It is precisely at this point that we enter what one might call the dimension of psychological realism. Again in the first pages of

Evelyn's book the basic position is made perfectly plain; the spiritual evolution of humanity, 'the unfolding of its tendency towards the Transcendental Order' is, as she says,

> as much a part of biology as the evolution of its stomach or its sense. In vain for theology to set this apart as alone the work of 'grace'. The action of 'grace', the spirit of love leading love to its highest expression, is continuous from the first travail of creation even until now (p. 6).

Hence the constant emphasis in her book on the analogy between normal psychic or mental development, and the unfolding of the 'mystic way', and the repeated references to this as an 'organic process' or an 'organic development'. What some readers of her book found especially offensive was the application of this view to the unfolding mystical consciousness of Jesus who, since he was the king and model of all mystics, could not for Evelyn be exempt from the consequences of what she calls 'that swinging pendulum of the unstable growing self, moving to new levels, which the Christian mystics call "the Game of Love".' Indeed the portrait of Jesus painted by Evelyn has more than a touch of 'the wild-eyed young rabbi' about him, that almost crazed apocalyptic genius beloved of another school of New Testament exegesis of the time, designated 'eschatological' because of the importance it attached to Jesus's preaching of the last times. This school of thought left distinct traces in the thinking of George Tyrrell and von Hugel but Evelyn's adaptation of it adds a dimension characteristically her own in turning the widely noticed psychological symptoms into the travail of a super-endowed spirit undergoing the successive purgations and illuminations, exaltations and self-abnegations, demanded in a lesser degree of all men impelled towards self-transcendence. The atonement of Jesus lies indeed precisely in the fact that he leads the process. Jesus's final '*Fiat volunta tua*', by which he expressed 'total submission to the Universal Will' is, as she says, 'the real atonement, the real return to the Divine Order made sooner or later by every evolving spirit (pp. 148-49).'

Very early in her book in fact the 'élan vital' ceases to be a philosophical concept and becomes a hermeneutical principle. Once so adopted it is used to expound the entire dynamism of Jesus and his disciples. It is the life the nurture of which is the sole aim of Jesus's so called 'ethical' teaching. It replaces the concept of grace and of the supernatural, the latter being designated at one point as 'our ridiculous phrase'. Translated into some kind of psychical energy the existence of which is abundantly demonstrated she claim in the remarkable ecstasies, illuminations, transfigurations, levitations, curative powers and, in a word, *vitality* of so many saints, the sacred élan becomes the explanation for many of the phenomena of the New Testament which hasty rationalists have supposed due to the myth-making fantasy of Jesus's followers. Or, if the supposed objectively considered events really do seem beyond credulity then the élan must be supposed at work prompting the profoundly mystical disciples to give symbolic expression to their 'experiences'.

It is not too difficult to see the impact of this novel kind of 'reductionism' on the historical framework of the New Testament story. Pious Christians like Arthur Machen and Jack Herbert seem to have supposed that Evelyn was bent on making of Jesus 'just another mystic'—even perhaps inferior to some of his followers in the quality of his experience; nothing in the New Testament, on her account, could it seemed, be taken at face-value any more; anything hard to swallow, the Virgin birth for example, could be attributed to the symbolic elaborations of the mystical consciousness (the evangelists all, of course, being mystics), true in intention but not literally ascertainable. The resurrection likewise, handled with great tact by Evelyn, became an experience to be handled, as she indeed had handled it, symbolically, as a 'great confused poem'. As she wrote:

a personal and continuous *life* was veritably recognised and experienced: recognised as belonging to Jesus, though raised to 'another beauty, power, glory', experienced as a vivifying force of enormous potency which played upon those still 'in the flesh'.

He was all gold when he lay down, but rose
All tincture—

says Donne, with the true poetic instinct for the essence of a situation (pp. 148, 149). Christ did indeed sacrifice himself, according to Evelyn's gospel, and he rose as a flood of new life immanent in the consciousness of his followers; he thus set on foot the transformation of the world, now no longer ignorant of the way, the mystic way, of integration in Reality.

It is not possible to leave *The Mystic Way* without remarking one characteristic piece of Evelyn's exegesis. This concerns the temptations of Jesus in the desert where he fasted for forty days and forty nights, and the devil tempted him. On Evelyn's account Jesus's departure for the wilderness under the impetus of the Holy Spirit is a natural result of his mystical sense of sonship of God, the swing of the pendulum from affirmation to negation. So far it was good. To wish to commune with the divine beloved in solitude after one's initial illumination (in Jesus's case this coincided with the ritual baptism of John) is a recurring and normal tendency of the mystic; such was the desire of Jesus at that moment. But in the desert Jesus was confronted by 'the unique and stupendous possibilities of his own nature' and he had to make a choice. His decision is described by Evelyn in terms which take us back once again to the theme of *The Column of Dust* and wholeness, which underlies her Christian philosophy of mysticism, in contrast, as she saw it with those of Platonists, Hindus and others:

The world-renouncing ascent to Pure Being, which Indian and

Platonic mysticism attempts and sometimes perhaps attains, was within His reach; as it has never been within the reach of any other of the Sons of Men. Yet this refusal of the temporal —the supposed interests of Eternal Life, this satisfaction of the Spirit's hunger for its home, He decisively rejected. In the full tide of illumination, knowing Himself, and knowing that Transcendent order in which He stood, He turned his back upon that solitude in which 'alone with the Alone' He might have enjoyed in a unique degree the perpetual and undisturbed fruition of reality. The *whole man* raised to heroic levels, 'his head in Eternity, his feet in Time,' never losing grasp of the totality of the human, but never ceasing to breathe the atmosphere of the divine; this is the ideal held out to us (p. 94).

Since *The Mystic Way* seemed to many to raise the question of Evelyn's orthodoxy from a Catholic Christian point of view it must also raise the question of her 'modernism'. Unfortunately in the present state of scholarship we are not in a position to say anything very useful about this. The relationship between Christian orthodoxy and the ubiquitous philosophical idealism and mystical immanentism of the pre-war years has never been properly studied. For many at the time it is fairly clear that modernism was *both* an attempt to iron out the more notorious incompatibilities between Catholic dogma and advances in contemporary biology, psychology and textual criticism, *and* a heavily philosophical re-interpretation of various Catholic doctrines in order to give them meaning and relevance for the informed opinion of the age. There was also, although it is infrequently noticed, a distinct mystical tinge to the thought of some so-called 'modernist' thinkers of the time to which corresponded a distinct anti-mysticism in the repression, as von Hugel noticed. No one it is true could well have been less mystically inclined than the Abbé Loisy whose utterances furnished the bulk of the propositions condemned by Pope Pius X in his decree *Lamentabili*. But others presented an utterly different picture, chief among them perhaps the Abbé Marcel Hébert, quoted with approval by Evelyn in *Mysticism*. Is Evelyn to be bracketed with the 'modernists' because she favoured an avowedly immanentist philosophy of mysticism and rode rather loose to the literal interpretation of certain 'dogmatic facts'? She herself vehemently defended her orthodoxy even when she accepted, in a sense, the label of 'modernist', and von Hugel was in much the same case.[12] Now that the change of theological fashion has gone against what was undoubtedly a narrow, repressive and authoritarian orthodoxy in the papacy, both she and von Hugel are more likely to incur honour than otherwise for the smell of bonfire which hung around them during the anti-modernist witch-hunt. As for the accusation of radical unorthodoxy it has yet to be lodged convincingly and does not therefore require an answer. Inge may have felt at the time that Bergson's philosophy was incompatible with belief in a transcendent God but Evelyn was far from believing this and, if Bergson's later statements have retrospective validity, so was Bergson.[13]

There is ample evidence that by mid-1914 the flood of interest in mysticism to which Evelyn had largely contributed seemed to be carrying all before it. A reviewer of the Quarterly Review, confronted by some eight 'mystical' volumes including Tagore's *Gitanjali*, *The Works* of Francis Thompson and no fewer than five volumes from the pen of Evelyn Underhill (two were the

12. One may maintain that von Hugel was radically unorthodox by the standards of 1910 and for that very reason a pioneer of modern theological enlightenment. Or one may defend the thesis that his orthodoxy was unimpeachable by any standard. No doubt similar stances could be adopted in Evelyn Underhill's case. But such a confrontation would be outside our scope.

13. Bergson's religious position was not made clear publicly and in detail until his publication of *Les deux Sources de la religion et de la morale*, 1932.

pseudonymous books of meditation *The Spiral Way* and *The Path of Eternal Wisdom*), readily adopted the suggestion of Dean Inge in his front page Times Literary Supplement review of *The Mystic Way* that a 'mystical revival' was under way. But such books, this reviewer said, were only

> the straws, sticks and logs floating on the surface of a much deeper and stronger current of interest and even enthusiasm for the phenomena of the spiritual life.

It was all partly a reaction to the material success and 'external ideals' of the Victorian age, he went on. Victorian optimism was a thing of the past and the Edwardian 'compromise with pessimism' was passing. Men were now becoming introspective and interested in 'the great question of the value of life which is bound up with the nature of consciousness and its relation to the universe'. This it seems was peculiarly the province of the mystic, the same mystic who could also lend a first-hand personal dimension to the current revaluation of psychology in so far as he presented himself as a pioneer or explorer of this recently opened-up territory. The mystic, too, was being discovered, along with comparative religion, as one who was in contact with an element common to all faiths and cultures and 'the only reality underlying them all'. The same reviewer had no doubt that Evelyn Underhill's *Mysticism* had 'done more to popularise the subject than any other single work'.[14]

Other commentators tended to dig rather deeper into the way in which the mystical revival expressed the aspirations, religious, philosophical and personal, of the age. Emma Hermann, for example, in 1912 could write:

> It is not too much to say that since Descartes there has never

14. 'The Quarterly Review', vol. 220 (1914) pp. 220ff.: *Modern Mysticism: Some Prophets and Poets*. By Leslie Johnston.

been a period in which the foremost elements in philosophic thought have fused so intimately not only with the religious aspiration of the universal soul but also with the theological and experimental interest in redemption. For the first time since the great metaphysical period of ecclesiastical dogma philosophy is tending once more to become a doctrine of redemption and the old cry, 'What must I do to be saved?' is whispering itself once more to the restless heart of a too early wearied age, and to the churning mind of an experimental and adventurous generation of thinkers.

Emma Hermann whose literary career runs for a time parallel to Evelyn's due to their common interest in mysticism and philosophy but without them ever meeting,[15] has much light to throw on the spirit of the age but the most accessible short description of the stage to which Evelyn had helped to bring public sentiment is probably provided by Dean Inge's review of *The Mystic Way* already referred to.

According to Inge in the Time Literary Supplement on 20 March 1913 (writing anonymously but the whole style and content of the piece shows it to be by him), 'books on mysticism are now pouring from the press . . . some sold by the thousand'. Chief among the latter was, of course, Evelyn Underhill's *Mysticism*. The Quakers, 'this once despised sect', are, Inge reports, experiencing a considerable increase in adherents especially from the ranks of Anglicans and Nonconformists. The new age indeed seemed to be dawning, that which George Tyrrell had foreseen shortly before his death when he prophesied that 'the Christianity of the future will be mysticism and charity'. But Maeterlinck too, had foreseen it when he wrote 'A book grows old only in propor-

15. A rather frosty exchange of letters took place between them later concerning passages of Evelyn's used in Emma Hermann's *The Meaning and Value of Mysticism* (1915) and insufficiently acknowledged.

tion to its anti-mysticism.' The recent successful visit of Rabin-dranath Tagore also served to underline the fact that 'mysticism in its essence is absolutely autonomous . . . (it) crosses all barriers'. Inge's more detailed reservations about Evelyn's position have already been noted and are merely repeated, fairly gently, here. He especially admired her commentary on the mass in *The Mystic Way*, finding it 'very interesting'; he follows this praise with the observation:

> It is tempting to speculate what the effect would be of a great mystical movement in the Church upon sacramental doctrine and practice.

This review has some incidental interest in quietly reversing Inge's view of the mystical *via negativa* which he had heavily criticised in his *Christian Mysticism*, then following the lead, as his terms indicate, of Walter Pater. Here he concedes that it has a purpose quite other than that of hyper-refining abstractions as he had previously maintained.

By 1914, then, Evelyn's position as a major figure in the contemporary religious scene seemed assured. Her books were very widely read and reviewed, and she herself was greatly revered and respected. In 1913 she was elected a Fellow of Queen's College for Women, as it was known. If the religion of the future was indeed to be strongly mystical in temper her own position in the van of its leadership seemed assured. But fashion in religious and philosophical affairs is as fickle as in most other departments of life. Even before 1911 the tide was beginning to turn against the philosophy to which Evelyn had pinned her colours. Theology was on the threshold of a major revolution in its categories. Europe and Great Britain were on the edge of a gulf which would make all the evolutionary optimism, mystical or otherwise, of the preceding decade seem unbearably facile and illusory.

7

Contemplation in Time
of War

OUR knowledge of Evelyn's reactions to the outbreak of war and of the way in which her life was affected by it is restricted by the apparently almost total failure to survive of letters or personal documents written by her during the period 1914–19. The development of her intellectual outlook is by comparison relatively easy to assess since the flow of published materials, books, editions, articles, continued unabated. For the daily course of her life on the other hand we have to piece together reports from her friends and from her father, and make the most of one or two hints she lets drop in later material and in some of her work published at this time. As we try to form a picture of her and her preoccupations from 1914 up to the eve of her return to communion in the Church of England in or about 1920 it may also be helpful to consider that other hitherto neglected fruit of her literary activity, her poetry.

Evelyn spent her war in London and had the company of her husband throughout. It is impossible to say what first-hand experience she had of the unmitigated horrors of war unleashed on the other side of the Channel. Though, as we shall see, no pacifist, she certainly writes of them in appropriate accents of abomination and distress. When such violence broke over London and bombs began to fall her father noted that she seemed to be enjoying herself, an observation which has to be weighed against his remark that he himself reacted by getting furiously angry while his wife remained 'calm but terrified'. Evelyn, we may conjecture, who was perfectly capable on some occasions of taking her colour from her surroundings, was equally capable on others of supplying the missing ingredient. Not that Mrs Underhill's alarm was entirely without justification. A direct hit was scored by the enemy on the house next door to their's while Lincoln's Inn, her husband's place of work, was similarly reduced to ruins at a relatively early stage of the bombing. Sir Arthur records in his *Memoirs* the deaths of two nephews at the front, Guy and Harold Thorne, only sons of his widowed sister.

Hubert appears to have pursued his profession at the bar. His personal and not insignificant contribution to the war effort was to turn his practical ingenuity to the invention of artificial limbs for the war-wounded in the Surgical Supply Workshop. One such gadget of his proved its worth and was widely adopted. Evelyn seems at an early stage to have engaged in work on behalf of the Soldiers and Sailors Families Association. This at least is the reasonable deduction of Lucy Menzies based on an article which appeared in the Saturday Westminster and which encapsulates the experience of visiting the families of absent soldiers and sorting out their problems. The work, which incidentally illustrates a curious transitional stage in our national development when genteel philanthropy worked hand in glove with an incipient state social welfare system, entailed coping with a wide range of reactions and attitudes among the wives and families of servicemen, from that of the determined exploiter building her case upon lies to that of the deserving but, alas, undocumented war 'wife' to whom the 'ladies' of the Association appeared to offer themselves as the only resource. Although Evelyn's piece, vivid as it is in a Dickensian sort of way, may now strike us as patronizing since we no longer approve of 'do-gooding', still less of writing it up afterwards, it does have value in bringing the scene to life and in reflecting the detached, humorous and businesslike way in which she practised her love of neighbour.

Evelyn also contributed to the war effort and to that, too, she contributed her spirit of gaiety. She was employed by Naval Intelligence (Africa), otherwise known as N.I.D.32, to prepare and translate guide-books. She found herself in congenial company for the same department had taken on another friend of this period, Emma Gurney Salter, and a brother and sister who were also to become fast friends of hers, Robin and Barbara Collingwood. With Barbara Collingwood, afterwards Mrs Gnospelius, Evelyn got on especially well and it is to her that we owe a further testimonial to Evelyn's joyousness as well as a physical description of her at this time, which she sent to Miss Margaret Cropper for her *Life of Evelyn Underhill*. Barbara Collingwood's candid yet friendly description reads in part:

> The astonishing thing about Evelyn in 1916 when I first met her, and when she was already a very well-known and respected poet and writer, was her gaiety. She was not certainly an impressive or even a striking object at first sight. She was smallish, stooping, and round-shouldered, her clothes definitely dowdy and her hair most unsatisfactory, though even in those days she wore her little lace caplet, which while giving her a cachet seemed less appropriate than in later years. But her creased little face, full of animation and very mobile, was an instant attraction; and as I remember it her face was always creased with laughter and twinkling with fun. She had a way of laughing up at you . . . . which, while endearing was, to the young and shy, just a trifle daunting. I had expected to meet a lady rather exquisitely withdrawn, but no one could have seemed less lofty and remote than Evelyn or more ready to meet everything and everyone with a bit of a grin, and a

splutter of laughter and a naughty irreverent joke. It was most refreshing (*Life*, p. 58).

The history of the 'lace caplet' which Evelyn wore for many years after this date, began during the visit to Holland in 1912. She did in fact buy several on that occasion, as her letters to Hubert make clear. The acquisition of 'cachet' via an article of clothing was no doubt incidental rather than the result of an elaborate design, yet the wearing of the odd little cap seems emblematic of her determination to be in the world and not of it, an outward sign of that inward detachment from the opinions of the worldly which many like-minded persons have adopted, witness the sacred thread, the saffron robe, the monastic cowl and tonsure, Fox's leather breeches, even perhaps the Christian Saviour's eccentric 'tunic', not to mention the weirdly decrepit headgear of this or that beloved pastor. Evelyn certainly seems to have approached the business of translating guidebooks in a detached enough spirit. She is recorded as having entertained her office by describing in detail a corner, presumably of Africa, which had no existence outside her imagination.

But life from 1914 onwards was not all gaiety for Evelyn, any more than it was for anyone else. Throughout the period of the war she kept up her writing, the only relatively slack period falling just after her publication of *Ruysbroeck* in 1915 and the publication of *Jacopone da Todi* in 1919. When not engaged on books she worked on editions, articles, reviews, introductions and, despite the apparent lack of surviving evidence, on writing letters. Since a certain amount of this writing bears directly on the war and its impact on her commitment to mysticism, this will come to be considered first. Some attention can next be paid to her poems, a last volume of which appeared in 1916. We can then glance briefly at the nature of her work and the evolution of her thought during the period as a whole.

The outbreak of war on 4 August 1914, besides catching the
Underhill family in the middle of a holiday on board *Wulfruna*
in the estuary of the Exe, also caught Evelyn putting the finishing
touches to her book *Practical Mysticism*. This book which she
describes in a letter of May that year to Herford Batsford of
B. T. Batsford Ltd, as an 'essay on Contemplation', had originally
been intended for Batsford's Fellowship Books series. Mr Batsford
had, however, to tell her that the series had not done well and his
firm could not continue it. His concluding remark probably
entitles him to be counted as the main instigator of *Practical
Mysticism* for he wrote:

> It is possible that the subject of 'contemplation' that you were
> going to work upon could be expanded and perhaps a higher
> priced book be issued which might have more chance of
> success . . .

a piece of advice which was adopted and a prophecy which was to
be amply justified by events, although it was not his house but
that of James Dent which reaped the commercial benefit.

Practical Mysticism, subtitled *A Little Book for Normal People*, was
intended as a plain man's guide to religious experience of a
mystical, or incipiently mystical, type. Its main features can be
looked at more conveniently later when we come to review its
context in Evelyn's thought. For the moment we shall notice it
simply in relation to the major events with which it coincided.
The war impinges on the dedication: 'The The Unseen Future',
as on the preliminary material, headed Preface 1914 and dated
14 September 1914, and very slightly on the concluding chapter
The Mystical Life. In her preface Evelyn sketches her first understanding of the turn of history against what she calls 'the "contemplative" attitude to existence'. On the one hand the 'dream of
a spiritual renaissance' must seem to have perished in the 'sudden
explosion of brute force'; on the other the efforts of all seem bent

on action, struggle and the practical virtues, thus putting at a disadvantage 'the passive attitude of self-surrender which is all' she says, 'that the practice of mysticism seems, at first sight, to demand'. Does not the harsh reality of war ruin also, she asks, men's belief in an immanent Divine Spirit in human souls? Her answer is that, certainly, the reality of war puts out of court 'superficially mystical notions' and, she insinuates, the rather trivial enthusiasm of the recent past. But mysticism has very much a rôle to play in a period of stress. It is founded on a profound experience of reality; de facto many have become mystics in periods of great conflict and have left their age the better for their experience. For mysticism is concerned with that vision without which the people perish, and which is absolutely necessary if men, or a nation, are to keep their grasp on a true perspective of the world, 'discerning eternal beauty beyond and beneath the apparent ruthlessness'. The result of such vision is to keep the rational soul 'active and vigorous' and its vision 'unsullied by the entangled interests and passions of the time'. 'Practical mysticism' therefore leads to 'renewed vitality' and it should be prized as men have learned to prize the mystically inspired labours of Joan of Arc and Florence Nightingale (Practical Mysticism, Preface, pp. vii–xiii). Even on the battlefield, she concludes in the last chapter, the contemplative, secure in his vision, will know that 'every aspect of life, however falsely imagined, can still be "saved", turned to the purposes of Reality: for all-thing hath the being by the love of God' (p. 155).

Evelyn's spontaneous reaction to the hideous evil of war is therefore two-fold. On the one hand the mystic is not prevented, rather the contrary, from being a vigorous upholder of his nation's cause; on the other hand he is possessed of a vision which assures him of the final resolution of all discords in a single beautiful harmony. Such an answer to such a problem thus succinctly expressed is not impressive. Very early in the war Evelyn had in

fact invited Anglican bishops through the columns of the Church
of England news-sheet called The Challenge, to give Christians
a lead in the matter. Since they were unable or unwilling to do
so except through individual warlike utterances in the correspondence columns of The Times she evidently felt herself con-
strained to give a more reasoned account of her views, which she
duly published in two articles, one in The Quest of January 1915,
the other in The Hibbert Journal for April of that year. The two
articles are complementary and both need to be studied to gain
a complete picture of her attitudes. The first, 'Mysticism and War',
devotes the bulk of the article to the equation mysticism = vigour
= true patriotism. The second, 'Problems of Conflict', studies and
advances the propositions that war though *apparently* a bad thing
is (a) 'part of the substance of life', i.e. inevitable, (b) only, after
all, a *realtively* greater evil that those we encounter daily and
accept without metaphysical heart-burn, even in peacetime, and,
(c) a 'constructive force'. From the standpoint of the convinced
Christian pacifist, which Evelyn later adopted, both articles make
painful reading, the former just more so than the latter. Neither
was considered worthy by her of being included in later collec-
tions of her scattered articles. As evidence however of the ease
with which apparently sublime doctrines can be diverted if not
perverted (from a pacifist's point of view) to sanction retrospectively if not to condone, what is objectively base beyond words
and irremediably tragic, these apologies of Evelyn have a certain
exemplary value relevant in our own day and, in any case, need
to be discussed and related to her general outlook.

The article in The Quest is largely devoted, as we have seen,
to developing the first of the two points made in the preface of
Practical Mysticism, to the effect that the mystic, far from being a
supine drop-out, as we should say today, is a person to whom his
nation's cause is dear in war and peace. The shape of Evelyn's
argument is not unfairly represented in a series of illustrative

phrases and sentences. Rejecting the popular misconception that the mystic is 'a secluded and anaemic creature' she advances to confront the confusion in Quakerism and, 'to a lesser extent' in Tolstoy, of mysticism and pacifism. Pacifism and Christianity have, she argues, nothing in common. Joan of Arc was led by her voices to the battlefield; the Christian, 'since the world as well as the gospel is for him a manifestation of the Divine Reason', in which Christ is perpetually re-born, is inclined 'to accept the ever-present fact of conflict as a part of the mysterious plan' (p. 208). There are two kinds of mystic, a good mystic, who is active:

> the struggling, fighting soul whom the Early Christians called an athlete of the Spirit; who grows by conflict, accepting his part in a world order of which effort is the very heart . . .

and the quietist:

> who resists nothing, risks nothing, conquers nothing, (and) who has been condemned again and again (p. 209).

Contemporary stress on the divine immanence and the brotherhood of mankind have sugared the ultimate realities of life and hidden them from many, breeding 'a charming but effeminate view of mysticism'. But what Evelyn offers is a 'true and virile mysticism'. This type acknowledges the virtue of loyalty, defined as 'the whole-hearted acquiescence of the individual in the acts and needs of the corporate life', and also has no illusions about the so-called triumphs of civilisation. Though the mystic acknowledges a divine spark in everyman his 'sanity' enables him to see that it burns 'with a stifled flame'.

At this point Evelyn reaches her central thesis: 'The mystic, then, accepts the fact of war.' It follows that the mystic throws himself into struggle and strife; his enhanced spiritual energy can indeed take a 'military form'—as it did with Joan of Arc and

General Gordon. Evelyn goes so far as to say that the mystic is not over-concerned about victory in battle, so long as courage and endurance are displayed 'in defence of the right'. Suffering in such a cause is redemptive. The mystics, who should be far from 'softness' and what she describes as 'a sort of cosmic amiability', all too prevalent in the world of 1915 apparently, are, on the contrary, bred up to accept 'suffering, effort, *cost*'. At this point Evelyn gives free rein to what a French lecturer on ascetics once described as a 'spiritualité de l'échec', a doctrine of the necessity and beneficial consequence of universal struggle, of which 'the deadly strife of nations' is a particular manifestation. To embrace such a cross is for our spiritual good. The article concludes on the theme: 'every activity amongst men is capable of being lifted from the dark to the light: and war is no exception to this rule'. Among benefits war confers are an undermining of 'our rampant individualism' and a 'quickened sense of corporate life'.

The article in the Hibbert Journal which follows this one concentrates on the theological justification of war in mystical-immanentist terms. Some of the same ground is covered but the tone is more metaphysical as became an article in a philosophical journal. The position is, however, no less committed. Man cannot transcend war—on the contrary, through war he may actually transcend himself for war has about it 'a religious element, a supersensual touch'. Perhaps, indeed, writes Evelyn, war is 'a medecine of humanity' as philosophers have argued. It is an inbuilt corrective, a condition of physical existence which 'we can hardly hope to transcend'. Having thus 'justified' war's existence, she does concede that militarism 'in its worst forms' must be considered 'a sordid and terrible sin'—war must be worked against just as disease and poverty, yet in the knowledge that, like them, it is 'inevitable'. At this point Evelyn changes tack and points out the stupidity of taking scandal at the existence of war in God's world when there are few of the horrors of war which do not 'find their opportunity in times of peace'. She lists cruelty, lust, squalor, revenge, the destructive effects of industrialism, 'the wreckage of vice and degeneration which underlies peaceful prosperity'. 'The Faith,' she argues:

> which can face these facts, and reconcile slum life, prostitution, sweating, the ravage of hereditary diseases, with the all powerful love of God, ought to be able to endure the cleaner, franker cruelties of warfare, wherein obvious evils are at least compensated by direct and obvious goods (p. 503).

Such an argument is purely *ad hominem*. The trouble with such arguments is that they tend to leave one justifying more than one had originally bargained for. In her final pages Evelyn is virtually taking on the whole problem of evil as she attempts to demonstrate how suffering and strife can be reconciled with the compassionate nature of God. Her standpoint is, she writes, one of 'transcendence'. But she does not use the word in the sense in which some at that time were already beginning to use it, to extricate the nineteenth-century immanent or monist deity from his works. *Her* transcendent God is still all too involved and compromised as, far from cutting him loose from the whole miserable business or setting him in judgement over it, she attempts to show how, though the suffering is ghastly, even the quantity of real evil diminishes with the forces of argument and so much as is left may not unbecomingly feature in the *realpolitik* of a God whom she aptly but with an unconscious irony compares to some hideous minatory quasi-divine destructive force in the Hindu pantheon. Warfare, she says, thinking back to Kabir, is but an episode in the divine game, the Lila of God. The nadir of the whole argument is reached in the paragraph:

> The question about war's ultimate rightness or wrongness then, must be, not 'How much wealth does it waste?' not 'How many simultaneous deaths does it occasion?' not even 'How

much innocent happiness and general well-being does it destroy?' but what is its effect on the national character?' (p. 508).

Evelyn was not alone in her attempt to justify the ways of man in the name of God. It is tempting to shift some of the blame for her twisted logic onto the shoulders of the dominantly monist philosophy of the age. For indeed, if God is so very present to and in his world, who is the believer to complain of the many and Protean shapes which an ever elusive divinity may adopt to test her? Yet others took similar attitudes without the benefits of such philosophical *a priori*, notable among them Friedrich von Hugel, whose patriotic extravaganzas while they certainly did not glorify war sought justification in God's name for one party alone. Few were those who, like another future director of Evelyn, the Anglican priest Reginald Somerset Ward, firmly rejected warfare as a tolerable way of settling political disputes. Given her standing as the authentic voice of mysticism at the time it is likely that Evelyn's views were echoed in the bellicose pulpit oratory of the early years of enthusiasm for the righteous war, and one can only regret the fact. Some sixty years later identical attitudes are struck under different inspiration and deploying different slogans, and yet with curiously similar types of argument and Christians appear to be just as much in the dark about the ethics of violence and the morality of engaging in generalised and massively destructive conflict. Evelyn herself did not return to the ethics of warfare until the problem again presented itself with actuality in the thirties when she took an entirely opposed view. Her tacit abandonment of these articles so far as later republication was concerned, suggests that she was not concerned about their survival. Their lasting significance, apart perhaps, from preparing the ground for her later pacifism, is to show how she was forced by the war to think about the relationship of the mystical vocation to the historical, cultural, political and social environment in which it is lived. The impetus to do this almost certainly comes from von Hugel's leaning on her 'Quakerish tendencies' for, as we shall see, she was beginning to face this question some time before war broke out. Its doing so added a particular urgency to the matter.

In 1916 Dent & Sons published *Theophanies*, the second of Evelyn's volumes of collected verse, the first having appeared from the same publishing house in 1912 with the title *Immanence*. By 1916 Evelyn's reputation as a poet stood a good deal higher than her reputation as a novelist if not as high as her fame as the exponent of mysticism. Her verse had appeared spasmodically in various journals from the turn of the century and no doubt a good deal more exists to be 'collected' than is known through these two slim volumes. Periodicals such as The Nation at about the time Rabindranath Tagore's name was beginning to appear in its pages in 1911, published her verse as well as her reviews and the existence of a 'mystical revival' could be deduced solely from the steady recurrence of so much rather indifferent celebration of the mystical theme in their pages. For Evelyn certainly was not alone in writing mystical verses at this time. She was indeed a leading practitioner but one has only to skim the pages of, say, the pre-war Quest or The Nation to see just how large was the appetite of a certain sector of the cultivated public for this kind of thing. It was a time which repeated with relish the story of W. B. Yeats's friend, the yogi, who, being invited to consider whether there was any reason he could think of why prose should exist, cogitated profoundly and replied that there was none.

Just as few things in literature are more absorbing than first-rate 'metaphysical poetry' so few things are deader than second-rate 'metaphysical poetry'. A man can play the fool anywhere, wrote Montaigne, except in poetry, and few things look more foolish than a self-conscious straining after mystical 'effects' in verse. This is the fault of the bulk of the verse of the

period. For one W. B. Yeats there seem to have been hundreds of
D. H. Lawrences—so far as mystical verse is concerned. Some of
Evelyn's fellow versifiers were collected into *The Oxford Book of
Mystical Verse* of 1917 where she herself is represented by *Imma-
nence* from her first volume of collected verse. In the same
Oxford Book one will find poems of, among others, Arthur
Waite and Aleister Crowley, Francis Thompson, R. H. Benson,
Eva Gore-Booth and Alice Meynell, 'A.E.' (George William
Russell), James Stephens, John Masefield, with all or any of
whom Evelyn's verse invites comparison. Of these, we already
know something of her relation with Waite and Benson. She
was later to write an Introduction to a posthumous collection of
verse by Eva Gore-Booth whom she seems to have known, if not
well. With A.E. she shared the honour of being published in
The Horlicks Magazine where A.E.'s 'The City', included in
The Oxford Book, first appeared. A.E.'s evocation of the mystically
transfigured tram in this poem suggests vividly the preoccupations of the 'school' to which Machen and Evelyn belonged,
as well as suggesting a course English poetry *might* have embarked upon successfully but didn't.

It is difficult to engage in critical dialogue about Evelyn's verse
since scarcely anyone these days reads it. Professor Hoxie Neale
Fairchild devoted a certain amount of his attention to her work
in his *Religious Trends in English Poetry* (volume V) but his treatment is inadequate if only for the reason that he totally ignores
the existence of *Theophanies*, omitting it even from his bibliography. Locating her verse without too much difficulty in the
immanentist poetic vogue of the period, he finds her theological
position ambiguous, ostensibly Christian, effectively pantheistic,
and derives in general an impression of 'excessive softness and
easiness' in her approach to the high mystery of divine immanence
in nature; so much so, indeed, that Christian revelation, the atonement, seems 'almost superfluous'. Professor Fairchild concludes

his remarks on Evelyn Underhill's poetry by linking her with Charles Williams, and observing:

As Christians Evelyn Underhill and Charles Williams are shielded from the temptation to feel themselves infinite. Even they, however, tend to think of God too exclusively as a guest in the garden or the bedchamber. They concede too much to the immanentist and 'inward witness' apologetics of their day. Also since this defect is much less apparent in their prose than in their verse, they are probably subject to the fallacy that mystical poetry should sound more romantic than mystical prose.[1]

Professor Fairchild's remarks, while they insinuate more than a grain of truth, are in one respect at least misleading. Evelyn didn't merely wish to *look* or *sound* romantic, she *was* romantic through and through; at the time when she wrote most of her verse she rejoiced in so being for that was abundant life and the meaning of existence. Moreover the prose of her novels scarcely lags behind the poems in this respect even when, as is certainly the case in *The Column of Dust*, she uses the plot to inculcate a lesson of spiritual realism. Even the special mystico-poetical language which she sometimes deploys in the poems, words such as 'sigil', periphrases such as 'the Only Fair', the 'Hidden Thing', the 'Master Builder' have their equivalents in her prose writing. Perhaps, taking a leaf from the book of Yeats's yogi, it would be more true to say of her early writing, whether in prose or verse, that according to the view it embodies all utterance that aspires to ultimate significance must, by that very token, aspire to poetry, i.e. to rhythm, symbolism, allusiveness and evocative power.

1. H. N. Fairchild, Religious Trends in English Poetry, vol. 5, New York and London, 1962; pp. 254—260.

Evelyn's poetry is without doubt immanentist in tendency. If we set aside all question of her sincerity, which is not at issue here, it would probably be true to say that the *only* poems of hers which succeed in conveying intensity of feeling, 'contact' as she might have said, are those in which a given experience of communion with God in and through nature or a natural scene, are conveyed. Such poems would be 'The Tree' or 'White Magic' (originally 'Divine Magic') from *Theophanies* (pp. 26, 67), which correspond to the scenes of mystical illumination in the novels. At most other times one simply has to take the poet's word for it, a lamentable state of affairs in most poetry and doubly disquieting when the poet has deliberately undertaken to insinuate the ineffable. It is difficult to know what to make, for example, of a poem like 'Nebula and Nest' (*Theophanies*, p. 19), written before her intoxication with the Bergsonian quasi-divine flux, in which the mystic quest is compared to a tour of the cosmos by a feathered being, the soul. At least that is what one thinks it is about, until one abruptly finds oneself sitting at the poet's window with God affectionately rustling at her from inside the nearby chestnut tree and the feathered soul, tired of acting the part of a sort of love-sick cosmic sparrow, settles down with an audible sigh of relief and the reflection that home—'nestling warm against a feathery breast' —is best after all.

Evelyn could never succeed in the epic vein. She would dearly have liked to translate into verse the white-hot passionate quest of the Plotinian soul for intelligible Beauty, the agony of longing, the joy of lovers' meeting, the wonder of the shared beholding. But her muse was not cast in this mould. Despite her attempts to kick against this particular goad she probably understood her limitation. Both her books of poems begin by suggesting the environment in which she did—to use the phrase for once with full deliberation—feel most 'at home'. The opening poem of *Immanence* (entitled 'Immanence') beings:

I come in the little things,
Saith the Lord:
Not borne on wings
Of majesty, but I have set My feet
Amidst the delicate and bladed wheat
That springs triumphant in the furrowed sod;
There do I dwell in weakness and in power:
Not broken or divided, saith our God.
(Immanence, p. 1).

And that of Theophanies, entitled 'Mountain Flora':

As the plant on the smooth of the hill,
That sees not the deep and the height,
That knows not the might
Of the whole . . .
I know not the terrible peak
The white and ineffable Thought,
Whence the hill-torrents flow
And my nurture is bought.
I am little and meek;
I dare not to lift
My look to his snow
But drink, drop by drop, of its gift.
(Theophanies, p. 1)

Such poems standing at the threshold of Evelyn's verse act as warnings not to expect too much in the way of mystical thrills. Small birds and flowers, trees and streams, field, garden and hedgerow, are her messengers and the natural focus of her contemplation. Her self-identification with lesser natural objects reminds one of the similar tendency of Ste Thérèse of Lisieux who, if one examines her work attentively could just as well be designated, if the proprieties allowed, 'the little bird' as 'the little flower'. Evelyn's muse tends to flag in proportion as her symbols increase in dimensions. Her poems evoking mountains suggest less than those set in fields and gardens. With a single natural object she can work a kind of minor magic but when she sets out to explore the cosmos she is lost.

It seems unduly censorious to describe her verse as 'pantheistic'. The temptation to seek out heterodox tendencies in so-called Christian or Catholic poets is one that critics often appear unable to resist. It is sometimes as though they wished to force a divorce between literature and its inspiration in an apparently harsh and uncompromising milieu to which they themselves feel alien. In Evelyn's case the suggestion of a divine indwelling of nature can be found on nearly every page. It is palpable in the verses above, especially in the last of the lines from 'Immanence' quoted, where 'Not broken or divided' recalls and is intended to recall, as the reference to 'bladed wheat' makes clear, Aquinas's eucharistic sequence celebrating the mystical indwelling of Christ in the consecrated bread:

> A sumente non concisus
> Non confractus non divisus
> Integer accipitur

'He is eaten whole and entire neither parted nor broken nor divided'. This notion of a sacramental indwelling of nature by God is not merely a quirkish assumption of Evelyn but a fundamental tenet of Christian theology with a long tradition behind it, to which Evelyn's title-page quotation from the ninth-century theologian, John Scotus Erigena, bears witness. Evelyn probably gathered Erigena's sentence from Inge's *Christian Mysticism* (p. 16). It reads: 'Every visible and invisible creature is a theophany or appearance of God', and is an accurate summary of the spirit in which she wrote a great many of her poems. But the doctrine is also, one might say, a commonplace of Christian poetry and meditational prose, beloved especially by the seventeenth-century Platonists and the English and American muse generally—Evelyn quotes or alludes to Walt Whitman almost as much as she does William Blake. When poets implicitly or explicitly choose to write in this tradition it seems rather too bad to accuse them of a theological position which would make nonsense of their intuition. To say that the tree or the mountain, the thrush or the flower is the message, mirror, vehicle, channel or 'duct' (to use Evelyn's word) of God is not at all the same thing as saying that all such natural objects *are* God. Evelyn herself would also wish to remind her critics of the elementary distinction between attempting to express a given 'feeling-state' in symbolic language and uttering propositions in precise theologically accountable terms.

She is in fact the last person one would choose to take as an example of a poet whose mystical intuitions confounded her theology. This is not simply because she was in perfect control of both her theology and her poetry but because her poetry is usually dependent for its effect precisely on a distinction between the symbol and that for which it stands. This can occur in a variety of ways. In 'The Train', for example, with its striking contrast between the blind onward plunge of life under one aspect, and its still God-centredness when seen under another, it is made clear that the still movement of nature is in the end, and relative to the only 'end' that matters, much 'faster' than that of the train. Natural progression is 'divine' compared with man's helter-skelter rush through 'the void', but only relatively so, only because nature in being itself is in some sense praying and seeking God as man ought, but hasn't time, to do:

> Where the long hedge leans to leeward
> One little sharp upstarting leaf I find,
> And deep within the hearted curl of it,
> Secret and strong as the wistful dream of a virgin,

> The bud that shall bear the immortal germ on its way—
> Small, humble, uncounted,
> Pricking the path the future shall tread to the light.
>
> (*Theophanies*, p. 10).

Nature for Evelyn is a veil of the divine, sometimes revealing sometimes concealing; in either case its rôle can only be defined in relation to that of which it is the intimation. What distinguishes her choice of subjects and may, indeed, sharpen suspicions of pantheism, is her tendency to exalt process as against completion, becoming as against being. This is apparent in the opening lines of 'The Tree' or of 'Dynamic Love', quoted earlier, and other poems. It is expressed in terms which allow for little misunderstanding of her aim although they lend themselves to the most heinous heterodoxy if interpreted literally, in, for example, 'Primavera':

> Who knows the Spring?
> He, when he lays his hands
> On any growing thing
> Discerns the pulse of God, and understands
> How that the Father's heart
> Thrusts forth in steady rhythm of charity
> To every part
> His life and energy. (*Theophanies*, p. 41.)

Such a poem is typical of those which owe all to the 'élan vital' of Henri Bergson, 'the holy thrust of living things' as she elsewhere transcribes it (*Theophanies*, p. 4). Such 'biology' certainly came handily for suggesting the participation of the created in the creator but it stops short of identifying the one with the other. The veil certainly is thin at times but its presence is indubitable and sharply felt when vitality flags, the light seems to fade and the beauty diminishes. Sometimes, indeed, Evelyn grows tired of such mediated vision and seems to plead for a sort of intellectual innocence, an indication perhaps of the way her active mind with its intellectualising schemata, seemed to her to spoil the artless directness of true communion with God. Thus some lines from 'Nature':

> I ask not beauty, but a little space
>> Swept clear for him;
>> Some naked place,
>> Intimate, dim
> Some haven where the fretted mind may rest,
> Where thy quick colour and inconstant sound
>> At last are steadfast found. (*Theophanies*, p. 56.)

It would be possible to corroborate a number of Evelyn's moods and preferences from the poems; Her association of sky and divine presence (*Theophanies*, pp. 2, 15–16; *Immanence*, p. 11), the mood of stillness in prayer (*Theophanies*, pp. 48–49, 67–69, 85), the anti-ecclesiastical note (*Theophanies*, p. 94), the suggestiveness of scents (*Theophanies*, p. v, 42, 48, 53, 74), the Mother and Child representing Maternal Life and the Soul (*Immanence*, p. 49). But such poems have little more than documentary value. The same is also true of her war poems in which she attempts to give voice to the feelings of patriotic womanhood deprived, as she was not, of menfolk, and beset by anxiety. Though she may genuinely have shared sympathetically the anguish of others these verses at the end of *Theophanies* have a forced air and suggest Evelyn felt her fame obliged her to express for others what they were incapable of expressing for themselves. The mantle of public poet did not suit her.

Evelyn was a deliberate worker for all her love of passion and spontaneity. We have seen how she announces her 'scale' at the opening of each of her books of verse. The poems which close them are no less significant. The last poem of *Immanence*, entitled

Transcendence, which the well-known Quaker historian, Rufus
Jones, chose to adorn the opening of his *Spiritual Reformers of the
Sixteenth and Seventeenth Centureis* (1914), suggests even more
clearly than 'Nebula and Nest', that the quest for God outside
the charmed circle of the daily domestic round is a waste of time.
God is here and now or he is nowhere and never. The effect of
the poem is, indeed, effectively to deny the significance of its
title. It is as though Evelyn's God, for all his Majesty and unutter-
able Beauty,—in theory—lacked the transcendental dimension
which would give the concept of exploration any validity in
practice. In theory, again, this dimension is fully allowed for in
Mysticism, and all the language of questing and seeking, exploring
and pioneering the trackless wastes of the divine wilderness are
seen to be occasioned (in that book) by the divine transcendence.
But in her verse there is no sense that this was ever Evelyn's own
experience. There the accent is predominantly on the homeliness
of God, his closeness and accessibility. It is indeed, as Professor
Fairchild says, all too easy. Any additional accusation that such
accessibility renders otiose the atonement of Christ can conveniently be left on one side for the present since it is one that Evelyn
did attempt to anticipate. So far as the collected poems of
Immanence are concerned it remains true that the last of them, as
the first, is characteristic of them all. But by the time we reach
the last poem of *Theophanies* Evelyn was ready to abandon verse
altogether and admit that she had not added much to the harmony
of the whole. As we have already remarked in connection with
her `examination of conscience it would be rash to assume so
clear-sighted a commentator did not mean her self-criticism—
even if Dante did write something similar at the conclusion of the
Paradiso. This last poem, entitled 'Invocation', ends:

> Yet since the humble lover can
> Ask all things, as thy seers have told,

> Within thy mighty metric span
> My faltering song do thou enfold:
> That in thy symphony of grace
> The note of failure finds its place.

Lucy Menzies records that when Evelyn was asked why she no longer wrote poetry she replied: 'Because it is too easy.' It is scarcely surprising that the woman who had never thought that the spiritual life should be easy or cosy, had experienced some of its difficulties and was to endure more and more of the sheer grind of it as life wore on, should find flowing, bouncy, almost school-girlish rhymes and rhythms about birds and flowers, mountains and clouds, inadequate to articulate her experience. Her poetic gift which blossoms, where it blooms at all, on the strength of her experience of illumination in both a man-made and a natural environment proved inadequate to the complexity of a still richer range of experience.

The Bar-Lamb's Ballad Book and the early doggerel undoubtedly left Evelyn with an unfortunate legacy of facility and a tendency to pastiche which peeps through sometimes even when she is at her most serious. It makes for example a painful appearance in 'Lila, the Play of God' which deliberately adopts the rhythms of Blake's 'Tyger' in order to underline the fact that it is attempting to grapple with the same problem. This poem is one of several which comment on the scandal of the existence of anguish and evil in creation and take us philosophically no further than the wartime articles already examined. They do if anything underline the inadequacy of Evelyn's analysis from which the notion of suffering as vicarious satisfaction is not absent. The notion that pain, 'Holy pain', has value as satisfaction in God's sight is conveyed in particular in 'Friday Night', a poem on self-scourging (Theophanies, p. 75). It was very much part of Evelyn's belief that sacrificial suffering is inscribed as it were in the very processes of nature where Christ is constantly being 'slain' in nature's cruelty. This idea is connected with the war in 'Any English-woman may' (1915) (*Theophanies*, p. 112).

Among other religious poets whose work finds its echo in Evelyn's lyrics are Francis Thompson (died 1907) whose 'Hound of Heaven' she greatly admired, and, occasionally, by an allusion of rhythm as much as anything, Herbert or Donne (*Theophanies*, p. 15; *Immanence*, p. 45). Thompson in particular looms behind her longer 'cosmic travel' poems such as 'Nebula and Nest', though he is hardly absent from a 'chase' poem such as 'The Backward Glance' in the rhythm of 'The Ancient Mariner', of the earlier collection. Thompson, who wrote so much poor or mediocre verse, some of it jingoistic to a degree, shows up the strong points of Evelyn's work. Her surplus of philosophical content seems preferable to his emptiness and if she never rises even to the heights of, say, Alice Meynell's 'The First Snow', she does have her moments as she is lifted, almost in spite rather than because of, trying so hard, 'beyond the Garden' to convey:

The strange and stealthy onslaught of the deep. (*Theophanies*, p. 64).

To turn from Evelyn's poems to Evelyn's work in the period 1914–20 is to become aware of certain differences between the later and the earlier Evelyn, between the enthusiast of *Mysticism* and Bergson whom the poems largely represent, and the scholarly editor of texts and lucid writer of articles and spiritual biographies who now presents herself. From a purely external point of view the change speaks for itself. In her three works, *Mysticism, The Mystic Way*, and *Practical Mysticism*, Evelyn had fully expounded her views as to what mysticism is, its consequences for its devotees and her own absolute commitment to the mystic way as the kernel of meaningful religious practice. In the same books she had also made accessible to a large public a catena of mystical texts drawn from neoplatonists, Sufis, mediaeval priests, monks and nuns, protestant illuminists, Catholic quietists and many others. She had also re-interpreted the fundamental documents of Christianity and she had written a plain man's guide to the practice of contemplation. The work that lay ahead was, logically, one of continuing the labour of vulgarisation by making some of her favourite mystical personalities and writings better known, while she also accompanied this work of palaeography and research with a series of reflective and philosophical articles in which she tried to define the status and rôle of mysticism more precisely. One aspect of this work we have already noticed in discussing her reactions to the war. Since our chief interest is in the development of her ideas, this aspect of her work from the publication of *Practical Mysticism* to the publication of the collected articles in *The Essentials of Mysticism* in August 1920 will, for the sake of orderly procedure, be treated second, after we have first looked at the biographical and editorial side of her work.

Evelyn worked hard to popularise the lives and writings of the mystics. In the course of working for *Mysticism* she had turned over a large number of mystical writings both printed and unprinted, both in English and in other languages. Probably no one else at the time had such an awareness of what was and was not actually or potentially accessible to the public at large. But almost no guides existed through this bewildering literature. Neither Inge nor von Hugel were greatly interested in the writings of the mystics as documentary evidence for mystical *lives*, considering them much more in the light of medieval and, indeed, contemporary metaphysics, ethics and theology. Others such as George Tyrrell or Edmund Gardner had also achieved something in this field but none equalled her in terms of quantity of output up to 1920. She was without doubt Great Britain's leading pioneer in this field. Evelyn was not greatly interested in abstruse discussion of any given mystic's stance in relation to, say, the poetry of

William Wordsworth or the philosophy of the contemporary professor, Ernst Troeltsh, however valuable that might be in its place and however valuable a given contemporary philosophy might be for making a mystical document more vivid. She looked for her mystic's reading of the place of love in the mystical life, his or her experience of prayer, sense of balance, attitude to the church, to ascetism, etc. In other words she looked for a characteristic psychology as well as a doctrine or a philosophy.

Her first published work of this type which appeared in 1911, concerned Ruysbroeck and the previously unpublished anonymouse treatise *The Mirror of Simple Souls*, work which was rapidly followed by a substantial article on Angela of Foligno (1248–1309) contributed to Paul Sabatier's *Franciscan Studies* (1912). What she saw in Ruysbroeck we shall consider when we come to the biography she devoted to him. As for *The Mirror*, she not only wrote an article for the Fortnightly Review summarising its literary history and contents, she also edited a selection of extracts. It was an obvious choice for her attention, in some ways more so than she realised. Over fifty years after her pioneer efforts to make it a little better known to the general public it has now been demonstrated that the book is the work of a woman mystic, Margaret Porette, of the late twelfth and early thirteenth centuries, who was burnt at the stake in Paris on 31 May 1310. The personality of the writer was to some extent concealed from Evelyn since she was concerned with an early English translation but, from the scholarly point of view, despite her ignorance of these details, her little introduction reads well, situating the work correctly as to date but shrewdly abstaining from any precise judgement as to milieu. Such positive indications as she does give are useful and the suggestions of a latent tendency to heterodoxy is born out by the findings of modern scholarship.[2]

2. Thesis, pp. 198ff.

The Mirror does not cut a great figure in the history of mysticism. The anonymous late fourteenth-century treatise, *The Cloud of Unknowing*, on the other hand, is one of the classics of mystical writing. Despite its patronage by the famous seventeenth-century English Benedictine mystical writer, Father Augustine Baker, who also wrote a commentary on it, the text of the treatise was not published until 1871 when the Reverend Henry Collins produced a defective edition devoid of any scholarly sanction. By 1912 this had long been out of print. Evelyn quoted the text from manuscript for the first edition of *Mysticism* and John M. Watkins issued her edition, based on a number of fifteenth-century manuscripts accessible to her in the British Museum, in 1912. It was another twelve years before Messrs Burns Oates issued the text of Father Justin McCann, which is now better known, and thirty-six years before a critical text of the Middle English original was printed. A comparison of Evelyn's text and Father McCann's, now available as revised on the critical text, shows her to have done good work to say the least. Here too, however, she was a pioneer and it was no doubt congenial to her modesty to drop out of the picture when a better text became available. It is only a pity she did not include with her text the *Epistle of Privy Counsel* of which she was an admirer, as Father McCann did.

Her other major piece of editing was *The Scale of Perfection* by the fifteenth-century Augustinian Canon, Walter Hilton. This appeared in 1924, making widely available in a satisfactory text another classic of English mystical writing which had been previously accessible only in Father Dalgairn's less ambitious little book published in 1908. A critical edition of Hilton's important treatise is still awaited but to Evelyn goes the credit of having suggested some of the problems which such a text will be expected to solve.[3]

3. cf. David Knowles, *The English Mystical Tradition*, London, Burns Oates, 1961; pp. 102–103.

Where Evelyn did not herself produce texts she was very happy to help others to do so and lend her name to their productions. Thus she wrote an Introduction to Frances Comper's somewhat modernised text of Richard Rolle's *Fire of Love* as translated in the fourteenth century by Richard Misyn, which was published in 1914. There is evidence in the unpublished correspondence that Evelyn thought at one time of editing this text herself. Rolle, for all that he seems rather a rough diamond among mystical writers, commended himself to Evelyn even in his eccentricities. As she summed it up: 'Passionate feeling taking artistic form: this perhaps is the ruling character of all Rolle's writings.' It is not remarkable that quotations from his outpourings in *Mysticism* outnumber those of the loftier more deliberate Walter Hilton for whom nonetheless Evelyn had the greatest respect. Evelyn in the pre-*Mysticism* days especially, could never resist a strong dash of personality in mystical writing and there was a time when she even became rapturously enthusiastic about the Quietist, Madame Guyon; this was almost at the very moment she was proclaiming her delight in the diametrically opposed personal accent of Meister Eckhardt (unpublished letter to Margaret Robinson). Mystical writing was for her a document of lived experience or it was nothing. It is improbable that she ever in her life turned over a scholastic manual of so-called 'mystical theology'.

This preference for strong personality in combination with mystical insight and, as she would have said, artistic genius, is apparent in her next choice of subjects for more ample treatment, Jan van Ruysbroeck and Jacopone de Todi; Ruysbroeck (1293–1381) whom she described in her bibliography to *Mysticism* (1911) as 'one of the very greatest mystics whom the world has ever known', was and remained her favourite of all her mystical fellow-citizens. In a letter to Margaret Robinson he is described as 'one of the truly illuminated'. In 1911 she could say categorically: 'Ruysbroeck is my own favourite of all the mystics' and even in 1940, after a lifetime of acquaintance with mystical literature, she was still able to write:

> Ruysbroeck's great passages on the 'fruitive unity of the Godhead' I have always thought to be among the most profound and inspiring writings of the mediaeval mystics.

If Ruysbroeck on hell made painful reading—well, one had to put up with it (*Letters*, pp. 68, 78, 122, 296).

Her biography of the great Flemish mystic which took up and developed her earlier articles in The Seeker, was published in 1915 and reveals how much common ground she felt she had with a man who evidently, like herself, combined in a high degree those two usually mutually exclusive ingredients of the human psyche, intellect and emotion. Thus Ruysbroeck as a writer is characterised by Evelyn as someone who 'forgets to be orderly as soon as he begins to be subjective'—an admirable description of what seems to happen in parts of *Mysticism*. As expounded by her, and this seems no less than the truth, his teaching is also typified by its insistence that 'the *whole man*' (Evelyn's emphasis), intellect *and* emotion, should be raised and transformed in his approach to God. If at times he speaks in terms of two lives 'We must remind ourselves,' Evelyn writes:

> that Ruysbroeck's theory of transcendence involves not the passage of one life to another, but the *adding* of one life to another: the perpetual deepening, widening, heightening and enriching of human experience (p. 117).

For Ruysbroeck, as for William Law, desire is everything and does everything—though, for once, Evelyn does *not* quote her favourite line from *The Cloud of Unknowing*, 'By love He may be gotten and holden, but by thought of Understanding never.' As Evelyn notes, many mystics have claimed divine inspiration but she felt that Ruysbroeck, who was no exception, came closest to vindicating the claim. She especially admired his earlier more dense writings, *The Adornment of the Spiritual Marriage* and *The Sparkling Stone*. It is to chapters nine and ten of the latter work that she refers in the letter of 1940 already quoted, chapters which she described in 1915 as 'the highwater mark of mystical literature'. It is perhaps unnecessary to emphasise that Evelyn was not echoing some widely received critical opinion As in most of her other judgements connected with the history of mysticism, she had found out and tested her conclusion for herself.

The second mystical personality to whom Evelyn devoted considerable attention was the Italian Franciscan tertiary, Jacopone da Todi (1228–1306). The large handsomely produced volume which Dent issued towards the end of 1919 was in fact a collaborative effort to which Evelyn contributed some 250 pages of 'spiritual biography'. The remaining half of the book was devoted to a selection of Jacopone's 'lode' on spiritual ballads, with facing text and translation, so arranged as 'to give some idea of his artistic and spiritual evolution'. Once again it is the personal note that Evelyn singles out:

> Jacopone was one of the most subjective of writers . . . His *laude* when we have learned to read them rightly, constitute a human document as complete as the *Confessions* of St Augustine, or the autobiography of Suso . . . (*Jacopone da Todi*, pp. vi–vii).

It was naturally her task to help would-be readers of this lively and ardent character precisely to 'read him rightly' and her account is still the best introduction to his life and work available in English. But the story of Jacopone would hardly be true to Evelyn if it lost anything in the telling, and one is fully prepared for the extremes of exaltation and self-abasement, hope and fear, joy and desolation, of 'emotional instability' in fact, with which Jacopone filled his lyrics as well, apparently, as his life. This was the living world of religion for Evelyn and she has no difficulty in evoking the

Italian scene of bustle and melody which she adored and in which she situates Jacopone for her readers. A scholar with less *parti pris* might have been less true to such a subject. For Evelyn might use and respect the dry-as-dust approach but that was not her own métier. She did not write original academic studies any more than she ever attempted to perfect a final critical edition. Her interest in her mystics and their writings was severely practical and personal.

Leaving Evelyn's efforts to publicise the lives and writings of individual mystics it is necessary to return once again to the other paths along which her interest in 'practical mysticism' led her. Since we have already seen how she reacted to the war—and surely the problem of how to react to war was a practical question if ever there was one—we may now turn to her treatment of other equally practical problems which one might describe as *internal*, perhaps even *integral*, to mysticism. But to provide a background to the discussion we should glance once again at the little book entitled *Practical Mysticism* which as we have seen was published at the beginning of the war.

This work is described in the sub-title as *A Little Book for Normal People*. Its tone is hard to capture today even if its intentions and spirit can only be admired by those who prize the traditional *via contemplativa*. But what is one to make, for example, of a book which addresses its reader in terms such as the following?

> For years your treasure has been in the Stock Exchange, at the House of Commons, or the Salon, or the reviews that 'really count' (if they still exist), or the drawing-rooms of Mayfair; and thither your heart perpetually tends to stray. Habit has you in its chains. You are not free. The awakening, then, of your deeper self, which knows not habit and desires nothing but free correspondence with the Real, awakens you at once to the

fact of a disharmony between the simple but inexorable longings and instincts of the buried spirit, now beginning to assert
themselves in your hours of meditation—pushing out as it
were, towards the light—and the various changeful, but insistent longing of the surface-self.

All that Evelyn says positively here is true and the milieu which
she assumes she is addressing still exists; but this milieu could no
longer receive a message couched in the language she uses and
pitched in the chiding, jollying key she chooses to speak in; the
very assumption that it might be receptive to such a message
seems to date the book beyond recall, to attach it for ever to that
'spiritual renaissance' which the Great War and the revolution in
philosophy blew to smithereens. This perhaps is the book's
greatest disadvantage today.

Yet Evelyn's point was and is a serious one. This book is
entirely in the mainstream of her preoccupations from beginning
to end. Looking retrospectively it takes us straight back into the
predicament of the heroes and heroines of her novels, Willie
Hopkinson, Paul Vickery, Constance Tyrrel, gradually awakening to an awareness of their ambivalent situation between Appearance and Reality. It is the book which should have been thrust
into their hands as they tried to adjust their infant spiritual eyes to
two mutually incompatible ways of seeing, neither of which
made them feel comfortable and neither of which seemed able to
get on with the other. The book has strictly nothing to do with
religion at all; 'religion' indeed is listed along with 'indigestion,
priggishness or discontent' as a cobweb which may 'drape the
panes' of the prospective mystical stock-broker. Like those books
of Plotinus which fell into the hands of the youthful Augustine
and helped to unseal his vision, the name of 'that Word which
was made flesh and dwelt among us' is not to be found in its
pages either. Yet is *is* a book which aims to do something almost

exactly analogous to that immortal 'Book of Beauty' composed
by Plotinus, which so fired Augustine and projected him one
might say on his flight path as one of the greatest luminaries of
the Western Church. Evelyn had little doubt, though her ready
exaltation of 'mystic types' and her constant appeal to the outstanding saints and heroes of the mystic way tends to obscure the
fact, that all of us, from Cabinet Ministers to scullery maids,
harbour within us in our deeper self, or Self (Evelyn uses upper
and lower case 'S' according to circumstance), the capacity for
self-realisation which her little course in practical mysticism seeks
to help towards fulfilment. It was fundamental to her creed
always that such re-orientation of the self towards God could be
effected in the most squalid or in the most homely circumstances.
Exercise in Attention, Recollection, Self-Adjustment (incorporat-
ing Fr Baker's Detachment and Mortification) and three gentle
grades of Contemplation bring the Soul to the illuminative stage
and there she leaves the matter.

Compared with *Mysticism*, *Practical Mysticism* is a small miracle
of condensation as Evelyn selects here and there from the immense
repertoire in the larger work those texts or similes which would
best illustrate the points she wishes to make. A fundamental text is
Blake's 'If the doors of perception were cleansed everything would
appear to man as it is—Infinite', adopted in the novels, several
times cited in *Mysticism*, never quite forgotten. There are some
new faces too. Evelyn had been reading Keats, and her genius for
lighting on what best expresses her ideas no doubt led her straight
to his 'O for a life of sensations rather than thoughts!' She also
shows her respect for a new friend, generally added to her lists of
this time, Florence Nightingale, quoted in the first chapter on
Contemplation as exclaiming 'I must strive to see only God in
my friends, and God in my cats', a sentiment which must certainly
have commended itself to Evelyn. An example of adaptation from
Mysticism is provided by the charming exemplary tale of Eyes

and No-Eyes and 'the other side of the hedge', where a passing metaphorical allusion in *Mysticism* is expanded into a parable. It is tempting to think that E. M. Forster derived the idea for one of his more Tolstoyean short stories, called precisely *The Other Side of the Hedge* from one or other of these passages.[4]

One important judgment on *Practical Mysticism* is to be found in Baron von Hugel's summing up in the revised bibliography to the *MysticalElement* of 1923 of Evelyn's development from 1911 to 1922:

> Evelyn Underhill: Interesting progress from *Mysticism*, 1911, full of breadth and charm, but lacking the institutional sense, after several excessively mystical works, to the *Life of the Spirit*, 1922, bravely insistent upon history and institutionalism, and furnishing a solidly valuable collection of papers.

In the Baron's terms *Practical Mysticism* was certainly, with *The Mystic Way*, one of the 'excessively mystical works'. It was nevertheless as great if not a greater success than *The Mystic Way*, and has lasted longer if the publisher's estimate of its sales value is anything to go by. But it was not the only expression of Evelyn's views in the year it was written. Indeed, as sometimes happens to other writers, at the moment she was expressing one view to a wide audience through a book she was already simultaneously surpassing it in addressing a more restricted audience through an article.

Evelyn's articles of the war and immediate post-war years prepare the 'brave' re-establishment of her position later. The general tendency of these articles is to break from a view of the spiritual life of men and women as uniquely 'a personal growth and response, a personal reception of, and self-orientation to, Reality', and to consider it as both fed by and feeding, even created by and creating, history and human institutions. It is not possible to do justice to all that she wrote at this time on this subject, but two articles in particular stand out for their new

4. E. M. Forster, *Collected Short Stories;* cf. *Practical Mysticism*, pp. 9–10.

orientation in this direction. The one, *Mysticism and the Doctrine of the Atonement* of January 1914 (in The Interpreter), takes up the story, as it were, from where *The Mystic Way* had left off, and attempts to show how Christ as the mystic *par excellence* should be thought of as creator of the Christian community. The other, *Mysticism and the Corporate Life* of January 1915 (also in The Interpreter), takes it on a step further by demonstrating how the mystic, the lover of God, should also be seen as entirely dependent for vital elements in his development on the historic community in which he happens to live.[5]

Evelyn plants squarely the problem of mysticism as she had been accustomed to think of it, and the doctrine of atonement. It is an indication of her own self-awareness, also perhaps of her openness to criticism, that she should thus immediately go to the heart of a problem which many would say is endemic in a mystical interpretation of the Christian Gosepl. For, if Christ is the one sufficient atonement of mankind and every single man and woman is in the last analysis saved by faith in his name, what room is there left for asceticism, purgation, the path of illumination and union, the whole 'apparatus' of mysticism? The question in various forms was an ancient one by Evelyn's day but had been given fresh actuality by the German theologian, Albert Ritschl, and a whole school of his followers, for whom the kind of salvation by immanence they considered inherent in mysticism was an affront to the evangelical preaching. Salvation could not rightly, on their view, be thought of as welling up from within as the fruit of a hidden communion; it is rather to be thought of as given from a transcendent height and given to men as a group rather than to individuals.

Evelyn's reply has some analogy with all Catholic answers to this classic accusation against apparently individualistic piety, an

5. Both articles may be found in *The Essentials of Mysticism*, pp. 44–63 and pp. 25–43, respectively.

accusation with its roots in the old argument about justification
and faith at the Reformation. The differences between Evelyn's
reply and most traditional Catholic ones is that she takes her stand
firmly on the primacy of actual direct experience of the divine
rather than the traditional Catholic doctrine of 'sanctifying grace',
and insists that all traditional atonement and reconciliation language is a metaphor for mystical self-realisation, accomplished
perfectly in Christ in order that it might be realised in each
believer according to his measure. The foundation of the Church
is, therefore, by analogy with the foundation of, say, a religious
order, the establishment in fellowship of all who would follow
the mystic path trodden by him they call master and lord, and
whose particular mystic 'way' is determined by *his* personality
and teaching.

Evelyn's doctrine makes a real effort here to give history the
preponderant role which critics of *The Mystic Way* felt was
lacking in her teaching about Christian origins. Speaking of all
Christians of whatever level of achievement she writes that:

> the Christian's achievement of God . . . is really and practically
> conditioned by the known fact and *character* of the [mystical]
> achievement of Christ. It is the addition of this fact, this dis-
> tinct historic happening, to the racial consciousness, which
> makes possible our special and Christian apprehension of God;
> differentiates it, say, from that of a Hindu or a Neoplatonic saint.

The story of Christ's life and death have entered Christian consciousness and radically condition, along lines known to psychology, the relationship of Christian men and women with God:

> Through love of Christ the Christian comes to the Cross and
> through the Cross he enters a spiritual region he could not
> reach in any other way (*Essentials of Mysticism*, pp. 51–2).

Because of the 'corporate character of humanity' it also follows that the achievement of Christ is an opening up of new levels of achievement for mankind, by analogy with for example the opening up of new aesthetic horizons by an inspired musical or other artistic genius. Atonement means that the atoner becomes for his fellow-humanity a pipe or canal of more abundant life. As he derives much from his cultural, social and religious milieu, so he gives very much back. He is a true bridge between the human and the divine.

Evelyn's mystical standpoint on atonement has its drawbacks no doubt from a theological point of view. If the 'apparatus' of mysticism remains intact, the apparatus of theology becomes largely otiose. Many would feel that the redemptive work of Christ requires an analogy of a different order to that which she draws with the work of a religious founder establishing her influence and leaving her impact on a particular 'way' of seeking union with God. Although Evelyn does verbally at least allow for a fundamental revolution in values achieved by Christ her categories of psychological realism somehow fail to match up to her theological expectations of them.

The second of these articles takes us a good deal further in exploring in detail the benefits to be derived for the spiritual life by integration in a believing community. The 'common opinion' she writes:

that the mystic is a lonely soul, wholly absorbed in his vertical relation with God, that his form of religious life represents an opposition to, and an implied criticism of, the corporate and institutional form of religious life: this is decisively contradicted by history, which shows us again and again, the great mystics as the loyal children of the great religious institutions, and forces us to admit that here as in other departments of human activity the corporate and the individual life are intimately plaited together (*Essentials of Mysticism*, p. 26).

Evelyn goes on to show how all, even the religious solitary, belong to *an* environment and it is as well for them and all bent on the mystic path that they should participate in a 'social consciousness' with a 'spiritual and religious tendency' rather than the reverse. Though the mystic's perceptions may greatly surpass those of his co-religionists, 'even so, it is better that he should be within a Church than outside it'. Furthermore it is good for him to be subject to corporate life for 'man is social through and through' and the attitude of 'self-giving surrender' it inculcates, the 'utter doing-away of the I, the Me, and the Mine', is an excellent preparation for union. To rebel, to strike out on one's own, is to risk personal eccentricity and loss of impact. George Fox and William Blake are examples of such a loss of balance, she claims. Of such extra-ecclesiastical or rebellious mystics she writes:

> To a greater or lesser extent they failed in effect because they tried to be mystical in a non-human instead of a human way; were 'other-worldly' in the bad sense of the word (*Essentials of Mysticism*, p. 32).

Christ did not set up his 'little flock' over against the official Jewish church but attempted to change the corporate consciousness from within.

Evelyn's change of emphasis in these articles may not seem to concede a very great deal for she still seems to dwell rather on the Church as a convenient breeding ground for mystical genius rather than as prolonging the life of Christ in humanity for humanity on Catholic lines. Yet she does go a long way even in this direction. As she writes:

> The Church represents a complete spiritual civilisation, a conserver of values; were it not for her, every new spiritual genius who arose would have to begin at the beginning, at the Stone Age of the soul. . . . Man needs a convention, a tradition, a

limitation if he is not to waste his creative powers (*Essentials of Mysticism*, p. 37).

Even going at the pace of the 'slowest sheep' is now seen by Evelyn to have some virtue. But the change is most noticeable in her attitude to the Plotinean phrase used to describe mystical adventure as 'the flight of the alone to the Alone'. In the first edition of *Mysticism* these are described as 'superb words'. But in the first of these two articles it is referred to as 'That poisonous phrase of Plotinus' and in the second as 'that dangerous and over-quoted phrase of Plotinus' (art. cit., p. 141; art. cit., p. 145). In the 1930 and subsequent editions of *Mysticism* the 'words' are indeed referred to but they are no longer 'superb'.

Compared with these articles the third and final one which falls for examination in this period, entitled *The Essentials of Mysticism* of January 1920 (published in The Quest) represents a definite falling back on old positions (*Essentials of Mysticism*, pp. 1–24). The reason is not far to seek. In the intervening period Evelyn had once more fallen in with her old flame, her first love, Plotinus, concerning whom she had written two lengthy reviews in the years 1918–19 when Inge's two-volume account of Plotinus' philosophy was published, together with Stephen McKenna's translation of part of the *Enneads*. Whereas before we had seemed to be moving in the direction of a specific Christian experience of God which might hypothetically and in the long run have been connected with a theology of faith and the centrality of Christian revelation, in this article we are thrown right back to the old language, as Evelyn asks of herself: What *is* the essential experience of the mystic? (her emphasis). 'What elements' she asks again:

> are due to the suggestions of tradition, to conscious or uncon-
> scious symbolism to the misinterpretation of emotion, to the
> invasion of cravings from the lower centres, or the disguised

fulfillment of an unconscious wish? And when all these channels
of illusion have been blocked, what is left?

What indeed. It is no wonder that Evelyn describes her inquiry as
'painful', it was a pain which, as we shall see, she really felt. For
her answer, 'What *is* essential is the way the mystic feels about his
Deity, and about his own relation with it . . .' was not really an
answer at all in so far as it, too, begged all the questions now apparently nagging at her mind. Having once more kicked away the
ladder—'credal forms', unsafe 'symbols'—she had seemed for a
moment to be putting some trust in, the best she can say of Christianity is that it enriches mysticism by insisting on charity and the
moral values, and 'filled up some of the gaps left by Neoplatonism'. Evelyn does not explicitly reinstate the alone with the Alone,
but the whole tenor of the article is to do just that; it culminates
in a celebrated quotation from Plotinus evoking the One as
Conductor of the choir of souls:

> all do not look towards the Conductor and therefore do not
> sing well. But those who do, sing harmoniously. Just so, to look
> towards the One is to attain 'the end of our existence'.

This achievement, says Evelyn, is the 'indestructible essence of
mysticism'.[6]

There is no reason why Evelyn's thought should have developed evenly and harmoniously. Her published work reflects
her life too well for us to suppose that such hesitation is merely
superficial. The contrast between the two earlier articles and the
1920 *Essentials of Mysticism* article which also headed the collected
articles published under its title later in that year, reflects a doubt
in Evelyn herself, which is confirmed from other sources to be
considered in due course. Perhaps the war period really had had a
disrupting effect. In any case, as we enter the twenties there is a

6. art. cit. p. 157, p. 166. *Essentials of Mysticism*, pp. 2, 23-4.

sense that something had to be done about an unsatisfactory situation. Evelyn duly acted. She became an active member of a Christian body, the Church of England and she placed herself under the spiritual direction of her old friend, Friedrich von Hugel.

8
Help in Time of Need

HITHERTO it has been possible to consider in detail the various documents which relate to Evelyn's life and ideas. On the other hand we have been saved the trouble of delving deeply because the books, articles and letters have been largely self-explanatory. We have in fact been saved a good deal of trouble by the very distance from her which the dearth of personal material has imposed. This has been especially true for the wartime period from which we appear to have no remaining evidence of her deeper, more personal thoughts and feelings. But the situation is very different for the decade we are now to consider, and especially for the period of three years or so from October 1921 to approximately the death of von Hugel in January 1925. This is due not only to the thick and constant flow of printed material which characterises this period, as it does the whole of the decade; nor simply to the fact that once again material is available from her correspondence. It is due primarily to the fact that we possess at least copies of most of the documents which passed between her and von Hugel when he became her spiritual director and also, though nothing from this source has hitherto been published, a personal collection of jottings upon her feelings and emotional state during the period down to 1930. Having hitherto been forced chiefly to infer and to guess we are now almost absurdly embarrassed by the accidental survival of so much that is relevant to Evelyn's biography.

It is easiest to begin at the outline, to speak of the outward events of her life, the literary production, the holidays, the various engagements, even her church allegiance. Since von Hugel looms so large in this period of her life her relations with him will figure largely even here. But it will also be possible and, at the risk of appearing to pry unduly, necessary to follow the growth of that inner experience which Evelyn to a large extent revealed to von Hugel but which she communicates more directly in the pages of the little green paper-covered exercise book, bought in the Paris store Bon Marché and appropriately adorned with a female allegorical figure of 'Scientia'. Acquaintance with this material may finally increase our awareness of just how little Evelyn's doctrine was for her simply an intellectual game or mere academic cannon-fodder, a matter of tongue and lips, and how deeply all she had to say which people found helpful in these later years was the product of her own suffering and experience.

Outwardly, Evelyn's life after the war cannot have been greatly different from what it was before. She and her husband continued to live in the same house, kept up by a suitable staff and housing a succession of much loved and no doubt deserving cats. The economic conditions of the time are never as such discussed by Evelyn. She and her husband were not wealthy in the sense that they had money to burn once the expenses of such an establishment as became Hubert's profession and station in life had been met. They never had a car grander than their second Austin called 'Monica', and, if they did afford holidays abroad, they travelled and lodged without ostentation. The greater part of their holidays in this period were in fact spent either in the English countryside or with Evelyn's father on the yacht 'Wulfruna'. Sir Arthur finally gave this up in 1930. It is clear from a remark incidentally let fall by von Hugel that Evelyn felt herself under some obligation to contribute financially to the maintenance of her own household and certainly considered herself to be earning her living. The legacy which came to her in 1924 on her mother's death should, von Hugel considered, have lifted some of this burden from her.

In fact it seems to have made no difference whatever. Among Evelyn's self-reproaches occur that of not giving away as much money as she might and that of liking the comfort of her home too much. We know nothing about how she cured the former of these 'vices'; as to the second the answer to that was indirect but final as we shall see.

By the time Evelyn applied to von Hugel to be directed by him in the autumn of 1922 the question of her ecclesiastical allegiance was already settled in her own mind. It is inconceivable that she would have written to him for such a purpose *without* first taking such a step, knowing how much he deprecated the 'Detached' situation and mentality—however polite and sympathetic he might be to particular 'D's'. As to why she joined the Anglican rather than the Roman Communion this is probably, in the last resort, a less significant question than the one surrounding her decision to join *any* religious institution. Certainly we are in a better position to answer this second question and to some extent have already done so, in tracing her attempts in the war to think about the mutual benefits conferred on each other by mysticism and religious institutionalism. Some later statements do however bring us closer in time to the moment when the decision was finally made; one of these at least is worth mentioning since it demonstrates how von Hugel's friendship and fatherly interest in her 'progress' was active several years before he became formally her director.

Evelyn and von Hugel cannot have been in very close contact during the war years if only because the first he heard of her more open attitude to a certain historical and institutional element in religion was via an article in the Cambridge Review of early 1916 which referred to a review she had written in The Harvard Theological Review for April of that year. His letter, hitherto unpublished, shows his interest in her and pleasure at her undoubted 'progress' from his personal point of view. This letter is dated 26 June 1916 and headed by von Hugel's address at 13, Vicarage Gate, Kensington. It runs:

Dear Mrs Stuart Moore,
    I have, now for a month, been deeply immersed in much con-
centrated reading for an Address—one of a series by some 8 lec-
turers—at Woodbroke Settlement on August 8th. And, until then
I must read and write/compose nothing but what goes to that.
    But in the midst of readings which, sometimes, had to be
most distasteful, I came suddenly across a little oasis amidst those
Dead Sea Marshes; which rejoiced me indeed. The Cambridge
Review of May 24th, told me that, in the Harvard Theological
Review for April, there is 'a singularly sane review by Miss
Eveline [sic] Underhill of two books on Mysticism'—a review
in which you are 'strongly insistent on the value of the historical element in Xtianity [sic], and on the danger of the attempt
to subordinate the historical to the symbolical or mystical
interpretation of formularies'.—This sounds indeed *most* satisfactory. I should be greatly obliged if you would lend me that
no. or this review of yours, for 2 or 3 days. I want to have it in
mind, and perhaps directly to quote from it at Woodbroke. As
you know I much prize the friendly appreciation, and the solid
kind offices, I receive from 'Miss E.U.'; and I have long felt
how large is your public—how many souls will be led right or
wrong by yourself, with your rare charm of style, large knowledge of literature, and delicate interestingness of character.
You only required just the sense which this reviewer finds in
this piece of work of yours, to be deeply and wholesomely helpful, I felt and feel. Hence I rejoice, I believe [,] more fully than
if I discovered some growth in myself—for you can and do
reach more people than I can ever expect to reach myself.

The letter ends with a request to pass on a message to the secretary of the Religious Thought Society concerning his address

'Heaven and Hell' at which he hopes Evelyn will be present. The letter ends 'Yours v. sincerely and delightedly F. v. Hugel.' The substance of this last mentioned address was the subject of another lengthy and rather technical letter from von Hugel to Evelyn of 14 December 1916. It discusses exhaustively a point she had evidently raised in a letter to him, and attempts to put the record straight concerning one or two points in his answers to Sir Oliver Lodge and Dean Inge. It appears incidentally that von Hugel was not above a little tail-twisting where the latter was concerned. Explaining how the Pope, who had not come into his original draft directly or otherwise, had crept into the delivered version, he writes:

> Dr. Inge is so rude and indeed childish about Rome, that grateful as I am to him for his great kindness to myself, and most sincere as is my admiration of various points in his convictions, I feel myself, in loyalty bound, if I speak under him, to bring in some in no wise bitter banter as to these my chairman's prejudices.

The books Evelyn was reviewing for The Harvard Theological Review in 1916 were *Mysticism and Modern Life* by John Wright Buckham, D.D., and *Mysticism and the Creed* by W. F. Cobbs, D.D. Each provided her with a standard against which she could distinguish her own position. Her criticism of the former rests almost entirely on the fact that 'the emphasis in his pages lies rather on self-fufilment than on self-surrender'. Dr Buckham seemed to her guilty of a 'glaring error of spirituality' in adopting:

> the conception which regards man as the first term and God as the second term, and which studies the mystical process with a view to the profit which man's soul can get from it: the way of illumination, peace, strength, holiness.

Evelyn writes that such

> advantages and many others in different spheres, listed by
> Buckham, are accidents of the spiritual life not its substance.
> They may incite beginners—that is all.

Dr Cobbs on the other hand is taken to task for reducing the
historic basis of Christianity to symbolism, and the creeds likewise. Such reduction of Christian dogma to perennial categories
may confer an 'agreeable spaciousness' on theology but is false
both to mysticism and Christianity. The former does not logically
entail the abandonment of the historical domain and the latter
insists absolutely on 'the primal value of historical fact as the basis
of . . . belief'.[1]

Similar points are made in an interesting article which appeared
in Everyman for 20 July 1918, under the heading 'The Future of
Mysticism', and from which it appears that Evelyn was by that
time logically if not actually committed to joining some Christian
communion. This article takes up the words of Inge concerning
a 'mystical revival' in his Times Literary Supplement article from
which we have already quoted. Evelyn doubts whether Tyrrell's
optimistic forecast of a religion of Mysticism and charity can be
supported. For such a turn of events two things are required:
outstanding individual mystics, and an environment favourable
to their development and receptive to their impact. Evelyn did
not see these conditions being fulfilled in the near future but she
thought it was worth devoting a little attention to them,
especially the second. 'The true mystical life' she wrote:

> flourishes best in alliance with a lofty moral code, strong sense
> of duty, a definite religious faith capable of upholding the
> mystic during the many periods in which his vision fails him.

1. 'The Harvard Theological Review', vol. 9, no. 2 (April 1916); pp. 234–8.

It assumes a freedom to concentrate on the spiritual world, to cultivate 'the art of prayer'. In fact mystical flowering supposes a Church and it is to the Churches that we must look if history is anything to go by:

> Divorced from all institutional expression it [mysticism] tends to become strange, vague or merely sentimental.

She continues:

> True mysticism is the soul of religion; but like the soul of man it needs a body if it is to fulfil its mighty destiny. This destiny is not merely individual; it is social—the disclosure to other men of fresh realms of the spirit, the imparting of more abundant life to the race.[2]

This article generated a somewhat irrelevant correspondence which dragged its way week by week to the end of that November. Evelyn herself did not intervene.

It is possible that Evelyn held these views in parallel with the apparently more intransigent views implied in 'The Essentials of Mysticism' article. Some attempt to relate the two can be seen in her introduction to Jacob Boehme's *Confessions*, 'compiled and edited' by her friend of long standing, Mrs Ernest Dowson (using the pseudonym of W. Scott Palmer). In this short piece, published on 25 March 1920, Evelyn is at pains to relate the rather eccentric early seventeenth-century mystical cobbler to his Christian context and to remind readers that he, too, was rooted in such moral virtues as patience, courage, love and surrender of the will. 'These evangelical virtues are the conditions of our knowledge of reality', writes Evelyn. Boehme was 'before all else a practical Christian, for whom his religion was a vital process, not merely a creed'. But he was also possessed of a will 'humbly set on the only rational object of desire', i.e. a dedicated mystic.

2. 'Everyman', vol. 12, no. 30 (20 July 1918); pp. 335–6.

We shall probably never discover what impelled Evelyn to return to communion in the Anglican fold. Apart from the philosophical or merely theoretical question it is possible that she was affected by the death of perhaps the closest friend of her middle life, Ethel Ross Baker, whom she visited daily when she was already dangerously ill in 1917 and whose last moments, in which she seems to have experienced remarkable religious consolation and illumination, are briefly evoked in a letter of October 1935. Ethel died an exemplary death in 1921 supported by the Roman Church she had joined fifteen years previously. It is curious how Evelyn turns to the experience of both of them in a review dating from 1919 of G. G. Coulton's *Christ, St Francis and To-day* (quoted by Lucy Menzies). In this she takes up her position in no uncertain terms against the pastoral imagery adopted by that Church in times of crisis, referring covertly to R. H. Benson as 'a distinguished opponent of Tyrrell and Loisy [who] was accustomed to tell converts afflicted with mental activity that 'the pace of the church of Christ must that of the slowest sheep'; Evelyn places herself shoulder to shoulder with Professor Coulton in opposing such an attitude and makes his views her own. The review continues:

This attitude of surrender to those forces of reaction which always drag at forward-moving life, represents the exact antithesis of Mr Coulton's religious attitude. He is concerned to enlarge the boundaries of the flock in order that those vigorous, independent, but still recognizably wool-bearing animals which now wander outside it, may enter, thus gaining the support of the community and conferring upon it a new briskness and momentum.[3]

3. The review is quoted by Lucy Menzies in her ms. biography, from which this passage is transcribed.

One takes the point; one also begins to see how Evelyn who described herself to von Hugel in late 1921 as 'a Christian . . . though in the modernist rather than strict orthodox sense' (*Life*, p. 74), should find herself drawn back to the Church of her baptism and confirmation, which she had formerly despised but in which she seemed to stand a fair chance of both being supported and of conferring some of what she had to give. She was in any case, as she said, a 'recognisably wool-bearing animal' and when von Hugel had explained the alternatives to her, she wholeheartedly rejected a 'fluffy and notional, instead of factual religion . . . a mere philosophy of value' and stated her faith in the historical basis of Christianity in unequivocal terms:

> The main historical happenings as given by reasonable N.T. criticism—and especially the Passion—are absolutely necessary to Christianity as I understand it. I never doubted their occurrence but they now mean a great deal more to me (*Life*, p. 92).

This was written in the midsummer of 1922.

Since it is sometimes stated that von Hugel was in principle opposed to exchanges of one communion for another and was therefore in some sense happy to connive at Evelyn's Anglicanism despite the claims of his own Church which, as a Catholic, he could hardly have denied, it is as well to set out in passing exactly what his attitude was in her case. The item 'Possible change of obedience' remains on the agenda between them during several of the exchanges of 1922–23, as readers of the texts printed by Miss Cropper will have noticed. Now in fact, of course, the question of Evelyn's 'obedience' had already involved von Hugel in 1912 as we have seen. At that time he did not think the moment a propitious one for any person of liberal intellectual sympathies rashly to cast themselves within the orbit of the Holy Office, then so busily engaged in furthering the objectives and methods of its

historic predecessor, the Holy Inquisition. Hence his 'discourage-
ment'. By 1922 things had changed, at least to the extent that the
panic had subsided. Von Hugel himself was no longer subject to
harassment but a respected if not much followed or imitated
figure in his own communion; he believed without reserve in the
fundamental justness of Roman claims to represent the centre of
unity. Under these circumstances he certainly did not 'discourage'
Evelyn from becoming a Roman Catholic. Indeed we may,
reading between the lines, see that he went out of his way to put
the issues squarely before her in elaborately setting out what he
conceived to be her moral dilemma vis-à-vis her husband's
objections even *after* she had firmly stated: 'Frankly I cannot at
present conceive the question of submission to Rome . . . ever
becoming a question of conscience'. She felt, she said, quite
satisfied as an Anglican and with people with whom she could
sympathise and work. She thought question *might* arise (her
emphasis) and if it did she would not draw back.

Von Hugel's reply, ably summarised in a sentence by Miss
Cropper, flows over more than three pages of quarto typescript
and is surely and deliberately calculated tactfully to disabuse
Evelyn of the view that fear of paining her husband and causing
him to think she was ruining her mind, would be sufficient reasons
for becoming a Catholic should she ever think this to be right.
His argument suggests she adopt Kant's principle 'can this my
impulse or conviction be so extended as to constitute a principle
of universal legislation' and apply it to her conviction that she
should not do anything to pain her husband if other considerations left her free to follow her attraction (which she had never
denied) to the Roman Church. What would have happened, von
Hugel asks, if all wives throughout the ages had adopted such
a principle of not hurting their husbands? Supposing Faustina,
'that frivolous minx', had felt a call to join the persecuted Church
of the second century—should she have hung back for fear

of hurting her husband, the great Stoic emperor-philosopher, Marcus Aurelius? 'Marcus Aurelius', he writes:

> was as fine a man as your husband & Marcus Aurelius was as dead against the Christians as ever can be your man against the clericals.

But where would Christianity have got if its adherents had been such as this (hypothetical) Faustina? He sums up:

> To my mind, the only quite satisfactory, just & balanced, definitely supernatural position, is to hold most firmly that all who in any way depend upon you—hence above all your husband—possess an inalienable right to be as much sustained & consoled by you, & as little pained by you, as is ever possible; that no mere preference of greater helps & consolations, religious or otherwise, can justify your inflicting grave pain upon your Husband; but if & when your conscience came to make you, after waiting & testing, to feel *bound* to move, you ought to do so, trusting to the same God, Who is determining you, to make it less of a pain & in some way a spiritual gain, for your Husband [sic] also, whilst you would yourself, of course, do everything possible to minimize that pain for him.

One could not very well tell a potential 'convert' more plainly that the mere pain or inconvenience of a loved one was insufficient reason for not following conscience. Von Hugel concluded this section of his advice with a reference to Mrs Lillie, an American lady with a husband also possessed of 'a horror of priests', who passed from agnosticism to the Church 'a year ago' and was received in the neighbouring Carmelite church:

> She takes her Catholic religion very largely and elastically, yet also very deeply; & her husband is now quite reconciled to what she has done . . .

He follows this with a warning to Evelyn against what he conceives as her 'amiable naturalism'—and there the matter rested between them. At least on this subject there could be no doubt for each of them about where the other stood. For her part Evelyn thereafter, having never apparently herself seen any absolutely compelling reason to join the Roman Communion, tended to associate doing so with what she called 'spiritual selfishness', i.e. just those 'reasons' which she and the Baron had agreed were *insufficient* to justify 'conversion'. This appears in her notoriously harsh words about Newman's departure from the Anglican Church (Letter of March 1933(?); *Letters*, p. 210). Similarly, reviewing in the Spectator Fr Vernon Johnson's story of his own road from Canterbury to Rome in 1929, entitled *One Lord, One Faith*, she concluded that 'the factor of intuition so completely outweighs the factor of thought' that Fr Vernon's 'reasons' were not of much consequence 'except for such as have to train Anglican priests'. There is every indication that Evelyn would have been hard to convince of Rome's preponderant claims as they were understood by Roman Catholics in her day. She plainly felt that Fr Vernon's sensational departure was occasioned by his 'encounter with holiness' at Lisieux as much as anything else. The Anglican Church could not, it was true, provide an equivalent for the Little Flower's skipping-rope (which Fr Vernon was there privileged to hold) but it could on her view remedy such intellectual maladroitness as he displayed and do what it might to favour the growth of holiness in its own ranks.

It is impossible to condense von Hugel's advice to Evelyn during these years into a few words. One or two points should, however, be singled out. His task was manifold and it is apparent that he handled it with skill; Evelyn had for example a decided tendency to that most painful and damaging of religious neuroses, excessive self-observation and self-reproach called 'scrupulosity' by older directors. And yet—indeed it was probably the obverse of the same tendency—she simply loathed the confessional. It 'tore her to bits'. A particularly horrific occasion was her attempt to confess in the Holy Week of 1922 when her self-torment led her to make a general confession to, as it happened, an evidently unsuitable and obtuse priest who 'devoted his time to smashing me up'. Nothing she realised afterwards *but* Christianity could redeem one in such a state of degradation as she then felt herself to be in. To make matters worse she found the very next day that two louts, 'two horrible insects' as she calls them, had been kissing one of 'her' slum children. This tore away the last shreds of her self-respect and filled her 'with horror and self-loathing'. 'I felt vile through and through', she continues:

> body & soul—just rubbed in the mud. And the queer thing is, it was then—when I couldn't look at or think of transcendent holiness—that I realised what the agonising need is that only Christianity *can* meet, by coming right down to you in the dust. St Augustine was 1000 times right. Plotinus can never have had to face his own beastliness—neoplatonism goes to bits when one gets really to the bottom & knows oneself un-mendably displeasing to God. I stayed at the bottom for weeks with occasional moments of peace but mostly suffocated by the inescapable sense of sin & utter rottenness.

The report of midsummer 1922 in which these lines occur is the only one to have survived in a manuscript fair copy in Evelyn's hand. It is the copy which von Hugel pored over, marking with his pencil the sections and phrases upon which to base his reply. The passage in question is, needless to say, scored in the margin and the reference to St Augustine underlined. This is not surprising. The point Evelyn was discovering experimentally in different ways recurs again and again in his counselling and instruction of her. He himself had sowed the seed of the realisation which struck her in her misery when he commented in an earlier report on her inability to understand 'the religious feeling of the need of a half-way house between oneself and God'. To this he replied, among other things:

> The human soul, upon the whole, in the long run, in its richest developments, certainly, I think, requires not a half-way house for it on its way to God, but *God Himself to come down to it*, not half-way but *the whole-way*. To put it in the most homely way: surely the infant does not feel its mother's breast *a half-way house*, a queer, artificial *intermezzo* between itself and its mother; the infant feels that breast as the self-giving of that mother, as a self-compression, a touching condescension, for bringing the mother's own life to the infant, & thus gradually to raise this infant to the mother's strength and stature. St Augustine surely, *surely* has got this point right in spite of the great attractions which, quite evidently a purely spiritual religion possessed for wide stretches of his mind. He felt that it was this condescension, *this coming down to us of God*, this appearing to us in human form & ways, which nourished love & ousted inflation. 'Quite, quite right! *That* alone, at least in some form & degree, will ever give us a religion sufficiently lowly, homely, humbling.'[4]

Such was the central pivot of all von Hugel's attempts to move Evelyn in the direction of what he called 'the more general and the bedrock principle of the Catholic mind'. It was his particular genius not simply to clear away irrelevancies on questions of principle about which she might have cause to hesitate, questions such as church-allegiance; not simply to pull her up over manifest indiscretions such as making a general confession without consulting him, but also to feed her mind with the kind of

4. This passage, transcribed from the typed copy in St Andrew University Library, differs in small respects from Miss Cropper, p. 79. The reference is to St Augustine's *Confessions*.

nourishment which would in the end bring about a complete re-
orientation of her perspectives and a new foundation upon which
to establish herself emotionally and intellectually. The Baron presided over Evelyn's long-term as well as her short-term interests
in a way that perhaps no one else could have done.

Von Hugel himself had been vehement. He could hardly help
noticing that Evelyn's own vehemence was one of the chief causes
of her discomforts and anguishes. Speaking of the division in her
mind and outlook between her tendency to 'pure mysticism' or
exclusive concentration on God on the one hand, and her growing
respect for Christ and institutional Christianity on the other, he
wrote:

> The tremendous—the appearance of tremendous logicality
> of mind of unbending principle which you give—I fancy
> sometimes even yourself to yourself—is, I am confident, very
> largely the result of oscillations, the doubleness in you which I
> have tried to lay bare.

Such a judgement which appears on the face of it to refer only to
Evelyn's intellectual situation could undoubtedly be broadened
to cover her whole emotional and spiritual situation. Devoted to
the pursuit of 'the one and only fair', subject even under von
Hugel, as he saw and she admitted, to 'strong inclinations to
revert to pure mysticism' she was nevertheless as much a creature
of her emotions, from one point of view, as her not infrequent
vividly phrased references to the subject would lead us to expect.
Most of us after all describe best what we have most reason to
know well by experience. Her whole approach to mysticism indeed, as we have outlined it, presupposes some such doubleness,
raises the problem of *how* precisely self-abnegation, self-mortifica-
tion, the stripping away of all mortal impediments, *custodia cordis*
or purity of heart, are to be reconciled with emotional self-
fulfilment, necessary and inevitable social, family and marital

self-commitment and room to breath a human atmosphere generally. Once again in fact Evelyn had to face problems she had faced all her life, those her fictional heroes, Paul Vickery and Constance Tyrrell had faced many years before. Only she was not being helped by a wild-eyed tubercular young Galahad from the hills but by a rather tired, deaf and seventy-two year old German Baron of the Holy Roman Empire with his home in Kensington.

Von Hugel surely epitomised for Evelyn all that she knew she was not but felt she must become, to be in truth a Christian and an effective help to others. What struck her especially about him was, curiously enough, his 'doubleness', but not a divisive, rending doubleness such as she experienced in herself, on the contrary a capacity for 'moving easily between the homely and the transcendental, the natural and the supernatural levels', a combination of 'a massive passion for God' with a 'profound and genial understanding of humanity' and love of creatures. Evelyn as she later traced the outline of the Baron's teaching perhaps inevitably dwelt on that aspect which had been particularly important for her: the Baron's distrust of the claims of 'pure mysticism' and his teaching that 'a humble recognition of the reaching out of the divine to the human, does more for the soul's best interests than any arrogant reaching-out of the human to the divine'. The former attitude had led to narrowness, one-sidedness, would-be exclusiveness in her own case, vices detestable to the Baron and which we can see at the root of her uncertainties and oscillations. The Baron's kind of doubleness was one of inclusion not exclusion and it was this kind she had to learn to make her own. In two departments in particular it seems did Evelyn suffer conflict as a result of her inability to reconcile the demands of the spiritual life and her own deepest longings; the one concerned her personal relationships; the other her life of prayer and the experience associated with it. In both cases her experience has exemplary value and is worth dwelling upon briefly.

The Baron commented more than once on the ardour of Evelyn's nature. The correspondence between them makes it evident that Evelyn, even before she began her jottings in the little green exercise book, had confessed to von Hugel that she suffered a fairly rampant egoism in her personal relationships, that she indulged 'claimfulness' and 'jealousy' and excessive vehemence. Von Hugel's diagnosis in his first approach to this problem is to situate it in the general context of Evelyn's one-sidedly intellectual approach to her religion. If she could balance her religious diet she might feel less emotionally starved and so suffer less from her 'hunger for the ardour of human affection'. Von Hugel did not wish her to drop her particular friendships but to attempt to control them from inside, as it were, to remain as loving as ever but to attempt to modify the fierce irrational or personal elements. His advice, not provided in full by Miss Cropper, is here transcribed from the copies at St Andrews. The emphasis where given is von Hugel's:

I want you carefully to discriminate between *your affections & your giving them to particular persons, & the claimfulness, jealousy, distractions, vehemence etc. which arise within, or on the occasion of, those affections.* I would have you not directly check those affections, though you should be slow & deliberate as far as you can without great strain in letting such affections begin, get established, with any new person. But I would wish you even more faithfully to drop, to escape from, the claimfulness, jealousy, vehemence, etc. This you should do, not by a direct fighting even of these passions, but by a gently turning to God, or to the thought of serenely loving saints etc. In this way you will practise detachment *within* attachment. You will thus grow much more fully than by concentrating upon attempts to keep out such materials & occasions. Try gradually to develop a sense that these passions are *impurities*—that they *degrade* love:

most true and most wholesome facts for you to get into your very blood.

Such a doctrine may appear 'cosy' to those for whom the advice of St Francis de Sales to utterly break off ardent personal relationships is the only satisfactory solution to their vexatious occurrence in the lives of would-be lovers of God. Yet von Hugel's advice is no soft option as Evelyn of course found out when adopting it in practice. His technique of indirect attack on her 'excesses' is illustrated by this example and is only part of a general strategy against her general tendency to self-preoccu-pation. Her oscillations had presented her with the alternatives: pure spirit—pure egoism. His indirect approach, which sought to re-unit flesh and spirit, even to give her emotional satisfaction in prayer, was incorporated into her *Rule* of Christmas 1921, based on the pages of advice from which we have quoted, and became a fundamental guide to her future examinations of conscience and, so we are assured by some of her friends who remember her, to her conduct. There was of course a long way to go and Evelyn's natural impetuosity which expected quick results from her new approach, received many a setback: 'I still find people attractive but can now take friendships rather less intensely' she wrote in 1922, but, she goes on, 'in many ways I am still absurdly over-sensitive & easily tipped off my spiritual balance by worries and vexation . . .' That 'still' bespeaks yet another 'excess' of which Evelyn had to become conscious. A few lines below this comes another 'excessive' sentence against which the Baron pencilled a cross and pulled her up severely in his reply:

It is a struggle to leave *all* one's professional vanity at the foot of the Cross—but unless I can do this, I may as well give up altogether.

The green notebook which consists chiefly of notes made on

the occasion of retreats between 1923–30 reveals in some detail the course of Evelyn's attempts to live a more deeply Christ-like love of those close to her, those who came her way socially, in the course of friendship or in the exercise of her ministry. She accuses herself of all the mistakes, sins and vices that one might reasonably expect: picking and choosing among those she is supposed to be helping, severity and coldness to the servants, irritability, impatience, giving rein to her satirical bent, making capital out of her poor people in ordinary conversation, the old claimfulness and jealousy, including envy of the success of other people's 'mystical books'. Such self-reproach is almost invariably accompanied by 'resolves', sometimes with reference to the Baron's advice. A characteristic example of the kind of advice she gave herself occurs under the heading *Notes from Baron's Letter to Gwen* in which she transcribes the Baron's description of what it means to help other people: '. . . The helping of other souls incurs suffering & renunciation to the helper: a perpetual death to self', etc. The suffering according to the Baron was caused by the inevitable gap between the particular vision, tastes, etc. of the 'light-bringing soul' and the particular needs and capacity of the 'soul helped'. The latter may well not take, may even spurn what the former holds precious:

> This means much detachment, unselfishness, even humiliation. It means yielding up one's treasures, & risking their being despised. It means forgetting one's self & fixing attention on the soul to be helped.

'Forgetting one's self' that certainly was the key. The trouble was that Evelyn's whole religious philosophy up to the time she met the Baron, while it might hold the doctrine of self-loss and self-transcendence in theory, was, in virtue of its strongly psychological and subjective bent, strongly focussed in practice on spiritual experience as a kind of value in itself. It is impossible to say anything further about her growth in love without grasping this particular nettle and attempting, if we can, to see a little beneath the surface of her inward restlessness. At the same time we shall also be confronting the anomaly that this writer on mysticism who exalted the part of feeling in religious experience as no-one before, became, as the Baron saw, emotionally undernourished and introspective, found herself trapped in a hole from which the only escape might appear to be ecstasy but in which every successive religious exaltation only seemed to anchor her more securely.

Evelyn at the time she applied to the Baron had intellectually come to accept religious institutionalism. It seems, to judge from her remarks at the end of 1921, that having lapsed from a fervent if not ecclesiastical religious practice in the course of the war she had also, shortly before writing to him, returned to regular prayer. She thus came to him on the wave of what Fr Baker might have called a 'second conversion'. As she explained to the Baron, during the war she had had 'several vivid calls back' but had not responded to them. Now she had returned she found it strange, indeed it made her 'nervous' as she put it, that, instead of having to fight her way back inch by inch, 'everything has been given back to me, and more'. Yet, writing on 21 December 1921, we find her once more questioning the significance and validity of her religious experience as she had done once before to Robert Benson shortly after 'the sort of conversion experience', as she calls it to von Hugel, which then seemed to establish definitively for her the truth of Catholic Christianity. This time she expresses her doubts together with her reasons for discounting them. The letter, as we have it in the typed copy, begins *in medias res:* the emphasis is Evelyn's:

> The chief point is, am I simply living on illusion? It seems impossible but all the same I feel I must be sure. I don't mean

by this any unwillingness to make a venture or any demand for impossible clearness of faith, but simply to be *certain* my own experiences are not simply imaginary.

She lists three reasons for accepting their validity: (a) *Givenness*, i.e. unexpectedness, entire non-earnedness, (b) 'Overwhelming sense of certitude, objective reality & of obligation,' (c) 'That I have never tried to either obtain or retain them, & know any such effort would be useless'. She adds characteristically:

> I leave out the emotional side as that is said to be no guarantee of genuineness. All the same it is difficult to conceive that a construction of one's own mind could produce such feeling.

Could, for instance, she asked herself, a construction from her own mind have produced the 'automatism' of nearly a year later? Evelyn reported this 'experience' to von Hugel most apologetically as though she had unwittingly offended good taste. But her description is graphic enough. The report in which it occurs exists in her rough copy. But the passage relating the experience is exceptional in bearing little sign of crossings-out and alteration. It runs:

> Probably I ought to tell you this. Last October, one day when I was praying, quite suddenly a voice seemed to speak to me— with tremendous staccato [this word is inserted] sharpness & clearness. It only said one short thing; first in Latin & then in English! PLEASE don't think I'm going in for psychic automatisms or horrors of that sort. It never happened since & I don't want it to. Of course I know all about the psychological aspect & am not 'hallucinated'. All the same, I simply *cannot* believe that there was not some thing deeper, more real, not me at all, behind. The effect was terrific. Sort of nailed me to the floor for ½ an hour, which went in a flash. I felt definitively called-out & settled once for all—that any falling back or leaving off after that will be an unpardonable treason. This sense has persisted.

She continues by saying that the experience meant an end to
'feverish banging-about' and she would not worry overmuch if
she has no more consolations. And yet she adds, 'derelictions are
more painful and trying than they used to be'.

The letter continues very much in this vein. On the one hand
a passage with many alterations describing

> new lights . . . sort of intellectual intuitions & quite clear of
> 'sensible devotion' . . . so quick and vast one can only retain
> about half,

or, alternatively, a more passive type of prayer in which she found
herself swept up 'to a kind of warm, inhabited darkness & blind
joy'. On the other:

> A terrible, overwhelming suspicion that after all my whole
> 'spiritual experience' may only be subjective. There are times
> (of course when one has not got it) when it seems incredible
> these things could happen to me, considering what I have been.

She points out that consolation and deprivation *are* very closely
linked to 'the ups and downs of one's nervous & even bodily
life'. She continues:

> There is no real test. I may have deceived myself right through,
> &, always studying these things, self-suggestion would be
> horribly easy. These doubts are absolute torture, after what has
> happened. They paralyse one's life at the roots once they lodge
> in the mind.

The little notebook fills in some of the details of these and
similar accounts. Thus one day in February 1923, some four
months before the report, she writes:

> Such lights as one gets are now different in type: All over-
> whelming in their emotional result: quite independent of

'sensible devotion', more quiet, calm, expansive, like intellectual intuitions yet not quite that either. Thus yesterday I saw
& felt *how* it actually is, that we are in Christ & He in us—the
interpenetration of Spirit— & all of us merged together in him
actually, & so fitly described as his body. The way to full
intercessory power must I think be along this path.

This section which clearly underlies the corresponding section of
the report anticipates also the report in expressing a desire to get
away from sensible consolations 'or at least their dominance'.
'They are entrancing and overwhelming,' she adds,

> but they don't really lead anywhere. It's the deep quiet mysteri-
> ous love one wants to keep; and gradually transfer focus to the
> will.

Her illuminations continued that winter. On 18 February she
describes a Sunday morning when she had not been well enough
to go out to Communion but read her 'Sunday prayers' in bed.
It felt wrong at first since she was used to make her hour's prayer
kneeling on the boards. Afterwards, suddenly,

> the Spirit of Christ came right into my soul—as it were trans-
> fusing it in every part. How *cd* I imagine this? I was not excited
> but deeply happy & awed. So intimate all-penetrating, humb-
> ling. Lasted a very little time. *Far* closer than even the best
> communions.

By 16 March, however, we have the background to the gloomier
parts of the report. Evelyn couldn't understand why she as a
beginner should experience this kind of thing; also she could not
understand how she did not immediately become 'better', i.e. less
irritable and critical. On her retreat from 4–8 May that year, she
wrote that she had felt no fervour, and had only just escaped
'another of those paralyzing fits of doubt'. She complains: 'I've

nothing at the present moment that the most ordinary small-beer piety cdnt contrive'. And so it goes on. A final example, dated Whitsunday, must suffice:

> More of those terrifying onsets of doubt when it all gets hazy & melts away & one feels, for a bit, it can't be real.

Von Hugel on grasping the problem wrote her two trenchant paragraphs of the utmost importance. If ever there was a 'turning-point' in Evelyn's life at this moment—she herself repeatedly claimed such turning points for this or that special prayer-experience—it should almost certainly be sought in the impact upon her of this and similar applications of fundamental theology. He wished, he said, to make two special points, the second, concerning mortification has for lack of space to be left on one side. But his first 'fundamentally important point' reads:

> I do not at all like this craving for absolute certainty that this or that experience of yours is what it seems to yourself. And I am assuredly not going to declare that I am absolutely certain of the final & evidential worth of any of these experiences. These experiences of yours are not articles of faith, are they? God & Christ & the need of our constant death to self, remain simply certain do they not, even if your experiences be mistaken ones? And for what are even the most probably genuine of such things given to us, than to help us further away from self & self-occupation?
>
> You are at times tempted to scepticism (who is not?) & so you long to have some, if only one direct personal experience which shall be beyond the reach of all reasonable doubt. But such an escape from scepticism would, even if it were possible (which it is not) be a most dangerous one, & would only weaken you, & shrivel you, or puff you up. By all means use such lights; by all means believe them, if & when they humble

and yet brace you, to be probably from God. But do not build your faith upon them; do not make them an end when they exist only to be a means. So practising you will escape one more entanglement, to which kind of *emberlificotage* you are prone.

Certainly it was time to tell Evelyn that she was a Christian and no longer, in the phrase she applied to one of her early heroines, a 'passionate amateur of experience'. It is not entirely surprising that the little Green Book begins at about this time to show a certain change in her 'lights'. While there is still that tendency to grasp out and clutch at the light given her, the burden of her reflections is more resigned, less possessive, more devoted to the great objective example of Christ's own love, less bent on reproducing some great 'Christ-experience' in her own soul. One example must suffice, dated 26 December 1923:

Looking back on this autumn, I feel I have chiefly learnt two things 1) A deep & clear sense of the all-penetrating Presence of God & of Love as His deepest nature—or at least the nearest *we* can come to it: & so, of any decent thing we do as not ours, but a direct activity on the one Love, passing rt [sic] through & [illegible] one, like the sea water supporting & passing right through a shell fish. Yet, all the time, one remains one's own beastly self! Great deepening & enrichment of one's sense of God at times—but it slips away, I can't hold it.

2) More and more I realize, the union with Christ one craves for can & must be only through union with His redemptive work, always going on in the world. If I ever hesitate before this, & the pain & stress it must mean for us wretched little creatures used as his instruments—then I draw back from Him and break the link. So the 'life of supremely happy men' is *not* 'alone with the alone'—its the redeeming life, now & in Eternity too, in ever greater & more entrancing union with

the Spirit of Jesus ceaselessly at *work* in the world. Only one must have the quiet times too, to consolidate that union & stretch out the house of one's soul, & feed on Him.

After this passage, the annotations continue spasmodically for a 1924 marked by 'ups and downs' and then give way to retrospective self-examinations and prospective resolutions made on the occasion of retreats from 1926–30. Despite a certain resigned mournfulness about her low state of prayer (she once in this period states her belief that she is undergoing the 'passive night of the senses') most of this material suggests a continuous and intense sense of herself as God's instrument, called to that total self-giving which is epitomised by Christ's cross, called upon to mortify all softness in her manner of life and all egoism in her relationships. The meaning of life as suggested by these meditations is essentially to be found in 'not being rescued and consoled, but being made into part of his rescuing and ever-sacrificial body', as she puts it on 24 May 1924.

It has not been possible to deal with every aspect of von Hugel's guidance of Evelyn. We have for example, said little or nothing about his gentle efforts to encourage Christo-centric devotion in her, efforts which the quotations above show to have been outstandingly successful. But to gain some general view of his dealings with her it is necessary to step back a little and consider Evelyn's total situation as he must have viewed it. To do this we cannot do better than take a passage which occurs towards the end of the second volume of *The Mystical Element* (p. 365):

The dominant and quite certain fact seems to be that, in proportion as the Abstractive movement of the Soul is taken as self-sufficient, and a Contemplative life is attempted as something substantially independent of any concrete, social, and devotional helps and duties, the soul gets into a state of danger, which no amount of predominance of the Director can really render safe, whereas, in proportion as the soul takes care to practise, in its own special degree and manner, the outgoing movement towards multiplicity and contingency, (particular attention to particular religious facts and particular service of particular persons), does such right, quite ordinary seeming, active subordination to, and incorporation within, the great sacred organisms of the Family, Society, and the Church, or of any wise and helpful subdivision of these, furnish material, purgation and check for the other movement, and render superfluous any great or universal predominance of direction.

Evelyn's situation before she came directly under von Hugel's influence undoubtedly corresponded closely to that of the abstractive or contemplative soul 'in danger', as he described it. The remedy was to give her a 'Catholic' approach as he defined it, in other words to lead her to accept her creaturely status, to accept that the economy of redemption like everything else of beauty or importance in human life is adjusted to the human scale and does not require man to jump out of his own skin. She was required therefore to see Christ not merely as an icon or epitome of man's psycho-mystical apotheosis but actually to seek and find him, his sacraments, his body, the church, as a living reality, source of nourishment, spur to practical charity. The primary factor had to become not 'experience' which raised one to the seventh heaven one week and cast one into an agnostic's Hades the next, but faith which involves both submission and commitment, both an acknowledgement of an overwhelming 'given' divine reality and of one's utter dependence upon it. In a sense we have seen it all before, for did not Constance's Watcher, Paul Vickery and Constance herself, have to humble themselves and consent to be redeemed. Yet as we look back over those 'redemptions' certain defects stand out. Paul's way of 'sacrifice' rather than 'ecstasy' is distinctly a *pis aller*: while in the case of the Watcher and Constance,

Evelyn allows herself the luxury of killing them both off so
that the apotheosis may be more striking. The sacrifice in their
case is the last, and the greatest, technique for inducing the vision.
Despite the evocation of heroic charity at the close of *The Column
of Dust* Constance's death has an air of convenience about it.
After all, for Constance to die was too easy. Most of us have to
live with our Veras as Evelyn certainly did with hers.

   Turning from Evelyn's private history to her public career we
confront once again that 'appearance of tremendous logicality of
mind and of unbending principle' noted by her director. In the
autumn of 1921 she was chosen to deliver the inaugural course of
a lectureship founded by Professor Upton and in the gift of the
Principal and governing body of Manchester College. It was a
notable event for Oxford as well as for Evelyn, she being 'the first
woman lecturer to appear in the University list' (Lucy Menzies).
These lectures were delivered later that same year and her preface
to the published volume is dated Epiphany, 1922. This suggests a
fairly rapid rate of production even granted that a certain amount
of the work only involved the adaptation of articles previously
published. These lectures in fact incorporate a good deal of
Evelyn's reflections in the preceding years and her very recent
'relapse' into pure mysticism as illustrated by *The Essentials of
Mysticism* leaves clear traces in the second of them. The fifth
chapter repeats and develops her now established views on the
need for religious institutions as in various ways essential to the
'full life of the Spirit'. The arguments demonstrating that it is
better for praying mankind to belong to a church than otherwise
balance individualism against gregariousness, conservation against
innovation, stability against mobility, freedom against discipline; but such considerations are possibly of less interest in the
context of Evelyn's total development than the great emphasis she
places in this chapter on the fundamental role played by the
'organised cultus' in the worshipping body and vis-à-vis each of

its members. This emphasis which follows logically after a chapter on Psychology and the Life of the Spirit gives to the chapter its particular flavour of dual inspiration: von Hugel on the one hand with his insistence on the need for an 'institutional element' as well as a 'mystical element' in religion; and, on the other, Evelyn's own subjectivist past. Evelyn begins at this point in her career as an Anglican to concentrate on liturgical prayer and action as *the* focal point of spiritual training and instruction of the Christian faithful.

Before leaving these lectures it is necessary to add that while they certainly give a foretaste of Evelyn's future preoccupations they also represent a high-point in her longstanding preoccupation—by now in fact very close to an obsession—with psychology and powers of suggestion. Once again the point cannot be elaborated but those who have weighed the implications of some of the statements in the chapters on Psychology and the Life of the Spirit already mentioned, in which prayer is assimilated, if not reduced, to auto-suggestion, will not be amazed to learn that Evelyn in her private notes in which she describes her struggles with her sceptical demon, could find herself moved to write: 'There are times when I wish I'd never heard of psychology' (report to von Hugel of June 1923). These lectures were thus 'brave' perhaps in more senses than that intended by von Hugel for in them Evelyn explores as deeply as she ever did on a philosophical level the condition and limits of man's capacity for God and God's accessibility to man. It was a dangerous enterprise at a moment when temperamentally and theologically she had yet to be stabilised in her new way of worship and self-perception.

Turning to other aspects of Evelyn's major published material in this decade we should first glance at her work *The Mystics of the Church* of 1925. The book was published by James Clarke in the 'Living Church' series edited by Dr John McFadyen, and serves as an eloquent witness to her new view of the God-centred life as fully embodied in the given historical Christian community. The introductory chapter recapitulates with specific mystical emphasis points from the Manchester College lectures. Having defined mysticism 'according to its historical and psychological definitions' as 'the direct intuition or experience of God' she goes on to relate this rather forbidding phrase to all religious experience which would make 'first-hand personal knowledge of God' and loving personal communion with him, the basis of life. In this scope she includes in passing 'not only the act of contemplation, the vision or state of consciouness in which the soul of the great mystic realises God, but many humbler and dimmer experiences of prayer, in which the little human spirit truly feels the presence of the Divine Spirit and Love'. As she takes her reader by the hand through the several epochs of Christian history she points out how the inspired individuals whose minds and hearts God so fruitfully obsessed acted both as transmitters of given traditions which they enriched and as prophets and innovators to save their communities from stagnation. Though the story is heavily biased in favour of the central Western Catholic mystical tradition, the testimony of other traditions is brought to bear in the persons of such as Luther, Boehme, Blake, Law, Woolman, etc. But once again the Cambridge Platonists are blown upon as mere visionaries and not practitioners. They are described as 'various types of gentle, cultivated, moderately fervent—in fact characteristically Anglican—spirits' (p. 221). Though the book closes with a reference to the life and teachings of the still living converted Hindu, Sadhu Sundar Singh, the story seems to culminate in the intensity of Charles de Foucauld (1858–1916), ex-aristocrat, dropout from society, God-obsessed desert dweller, who yet proclaimed himself the 'universal brother' and devoted himself to serving and evangelising, single-handed, remote areas of the Sahara. The words she quotes from him express well the perception she admired in varying degrees in them all:

When we love . . . we live less in ourselves than in that which
we love; and the more we love, the more we establish our life
beyond ourselves in that which we love; We feel when we
suffer—we do not always feel when we love; and this is an
added suffering. But we know that we want to love; and the
want to love is to love! (p. 252).

What would von Hugel have thought of *The Mystics of the
Church*? The question is not without interest and all the more so
for not being amenable to any satisfactory short answer. It will
have to suffice here to say that it is not the kind of book von Hugel
himself could, or more accurately, would have written. The fullest reasons for this would take too long to recount. In the first instance for example, von Hugel was not in the habit of writing
vulgarizing books of any kind. His personal style and habits of
thought precluded the fulfilling of such aspirations if he ever
had them. But more important than this, there is also the analytic
tendency of his thought, which was on the whole less prone to
bring together what individuals of very diverse antecedents and
background might have had in common than to discriminate the
nuances of distinction such diversity might occasion, and to use
their opinions to make up the fullest possible spectrum of philosophical contrarieties according to what Joseph Whelan calls his
'radically inductive approach'. And the major reason why von
Hugel would never have embarked on such a book as this one of
Evelyn's lies precisely in the fact that where religious experience
and the *Church* were concerned his analytic tendency was nearly
always at its most marked, at its most 'discriminating', to use his
favourite word. For von Hugel, consistent with his acceptance of
what one might call the cultural-relatedness of religious experience generally, believed profoundly that men's religious and
mystical experience, in itself and as reported, could vary greatly
according to their religious denomination, and a good deal of

literary labour was expended by him in correlating as exactly as possible different 'types' of religious experience with this end in view. Since from his vantage point the Roman Church offered in principle *the* most satisfactory, all-round, balanced environment for the development of religious experience it would follow that to attempt impartially to distil some sort of universal Christian experience irrespective of this fact would be unrealistic and doomed to failure, *a fortiori* if one sought to distil a Christian experience linked to Church membership.

Evelyn in her book seeks to do just this, drawing her examples from all shades of ecclesiastical opinion in the Christian spectrum. If one approves of such a procedure one may designate it as synthesising and interpret it as an endeavour to compare like to like and seek enlightenment where previously only opposition seemed to show. If one is against, one calls it eclectic and, usually, shallow. Whether Evelyn is justifiably synthesising even eirenic, in her attempts to show how representative mystics from widely differing and even antagonistic Christian groups are in the last resort sharers in a *common* spirit of dependence and self-dedication vis-à-vis their respective communities, or whether her thesis is 'shallow', is too large a question to argue here. But whatever the verdict as to the success of her enterprise the very undertaking of it reveals her as no mere echo or disciple of her spiritual master von Hugel. At least we can say that although the book has its faults it would certainly not have received from him the reception meted out to it by an unsigned review in Blackfriars for November that year, in which 'Catholics' were warned of its dire heterodoxy with a mixture of quarter-truths and unsupported innuendos. It was a review which was intended to hurt and did. Evelyn described it as 'pure spite' (*Life*, p. 135).

Evelyn after becoming an Anglican, although she did occasionally pray in Catholic churches as we have seen, also displayed a certain Anglicanism in principle in, for example, seeking out

Anglican places of worship when abroad. At least she did so during her holiday with her husband in Italy in 1925. In Cortina she could savour fully the less pleasant aspects of belonging to a non-Catholic body, as she described to her intimate friend, Clara Smith:

> There was a most horrible English Church, so I had to go to it: all the rigours of Continental Anglicanism—the parson [here a passage is omitted by the Anglican editor of the *Letters*] with a bushy moustache—points which a rather nice R.C. woman who had made friends with me, took pleasure in emphasizing! She went to mass at the parish church with lots of nice creatures in Tyrolese dress (*Letters*, p. 166).

In Venice shortly afterwards she also went out of her way:

> There is an English church in Venice and by catching the 7.20 steamer to-morrow morning I can manage it, so must . . .

This expedition to the Chiesa Anglicana was not, in the event, without its rewards (*Letters*, p. 167). In any case she followed it by attending High Mass at San Marco as of old.

This holiday was especially notable for at last effecting a meeting between Evelyn and an Italian woman correspondent she had known since 1919 through a mutual friend, Miss Turton, the Sorella Maria who had established a small contemplative community of women in the spirit of St Francis of Assissi. Evelyn wrote up the little hermitage, called the Rifugoi di San Francesco at Campello-sul-Clitunno—without of course giving away its exact whereabouts—for The Spectator. She much appreciated the simple ecumenical spirit of this little spiritual family in which clearly she was welcomed unreservedly and with open arms. It was with this group among others that she had established her Confraternity of the Spiritual Entente in 1920, designed as an ecumenical body to unite members of various denominations in a common spiritual aim of realising in their lives and prayers the charity of Christ. Membership of such a group may even have seemed to Evelyn at one time a possible alternative to accepting a communicant status in an existing visible church.

Back in England, once it became known that she was an Anglican, Evelyn began fairly swiftly to feel somewhat at home. After the publication of the Oxford lectures and the news of her allegiance had filtered out it is evident that a gradual rapprochement began to take place which led to a climax of activity on the Church's behalf in 1924. But before that she had been to Pleshey Retreat House for a retreat given by Canon Henry Monks in March 1922 and felt greatly refreshed and encouraged, as she told her friends, by the spirit of Christian kindliness and devotion she met there. The Retreat House, having the air and much of the charm of the larger type of Essex village house and deeply secluded in a little known but picturesque corner of countryside near Chelmsford, and surprisingly close to London, was at this time just beginning to establish itself in its new rôle after a previous career as an Anglican convent. It came to occupy a special place in Evelyn's affections, but even in June 1923 when she had only been there twice she could write to Lucy Menzies with a certain finality: 'The retreat house I always go to is Pleshey' (*Letters*, p. 316). She gave her first retreat in the house in March 1924, a retreat for which she had been carefully prepared by the Baron. Her page or so of description in her notebook reveals how keyed up she was for it and how doing it seemed to reveal her in some ways to herself. The experience of doing such work almost as it were in spite of herself, led on by a 'strong unwavering power', confirmed her sense that she was to be used as a tool for God's work. The paragraph concludes:

Objects of my life towards God is not, I am now convinced, any personal achievement or ecstasy at all but just to make one able to do this kind of work.

Lucy Menzies whom she seems to have introduced to the place, was later, in 1928, to succeed in office Mrs Annie Harvey, the warden from the foundation in 1919. Concerning Lucy, with whom Evelyn had corresponded since 1917 and whose director she became, nothing more will be said here save to remark that they did not in fact meet until 1923 when Evelyn went to lecture in Scotland.

An older friend upon whom Evelyn called that same year was Eva Gore-Booth. An entry in the notebook dated 16 March 1923 runs:

> Went to see Eva Gore-Booth. Found with joy and amazement *she* had become vividly Xtn. 'What a fairy tale of a life it is!' she said. Nothing *really* given in any other way. Each new light she thinks must *at once* be handed on—that's the condition. *No* separateness. All vision of truth is in Him thr[ough] love.

Eva, who had been a considerable suffragette campaigner in her day, a poet and author as well as a 'white hot Neoplatonist' like Evelyn herself, and at about the same time, died on 30 June 1926. Evelyn in that year wrote the introduction to a posthumous collection of her verse entitled *The House of Three Windows*, in which she placed her friend in the exalted category of mystics and artists, mediating between unseen and seen realities. But it is as she speaks in general terms of the two different ways in which all mystics tend to develop that she seems to speak for them both, both being evidently examples of the second type of evolution referred to:

> It is generally true to say of the mystics that they follow in their growth one of two opposite courses. On one hand they may begin with a vividly personal, often anthropomorphic conception of the Divine, and thence move to an evermore abstract and formless experience of God: 'stripping themselves' as they

often say, 'of all bodily images' and therewith of the very means by which men and women still in the body may actualize reality best. On the other hand, they may begin with the diffuse and impersonal—with some sort of 'cosmic consciousness' or 'nature-mysticism' or other type of philosophic abstraction—and thence move to a more and more concentrated, concrete and personal, and thus more rich and fruitful relationship.

In April 1924 Evelyn lost her mother who died after a short illness. As von Hugel in his letter of condolence put it with his customary tactful honesty, the fact that mother and daughter had for long had different if not opposed outlooks on life probably added to Evelyn's 'discomfort'. Her father was sorely afflicted and for a time that year there was every possibility that the Stuart Moores would give up their home and move to No. 3. There is at least one gloomy resolution written into Evelyn's notebook to the effect that if God asks this of her she will give it. In the event things were otherwise arranged—Hubert certainly had even less desire to move—and Evelyn helped her father out by acting hostess for him either at home or in Lincoln's Inn.

In January 1925 Friedrich von Hugel died. His last days were characteristically calm, laborious and prayerful. Evelyn, who knew his family and home, especially his niece, Gwendolen Plunkett-Greene, to whom she refers in her private notes as among those upon whose spiritual support she most relies, would have been kept fully informed about events. In the final year Evelyn was due to send a report in June. In fact, because no doubt of the Baron's health and preoccupations with other work, she sent him a letter. This, her last 'confessional' document was not available to Miss Cropper but has in fact survived in the little green notebook transcribed rather incoherently by, presumably, Evelyn's later friend, Marjorie Vernon. The order in which it should unfold is not altogether clear in Mrs Vernon's copy which is most probably based on a preliminary draft of Evelyn's, but the best reconstruction seems the following:

This letter is instead of my 'spiritual report' ordinarily due this week. I had intended to pass it over, being sure you need all your time & strength for yr work, but Gwen says you will expect me to write. Of course I expect no answer.

All is now more difficult. My normal state is a quiet peace of the will without sensible consolations. Its true I've learnt more about myself and *far* more about the Cross, and have been given a bigger deeper sense of God. There have been times when one seemed immersed as it were in an ocean of spirit & when one opened one's soul it poured through. But lately circumstances have constituted a standing temptation to my worst passions. I am in constant conflict with hateful feelings of claimfulness, bitterness, jealousy, uncharitableness wh. swamp my soul in spite of desperate struggles. I never knew what temptation really was before. Its like a devil. If I cd fully & generously accept the situation (as any real Xtn easily could) it wd exactly mortify all my ruling faults, but it means a death to self of wh. I still seem incapable. Its crushing to find they are still as violent as ever. There seem 2 natures in me, & the bad one is still the strongest. I keep making acts of renunciation & again slipping back to sinful thoughts. Sometimes God comes fully back in a golden silence & peace & one sort of melts & vanishes & doesn't count & He alone remains. Then I realize what a food as well as a beast I am to mind about *anything* else, but I can't keep it up. If I fail in this test its all up with trying to work for Xt.

Oh my dear friend & saviour, I'm so sorry & ashamed to have to write so unsatisfactorily after all you have done for me. You'll see no evidence of growth here. I did so want to be able to say I'd got nicer, but seem as awful as ever, only now I know it. I realize far worse than before the depth of holiness & penetrating everywhere goodness & beauty & peace. I've seen it all once or twice in different ways, and the craving for God & self-abandonment never ceases. But insights count for *nothing* beside these horrible failures in love. I know I shall never *really* achieve much—the best I can hope for is to stick at the foot of the ladder & show people the way up. But I am going on with the struggle.

Von Hugel's brief but weighty reply to this outpouring is given by Miss Cropper. Unfortunately the central paragraph dealing with the underlying causes of Evelyn's distress is there misprinted, so confusing the advice given. It is here transcribed from the typed copy at St Andrews:

I notice how well you are aware that self-satisfaction—or even simply the appearance to our own eyes, of your state of soul as satisfactory, are no genuine tests & measures of solid spiritual advancement. And yet, I think, that you allow yourself to attend to, or at least to notice vivaciously this sight of yourself in your real condition of spiritual misery. I should like you *gently*, to try to alter this—not the appearance of your soul to your own eyes, still less (in any direct way) the substance of this your soul, or your estimate of such substance: but simply the *vivacious irritated or confusing attention* to these things or impressions. Drop, gently drop by a quiet turning to God & Christ & the poor: & you will grow in peace & power.[5]

This final attempt to lead Evelyn away from excitement about her own states towards a Christian self-forgetfulness epitomises the Baron's message to Evelyn. His death itself reinforced his final message to her. Gwen (Gwendolen Plunkett-Greene) wrote down

5. Emphasis von Hugel's, cp. *Life*, p. 124.

the last talk she had with him in which he expressed his desire to give himself in answer to God's generosity, and gave it to Evelyn who attended the funeral on 30 January. Evelyn contributed an anonymous appreciation of him to The Guardian in the week following which was subsequently re-printed in *Mixed Pastures*, entitled *Baron von Hugel as a Spiritual Teacher* (pp. 229-33). It is this piece which recalls von Hugel's standard reply to effusions of gratitude: 'One likes to help people'.

The last letter Evelyn received from von Hugel expressed the wish that she should undertake about two-thirds of the work which, on average, she had been doing over the past ten years. It is clear that he saw in her signs of strain and over-stress of which she was largely unaware in her rather desperate attempts to escape the sense of her own spiritual privilege and comfort which sometimes possessed her, and which she did all in her power and beyond her power to counteract. She was, she wrote to herself at one point in her notes in early 1923, a Glaxo-baby, a typical product of patent spiritual foods,—'may look plump but deficient in bone'. To achieve 'bony hardness' she then believed she needed mortification, even the self-inflicted kind as suggested by the example of the then notorious self-mascerating Jesuit, Fr George Doyle. Von Hugel's dissuasion and her own experience taught her eventually that the best mortification is self-renouncing self-forgetting *work*. For, as she well knew, the best way to *become* more loving is to *be* more loving. In fact she probably should have taken the advice to let up; one can see that to have done so would have been almost the ultimate mortification so that her egoism, too, would have been lessened by such due attention to her health. In the event she did nothing of the sort and went on until checked by sickness.

From one point of view it was natural that Evelyn should be asked to give retreats to Anglicans. After all she was an established champion of contemplative values and known to be a disciple of a Roman Catholic philosopher whom Anglicans could respect unreservedly. It was almost too good to be true that she should be a practising Anglican too. In retrospect it seems amazing that her services were not more used, especially in giving addresses to clergy at which, to judge from the samples provided by the one which was published in full, and miscellaneous 'quiet day' addresses, she excelled. In the event she gave an example of what she could do for the Liverpool clergy which was later published as *Concerning the Inner Life* in 1926. The gist of her advice will be considered in the next chapter in the context of her religious doctrine generally. The first book of her retreat addresses to lay people was *The House of Prayer* (1929), and shows her fully fledged technique as deployed at Pleshey and elsewhere. Discussion of this too must be left over for the moment.

The book which best represents the kind of thing she was saying up and down the country and over the northern border is *Man and the Supernatural* (1927) which incorporates material from some ten papers, lectures and addresses delivered from 1922–1927. Despite its resulting 'pot-boilerish' appearance which leads to repetition the work has a striking unity of theme and convergence of views, marking a certain advance on the earlier Oxford lectures. It sometimes also adopts a more polemic tone than one is accustomed to find in Evelyn's books. A spirited attack on what is called 'social Christianity' in particular has some hard things to say about progressive anthropocentrism and a general tendency to pragmatism among Christian thinkers and activists (p. 61). This stance should be compared with the kind of thing she was saying at times to the Conference on Politics, Economics and Christianity and similar bodies, such lectures as *The Christian Basis of Social Action* and *The Will of the Voice*, both COPEC addresses published in the quarterly, The Pilgrim, in 1923 and 1924 respectively. It is clear that right from the start Evelyn presented her Anglican audiences with an uncompromising summons to return to loving contemplation of God as true source and guarantee of Christian love in conformity with her doctrine outlined in the Manchester College lectures:

> We must *be* good before we can *do* good; be real before we can accomplish real things. No generalised benevolence, no social Christianity however beautiful and devoted, can take the place of this centring of the Spirit on eternal values; this humble deliberate recourse to Reality (*Life of the Spirit*, p. 42).

The mystic is the model even to the 'social' Christian in so far as he alone can really bring a vision to the people and do God's work, being to God 'as a man's right hand is to a man', for:

> the more purely the flame of contemplation burns the more is it found in the end to inspire saving action. . . . We cannot sit down and be devotional, while acquiescing in conditions which make it impossible for other souls even to obey the moral law (*Mixed Pastures*, p. 101. Address of July 1925).

William Temple, chairman of COPEC and editor of The Pilgrim which published some of these addresses, evidently esteemed Evelyn's witness for she spoke a good deal thanks to his invitation in these years.

Evelyn was involved in another subject of considerable church concern in 1927 when the topic of Prayer Book revision was much in the air. Evelyn, who seems to have realised early and as a result of intimate acquaintance with some of the personalities involved, that ecclesiastical politics is as much an art of the possible as any other kind, was afraid that the whole exercise of revision would be sabotaged by the antagonisms of extremists—not so much, clearly, because they disagreed with each other as because of their combined refusal to accept compromise. Probably her contribution to the debate, a piece published in The Spectator on 19 November 1927 and entitled *The Hill of the Lord*, only provoked dissatisfied mirth among those concerned—if they had time to read it. It is clearly an attempt to get all sides to see the subject *sub specie aeternitatis* and remind everyone that they are after all discussing God's medium for communicating with man. Having guyed all the parties to the conflict in terms of an extended mountaineering metaphor in which their opposing views are compared to alternative (and equally valid?) routes to the mountain-top, Evelyn ends by evoking the fifteenth-century mystical theologian Nicolas of Cusa (she was then writing the introduction to a translation of one of his works), who said that 'the wall of Paradise is built of contradictions'. We must conclude not only that Evelyn was not at her best in such 'political' matters but also that her article expresses beneath the apparent smugness, a worried sense that the discussion was *not* being conducted in the light of first principles—anyway certainly not what *she* regarded as first principles.

In the last years of the decade Evelyn added to her retreats, lectures, publishing of articles and reviews, activity on committees, looking after 'cases', corresponding with disciples and other interested parties, twice-weekly slum visiting, entertaining, study, gardening and praying, the post of religious editor of The Spectator to which she had already been an occasional contributor for some time. The task became very much a major preoccupation of the next four years and we shall have to give some account of her stewardship in the following chapter. During this period her director was Walter Howard Frere, Bishop of Truro, whom she seems to have asked to take her on after some eighteen months without direction following von Hugel's death. Of him also something more must be said. In the meantime we may perhaps take leave of the Evelyn of the twenties still wrestling with herself as she makes her retreat notes at Marden in June 1929, caught between her 'inordinate' dependent affection for one of her women friends and struggling to bear up under the tense over-dependence and emotional demands of another. Still accusing herself of seeking her own comfort and preferences and other old familiar vices, she yet remembers the Baron's injunctions to purify love and to try to moderate 'all vehemence and strain'. 'Fraternal Charity' she writes:

the index of all love of God. . . . Nothing in my practical life can be a genuine reason for shirking the service of God, saying 'I cannot come'. Must be ready to *act* not always wait till pushed. *DO* the will more, not be just devotional & to do it in little humble loving ways. Great gentleness in all relationships never exacting. Never trying to get my rights. Definitely try to take lowest places, force myself to do it. Have been spoilt child. Now must genuinely grasp the Cross.

All very mundane in a mystic no doubt but not altogether un-expected in a Christian.

9
Death in a Thin Place

By May 1930 when Evelyn made her annual retreat at St Mary's Abbey, West Malling, she foresaw that ill health was likely to be with her to the end. This prospect thus becomes the subject of the fourth of her retreat resolutions for that year which reads:

Since it appears likely I will have indifferent health for the rest of my life, must face this quietly & gratefully, determine that it shall be the least possible worry & detriment to others, & fully used to purify & subordinate me to God's will. Steady effort to avoid dwelling on own physical state, getting into centre of picture, & accept the fatigue, weakness, monotony, & humbling details of illness with JOY.

Chronic asthma from which she began to suffer increasingly at this time, was chiefly responsible for this estimate of her prospects but to it must certainly be added the steady pressure of study, writing, giving retreats, and visiting, on top of her normal domestic and social duties, all of which added up to a burden which became well-nigh intolerable by 1935 when she reached her sixtieth year and was in the throes of producing her second major work, *Worship*. The general state of her health was not helped by a motor accident in February 1934, resulting in 'mild concussion' and bruising which left her nerves in a raw state for much of that summer. But one who was a close friend of Evelyn at the time believes that it was the unremitting labour of *Worship* from 1934 to 1936 which most grievously wore her down and contributed to her relatively early death at sixty-five. The best authority for

241

all aspects of Evelyn's life at this period is Miss Margaret Cropper, who knew her personally from 1931 as friend, disciple, hostess and collaborator, and has given a very full account of her activities in *The Life of Evelyn Underhill*. Detail supplementary to this account should be sought in that work and in the invaluable *Letters* edited by Charles Williams.

Apart therefore from her work and doctrine, there is as usual little of outstanding importance to relate. The Underhill family seems to have weathered the economic storms of the period like most other British middle-class families and if Sir Arthur Underhill made no secret of where his sympathies lay in the various industrial struggles and trials of the time, the same cannot be said of his daughter whose opinions on these matters are totally unknown to us. Nor is there any particular reason why they should be. Evelyn had, she felt, been given her work to do, useful work and work that needed doing. She would surely not have felt it her place to appropriate the platform she had been entrusted with in order to propound particular political nostrums or theories, even if she had any to advance. Although in 1920 and afterwards she had hinted that the 'spiritual oases' of devout souls she then envisaged *would* have much to say on current affairs, economic as well as diplomatic, her suggestions do not seem to have been followed by practical consequences, not that is to say until once again the course of events seemed to be leading inexorably to war. No doubt public affairs are tacitly and as it were *a fortiori* included in her general statement of her position with regard to polemical subjects set out in a letter to Conrad Noel in March, 1933:

Thank you so much for your letter. I am terribly sorry that I am entirely snowed under with work at present: and could not write anything for your Crusade, as you so kindly asked me to do. Also, to do this would rather conflict with my fixed policy

of not identifying myself with any particular parties or movements within the Church: more especially those of a religious-
political character. You see I do feel that my particular call,
such as it is, concerns the interior problems of individuals of all
sorts and all opinions: and therefore any deliberate labelling of
myself beyond the general label of the Church, reduces the
area within which I can operate and my help is likely to be
accepted: but telling *you* what I think is quite another matter!
(*Letters*, p. 209).

The last remark in this paragraph is enough to show that Evelyn
did not regard ministry as ruling out the holding of very definite
opinions. But only the greatest need and pressure would lead her
to adopt a polemical stance in public. Perhaps if more of her
private letters come to light it will be possible to chart more
exactly the direction and intensities of her political preferences.
In the meantime it is no use guessing.

A number of people remember well the Evelyn of the thirties.
All seem to agree that she had something about her which was
a little out of the ordinary. Calmness, serenity, charm, vivacity
and, inevitably, 'aura' or 'light' are normal ingredients of such
descriptions: 'I can see her still,' writes one:

a slight figure in black evening dress, wearing a silver snake
waistband (snakes actually attracted her!)—a sort of quaint
white Dutch bonnet, which was most becoming. Hers was a
sensitive, humorous and spiritually beautiful face, and she had a
fascinating way of laughing with her eyes. It was charm of
personality rather than actual beauty that distinguished her.

The same writer, Mrs Jennie Boydell, goes on to relate how
Evelyn was, by her own account, accosted by an unknown woman
on top of a bus, who leaned forward and said to her 'Forgive my
telling you, but you have the most lovely aura!'—an incident

which, by all accounts, Evelyn found highly amusing. Another acquaintance writes:

> She gave out a feeling of peacefulness, almost like a Chinese sage or a Benedictine monk. . . . I used to go and see her sometimes at her house in Campden Hill Square, and was sometimes startled by the impression of *light* that came into the room with her. Nothing you could see with your eyes of course: but a sort of analogue of light.

Not that Evelyn made the same impression upon everybody. Rose Macaulay, for example, having once met her, described her cryptically in later correspondence as 'not quite so good as her books', though she admitted that these had interested her greatly and were written from a point of view (the psychological) which she found congenial. Amidst thoughts on the vulgarity of emotion in religion she observes of Evelyn in her writing that 'she is never merely emotional'.[1]

A curious and, according to at least one of her friends, re-markably accurate witness to Evelyn's character is to be found in the following analysis based upon her handwriting, which was undertaken in complete ignorance of her identity as writer of the sample in question. The resulting observations are here given in the staccato form in which they were first written down and make no pretence to scientific finality but are offered rather as a further and, perhaps, corroborative evidence of what we already know concerning her:

> An unusual sort of person. Imaginative. Strong sense of

1. *Letters to a Friend from Rose Macaulay 1950–1951*. Ed. Constance Babington Smith. London, Collins, 1961, letters of 12 March 1951, 29 July 1951, 3 August 1951. Rose Macaulay mistakenly identifies Evelyn as a 'sister' of Fr Francis Underhill, Bishop of Bath and Wells and author of several devotional works. Evelyn and the Bishop were only distantly related and never met.

humour (this is a leading characteristic). Completely unself-conscious—even astonishingly so. Warm-hearted and affection-ate. Wonderfully *un*-methodical. Doesn't like being hurried. This is a person able to see round a problem. A person who would see 'more things in Heaven and Earth than' etc. Might be interested in psychology (but not from the scientific point of view) with a wonderful understanding of people. Had a conventional upbringing but had broken away from it in part, though continuing to wear gloves on the right occasion. A person who might be suddenly inspired. Would put a lot of work into anything she thought mattered and ignore, probably, anything she thought did not matter. A lot of vitality—would be noticed in a crowd. Never got into a rut of any kind, would continue going always. Very full of sympathy. No business or political aptitude. Might not appear moody, but actually a person of very variable moods.

'A person of very variable moods'—it is not surprising that Evelyn felt after eighteen months without a spiritual adviser the need for someone to support her in her continuing mental and emotional ups and downs. After the death of von Hugel there was, as we have seen, an interval of eighteen months without a director. In one sense, clearly, Evelyn who was herself directing other people and had been for years, 'knew it all already', a fact of which those to whom she appealed warily reminded her from time to time. And yet, having been taught by von Hugel the necessity for creaturely ministrations, having also experienced the beneficial results of strong direction on his part, she naturally came to prize the value of experienced, detached and preferably, firm, even sharp, advice from an outside source. Walter Howard Frere and Reginald Somerset Ward were the two Anglican directors who succeeded von Hugel. There are indications that at one moment she would have liked to be taken on by Abbot

John Chapman, though nothing came of this. Her relations with each deserve to be summarised briefly.

Frere at the time Evelyn came to him had been Bishop of Truro since 1923. He was a member of the Mirfield Community and had by no means renounced the external simplicity of life demanded of a religious, on becoming an Anglican bishop. But his chief claim to renown rested, and rests, not so much on his skill in the direction of souls as on his work as scholar, historian and musicologist; he distinguished himself in a distinguished generation above all for his work of editing and glossing then very obscure and little known liturgical texts. How Evelyn came to ask for his help is unclear. Frere was an industrious, humorous and supremely good-hearted pastor, known for the solidarity of his intellectual achievement and for what used to be called 'devout living'. Perhaps that was enough. In many respects he was a complete contrast both to the Baron, his predecessor, and to Evelyn herself, for he had no speculative or metaphysical curiosities that one can discover and was entirely innocent of any interest in the type of experience generally designated 'mystical'. His cast of mind was pre-eminently factual.

He seems to have directed Evelyn from 1926 until 1932 when he was succeeded by Fr Somerset Ward. A few of his letters to her survive. They are warm, fatherly—and brief. The evidence of Evelyn's private papers is that she was continuing during these years to suffer considerably from the alternations of vivid consolations and deprivations in her prayer, continuing also to reproach herself and to worry about her failings in love and her privileges. But Frere did not expatiate as von Hugel had done. He seems to have liked to mull over her letters for weeks at a time and then send a fairly gentle word of expostulation on two or three sides of rather formal writing-paper. Which is not to say that his advice was not to the point. An example or two must suffice. There is a letter for instance of 9 March 1927, clearly written in reply to one on the theme of self-reproach, which illustrates the modesty, gentleness and directness of Frere's approach:

My dear Daughter,
A month's reflexion (at intervals) on your problem brings me only one small & trivial result—a suggestion as to remedy. Clearly not your own struggle—so I won't say *Try harder.* Clearly not a process of reasoning—so I won't say *Think how foolish it is.* But see if this is not a sort of moral cancer: & curable by a Divine 'ray', as we seem to find these physical internal growths sometimes to be curable in such wise. Say to God that if this is true you ask to have it healed & will welcome whatever pain is involved in ironing out the mischief.
And then don't bother about the symptoms, but only about the cause: & about that—only so far as to ask God to remove it. If He will, He will do it His own way: & as to that I am speechlessly ignorant. But there is my little suggestion as far as it goes. If there's anything in it, may He bless it.
Best wishes for your coming work.
Yours very sincerely W.T.

Evelyn did not see a great deal of Frere. She and Hubert went down to Lis Escop, the episcopal residence in Cornwall which Frere had turned into a kind of monastic enclave, in the summer of 1928, and the Bishop evidently visited them in London at least once. Even when, for reasons unknown but possibly due to Evelyn's desire for 'strong' direction, the relationship of director and spiritual daughter had ended, they remained in touch and Frere helped oversee the writing of *Worship* a few years later. He retired from the bishopric in 1935 and died in 1938. A volume published in 1947 devoted to various aspects of his career and personality contains the bulk of a memoir written by Evelyn entitled by the editor of the book 'Spiritual Life and Influence'. Amidst much that is complimentary one or two sentences seem to

sum up the kind of help Frere gave her and the distance between
their outlooks:

> Like all great Christians, he was a realist but Christian realism
> has many forms of expression. For Father Frere I think his
> religion was above all a personal relationship: it seemed indeed
> to have little or no metaphysical side, and I am sure that he
> would never have agreed with von Hugel's definition of it as a
> 'metaphysical thirst'—Though in the technical sense he could
> not be called a mystic, he certainly lived in the presence of the
> Invisible and in constant and dutiful dependence upon the
> action of God. . . . The combined common sense, actuality and
> spirituality so characteristic of St Francois de Sales, was promi-
> nent in his teaching. It was not, however always easy to get
> definite advice or opinions from him, for his humility always
> made him diffident and tentative in his approach to other souls.
> But if there was a real 'spot of trouble' demanding help and
> care he sprang to attention at once without any consideration
> for his own convenience or arrangements, like a skilful surgeon
> confronted by a case for immediate operation. Then he spoke
> and advised firmly and with an absolute certainty . . .²

A sign that Evelyn was not entirely satisfied with the rather thin
if healthy gruel coming from Cornwall is to be found in her
correspondence with Abbot Chapman partially published in her
own *Letters* (pp. 195, 198), and in the Abbot's *Spiritual Letters*
under the heading 'To a Married Lady' (pp. 103–107). The letters
mentioned or included in these sources date from the end of 1931
and the correspondence seems to have continued until late 1932.
Unfortunately the printed material gives us only a glimpse of the
exchange which, beginning with generalities and Evelyn's
compliment to Chapman on a paper of his she had heard, fairly

2. *Walter Howard Frere Bishop of Truro*. A Memoir by C. S. Phillips and others.
London, Faber & Faber, 1947; pp. 181–2.

soon became personal on Evelyn's side with a clear appeal for advice on one or two of her perennial problems. Not that Evelyn was writing 'into the blue' since she had had an opportunity to meet Dom John on a visit to Downside in 1929, the year in which the community elected him its Abbot. This had been an occasion she almost certainly used to visit the grave of von Hugel, buried in the graveyard of the local Roman Catholic parish church (not, as is sometimes stated, in the monastic cemetery). What she thought of Downside or of her erstwhile director's very modest tomb we do not know. But it is certain that she came away delighted by Chapman's personality and wisdom, and ever after added him as 'my Abbot' to the pantheon comprised by 'my beloved Indian Prophet' (Tagore), 'my old man' (von Hugel) and 'my Bishop' (Frere).

Although she did explain her ecclesiastical 'position' to the Abbot there is no evidence that she was seriously unsettled about it at this time. Her experience with von Hugel amply demonstrated to her that direction was possible across and in spite of ecclesiastical frontiers. Chapman, son of an Anglican archdeacon, began his ecclesiastical career at Cuddesdon whence he moved as a deacon to a slum parish in London. He did not receive priest's orders in the Anglican Church but was 'received' by Rome and became a Benedictine monk, first in a German foundation at Erdington in Birmingham and finally, after seeing active service in France during the war and doing a stint in Rome, among the English Benedictines at Downside. Chapman was a scholar with several publications behind him when he met Evelyn; he was brilliant with a controversial edge to his mind not uncommon in 'converts'; a man full of wit, given to theological speculation and above all, possessed of a devouring curiosity and practical interest in the nature of prayer and the spiritual life. So far as his relations with Evelyn are concerned his advice opens on the subject of activity and passivity in prayer and moves on, in June 1931, to the question of rebellion against suffering. Evelyn was clearly, as Chapman himself puts it, 'worrying at being worried'. Chapman argues that suffering inevitably produces the kind of turmoil which reveals our weakness and lack of abandonment to God at their starkest. Yet even as suffering, 'God's medecine', seems to stir up 'bad thoughts, feelings, desires, emotions' and we feel less and less 'abandoned', one important question always asks for an answer:

> which do we *identify ourselves* with, the revolt or the 'abandon'? If with the centre of the soul you hold on to the almost impercept-ible acceptance of God's will (manifested not only in circum-stances, but in your state of feeling) then that almost imper-ceptible acceptance is the real 'you'. It is a question of living in the 'fundus animae', or apex, or centre (or whatever you like to call it) which seems a very frail life-boat in a strong sea. But provided we stop in the boat and not in the sea, it is all right (*Spiritual Letters*, p. 106).

It was the kind of advice that Evelyn needed to have repeated to her. The fact that it *was* repeated to her from so authoritative a source no doubt did help even if Chapman was in a sense right in saying at the close of this same letter: 'You know all this as well as I do, and you could express it much better.' To seek reassurance after all is human. That it is ultimately available to those who seek it, is a fundamental tenet of Christianity.

Evelyn once or twice mocked at the kind of person who swears by Father so-and-so and in so doing exhibits childish symptoms of dependence and inadequacy. Yet Evelyn herself needed a firm background figure. As we know little of the beginning of her relationship with Chapman so we know little of its end, and we are ignorant whether the question of regular counselling ever came up. To the curious the printed correspondence inevitably ap-pears woefully truncated by the two editors concerned. Chapman,

like most of his community, was in any case a fearfully busy man
and died towards the end of 1933.

It was thanks to her friend Margaret Cropper that Evelyn met
Fr Reginald Somerset Ward who in fact succeeded Bishop Frere.
Exactly how and under what pretext the transfer was effected we
do not know. Frere was still well, if rather overworked, in these
years and only resigned his charge in 1935. But on 8 December
1932, shortly after her last letter to Chapman, Evelyn had already
consulted Ward and reported to Miss Cropper with enthusisam:

> My dear Margaret—I *must* tell you I have just had a wonderful
> day with Mr Somerset Ward. I think he is the most remarkable
> soul-specialist I've ever met since the Baron—& the thrilling
> thing is, that tho' apparently so utterly unlike, their method of
> direction & point of view is *very* close. I ended by having a
> highly personal talk with him as he refused to answer my
> questions without knowing surrounding circumstances, which
> led a good way. He has amazing insight not only spiritual but
> psychological in fact I was much astonished to find how psycho-
> logical his method is. He certainly cleared my mind a lot— &
> concluded by suddenly observing that he was very dissatisfied
> with my nervous state, & delivering a rousing & fatherly
> lecture on the well-known subject of over-strain & the need for
> a Day Off. One felt absolutely in the presence of a specialist
> working for the Love of God, & brimming over with common
> sense!

Reginald Somerset Ward, who died in 1962 at the age of
eighty-one, was the only one of Evelyn's directors to be younger
than herself. He was also probably the only one to be her regular
confessor. About his doctrine, personality and style of direction
we know unfortunately all too little from printed sources though
many it would seem are those with cause to be grateful for his
guidance in the course of a ministry lasting some fifty years. He

was indeed that rather rare phenomenon in the Church of England, a full-time spiritual adviser and one whose cure of souls was designated by Dr Eric Abbot, preaching his panegyric, as 'charismatic'. It can be seen in retrospect how ideally suited he was to become Evelyn's director at this point, sharing with her entirely as he did, a belief in the fundamental importance of prayer and self-forgetfulness, dedicated like her to leading others to learn of God himself and enter ever more deeply into communion with him. No one who has read even summarily some among the many hundreds of 'Instructions' or short eight-page exhortations Ward was accustomed to circulate among his spiritual sons and daughters, can have any doubt about his depth and articulateness, nor indeed about his preparedness to face up to current problems. We have Bishop Morgan's word for it that he believed in 'strong' direction and despite the occasional faux pas on his part there can be no doubt Evelyn appreciated this.

Letters between them do not survive. Ward made 'tours' some three times a year at this time so that his penitents could meet him by appointment at strategic points round the country. Evelyn saw him at least once in Oxford and of course in London, besides going to visit him and his wife regularly at Farncombe in the South of England. Ward, like von Hugel, believed strongly in the value of 'outside interests' and had himself engaged in historical research. It is curious that both he and von Hugel shared with Evelyn at some stage in their lives an interest in book-binding. One at least of his observations indicates that he knew what to expect in his intense new penitent. As he put it in one of his addresses, 'Overwork among conscientious souls is a far more real and frequent sin than laziness'. As for his precise influence on Evelyn—this is difficult to estimate. The fact that she was content speaks for itself. Physically he resembled Abbot Chapman, being as it were a somewhat denser, less effervescent, less intellectual but equally percipient and down-to-earth Anglican analogue of the learned Benedictine. Both contrast with the more ethereal, if erudite Bishop; while von Hugel seems somehow to include and transcend them all in the width and depth of his learning, sympathy and simplicity. It may be that the modern age has learned to look askance at the institution of the 'spiritual director' and recoils at Eveylyn asking Ward's permission, for example, to cancel retreats or to take up an assignment such as *Worship*. It is true that the old value of 'liberty of spirit' has claimed much territory which formerly was matter for docility and sacrifice. Yet Evelyn's relations with her directors and advisers was no luxury for *her* and many, like her, have felt more free because they accepted as determinative the friendly word of a fellow Christian. But she was fortunate perhaps in having advisers who believed, as she herself did, in von Hugel's maxim, 'The best thing we can do for those we love is to help them to escape from us.' (*Letters*, p. 230.)

In between writing and her other activities Evelyn gardened, took holidays with her husband at home or abroad, and attended the odd exhibition. We do not read of her going to concerts and it does not appear that music played a large part in her life. An incidental reference towards the end suggests that she was fond of listening to the music of J. S. Bach—that is all. Sailing holidays with her father ended in 1930 and she and Hubert took their holidays in Norway every summer between 1931–35. She had been going to accompany Lucy Menzies to Palestine in the spring of 1934 but the motor accident put an end to that idea. Lucy was very keen indeed on this expedition or pilgrimage. Evelyn a good deal less so, as she confided on 30 January of that year to Margaret Cropper:

Lucy and I are definitely (so far as we know) going to the Holy Land ... getting to Jerusalem early in Holy Week. I can't quite believe it! She is very intense about it. I always have such terrible difficulty in feeling nearer God in one place than another

(voice from the wings 'Quaker!') that I'm a little frightened of
anti-climax & the destruction of my intensely open-air con-
ception of the new testament by the imprisonment of sacred
sites in frowsty churches.

By the following year she was up to her eyes in work on *Worship*
and Lucy went to Palestine by herself. Perhaps Norway was
everything that Evelyn dreaded Palestine would not be—anyway
there is no doubt that she and, apparently, Hubert, thrived on their
open-air holidays among the lakes and mountains of that country.
The higher they could climb the better she was content; certainly
the thin atmosphere of higher altitudes suited her asthmatic
condition but she had always loved mountains and became well
acquaintained with the flowers and little wooden churches of
Norway's undiscovered, welcoming countryside.

Evelyn's circle of acquaintances in the thirties was wide and
varied. To mention only the better known she was in fairly close
touch by correspondence with people of similar interests to her
own such as the Catholic philosopher E. I. Watkin or the well-
known student of Islamic mysticism, Margaret Smith. It was quite
natural for Friedrich Heiler, widely celebrated for his book,
Prayer (Das Gebet), to drop in on her for tea while in London.
She visited and received visits from T. S. Eliot for whom she was
steadily contributing reviews to the Criterion of which he was
editor. She encouraged, helped and was helped by Margaret
Cropper, author of several religious dramas and useful works of
popularisation in the history of religion. Maisie Spens, writer of
several dense works of spirituality, was another of her friends.
Through her interests in the Eastern Church, contemporary
disarmament and peace movements and, above all, her journalistic
work she was also in touch with several worlds which probably
had little contact with each other. And outside the public involvement there was the circle of correspondents, some writing

odd letters as a result of a retreat or a book, some 'regulars' and forming part of what she called her 'family', some constituting what she called 'cases' and needing remedial care. But the scope and extent of the correspondence is very difficult to define since the total picture is unknown. We are unlikely for example ever to know what or why Evelyn wrote to a Carmelite nun, Sister Mary of St John, living in the Carmel at Exmouth. We have only the sister's side of the correspondence, some two dozen letters written between 1935–41, and it is clear that Evelyn kept her informed of all that was going on, sent her own and other books as well as alms for the support of the community. The sister addresses Evelyn in a number of letters as 'my dearest step-daughter' and several of them contain advice concerning self-dedication and submission to the divine will, subjects on which the Carmelite who became prioress of her convent (since closed down) was no doubt well qualified to advise her. The Italian Sorella Maria perhaps fulfilled a similar role as confidante, moral support, intercessor and fellow pilgrim before God.

Nor can we omit from this list Laura Rose, an invalid of humble background whom Evelyn had first met while 'visiting' in a poor district but who shared her interests and was always involved in her activities through being told about them and asked to keep them in her prayers. Evelyn certainly did not believe the communion of saints was something which could only be realised 'up there' and she would have been the first to acknowledge that she received as well as gave help.

As we turn to Evelyn's work in this period we find it dominated in the earlier part by her journalistic activity which we shall consider first; by retreat-giving, and, later on, by the writing of *Worship*. Evelyn, as we have seen, from her girlhood was no stranger to writing for the papers. Indeed, it is safe to say that she contributed either poems, articles or reviews to various journals from the age of fifteen until the very end of her days. Once again much research remains to be done and we are nowhere near having a complete picture of all that she wrote of this nature for such journals as the Westminster Gazette (during and just after the First World War) or John o'Groats Weekly, Time and Tide (middle and late thirties). Yet in this department of her activity her work for the Spectator stands out beyond all the rest and deserves to be at least briefly described here.

Evelyn was appointed religious editor of the Spectator early in 1928 and stayed in the post for four years, She had periodically published reviews in its pages during the previous three years and her growing reputation in Anglican circles ensured her a respectful hearing should she wish to make her own views known in its pages. In fact she took this opportunity relatively infrequently, publishing only some five articles properly so called, as distinct from reviews. Of these a constant stream appeared in the course of the years, during which many dozen of theological, devotional, mystical, hagiographical and related publications passed through her hands and, after appropriate scarification or applause, were duly nodded through the columns of the Spectator. Taken all together this work provides an excellent index of her likes and dislikes in the field of contemporary religion and theological discussion, offering for example her views on the famous conversations at Malines (1921–25) (review of 28 January 1928); on various posthumous publications of von Hugel (see bibliography), on the monism of John Middleton Murry (Literature and Dogma, a review of Murray's *Thing to Come* 23 June 1928) and on many lasting works published or re-published in the period such as Otto's *Religious Essays*, Bremond's *Literary History of Religious Thought in France*, F. V. Hicks' *The Fullness of Sacrifice*, Joseph Maréchal's *Studies in the Psychology of the Mystics*, some of which had considerable influence on her own work and outlook.

It is not possible to do more here than illustrate her attitude by a few characteristic remarks. There is a certain richness for example in her taking Dean Inge (*Christian Ethics and Moral Problems*) to task for his anti-institutional attitudes. His notion of a spiritually purified Church is characterised by her as a 'beautiful dream' and leading to nothing more in the end than 'a coterie of spiritual aristocrats' (20 September 1930, p. 386). A favourable review of Father R. H. J. Stewart's *The Inward Vision* and Gwendolen Greene's *Mount Zion* laments the 'incurable mediocrity' of most contemporary spiritual literature—among which these are exceptional. *My Hopes and Fears for the Church*, a collection of essays edited by H. R. L. Sheppard, published in view of the forthcoming Lambeth Conference, towards the end of 1930, provokes a hostile comment, frequently repeated in these years:

> The point of view is almost uniformly anthropocentric. The church must provide what the people want; must hasten to adapt itself to new social conditions, bring its conceptions up to date. There is little here of that noble other worldliness which is the life-blood of religion; of that note of adoring worship, the call for utter self-donation to a Reality beyond ourselves (p. 788).

A review of J. S. Haldane's Gifford Lectures, *The Sciences and Philosophy*, produces the suggestive observation that 'Dr. Haldane, like most scientists who are concerned with ultimates, is a monist' (June 1929, p. 935).

It is tempting to stay longer with Evelyn's reviews; however, to do so would tend to distract from what was after all the major part of her work on the weekly, namely to attract a steady series of relevant and readable articles on religious topics into its columns. This she succeeded astonishingly well in doing. During her editorship the Spectator was distinguished by several long-running groups of contributions to which many among the best known contemporaries offered their services. One in particular

'The Challenge to Religious Orthodoxy' (late 1930) she contrived
so that the Spectator's readership should have the benefit of a
confrontation between opposed viewpoints; as she explained, in
her editorial capacity, there would be a 'new series of articles in
which men and women of the younger generation have been
invited to express their criticisms of organised religion. Each
article will be answered the following week from the Christian
standpoint' (18 October 1930). The series ran throughout the
autumn of 1930 enlisting J. D. Bernal, Bertrand Russell, C. E. M.
Joad, among others, on the critical side, and N. P. Williams,
W. H. Elliott, C. C. Martindale among those writing the 'replies'.
It is a pity perhaps that this style of considered debate is not more
common in the more serious weeklies. Evelyn herself summed up
the arguments and counter-arguments in an article *Pax Domini* of
27 December (p. 1003), in which with characteristic unpompous
frankness she asked her readers for ideas and suggestions about
further series. The four other series she inspired were In Defence
of the Faith (1929), composed of twelve articles assembling
William Temple, Vernon Storr, Edwyn Bevan, Algar Thorold,
Rudolf Otto, Cuthbert Butler and others; Problems of the
Christian Conscience, in which the technique of confrontation
was again used to debate such questions as 'Riches and Poverty',
'Marriage and Sex', 'Should a Christian fight for his Country?'
etc. (autumn, 1931); Studies in Sanctity (autumn 1932), drawing
on talent from several parts of the religious spectrum in the
persons of Violet Hodgkin (Quakers), Sheila Kaye-Smith, Olive
Wyon, G. K. Chesterton, Cuthbert Butler, Lucy Menzies and
T. S. Eliot; and, finally, a very brief foursome entitled A Christian's Faith (December 1932). To the series on sanctity Evelyn
contributed an article on Father Wainwright (9 April 1932,
pp. 502–3), a devoted Anglo-Catholic pastor in the London
dockland area whose biography was later (1947) published by Lucy
Menzies. After such excellent work Evelyn's departure from the

Spectator at the end of 1932 seems rather abrupt. Her own account was that a change of editor and editorial policy was responsible (cf. *Letters*, p. 233; *Thesis*, p. 50). She continued to send him occasional reviews but thereafter the bulk of her journalistic writing appeared in Time and Tide.

Beside Evelyn's journalistic work two less easily categorisable but equally in their way important achievements have to be placed on record, First the revising of *Mysticism* in 1929–30 for its twelfth edition, no easy task for an Evelyn who had so largely re-orientated herself in the intervening twenty years; second, the expert short summary, *Medieval Mysticism*, which she contributed to the Cambridge Medieval History (volume vii) in 1932. This latter need not detain us long. It is chiefly significant as her final contribution to the task she had made so peculiarly her own, of making better known the mystical writings of medieval Catholic Europe. Besides being a useful summary of information, the article contains perhaps her best summary of what in 1932 she thought the peculiar intensity of a mystically orientated personal religion owed to and could contribute towards historic institutional Christianity, an area in which she is clearly very much at one with von Hugel. The whole article is, as she says, concerned to study mysticism as 'a religious and social phenomenon' and although it has now been surpassed, particularly on the side of that 'intensely spontaneous element' which, when 'out of its harmony with its environment', is associated with revolt and heresy, it still has value as an introduction to the subject. Historical introductions, after all, achieve little if they do not stimulate questions in the minds of their readers. It is difficult, to take a trivial example, to resist investigating her reference to the far from well-known English saint Wulsi of Evesham, whom she describes as 'one of the chief spiritual influences of the West'. This judgement she appears to owe to Rotha Mary Clay's *Hermits and Anchorites of England* (p. 37), published in 1914; it is one which

contemporary scholarship has so far singularly failed to corroborate.

Of greater interest in the picture of Evelyn's development is
the 1930 revision of *Mysticism*. Her own 'preface' makes the chief
points about this in a paragraph:

> Were I now planning this book for the first time its argument
> would be differently stated. More emphasis would be given (a)
> to the concrete, richly living yet unchanging character of the
> Reality over against the mystic as the first term, cause and
> incentive of his experience; (b) to that paradox of utter contrast
> yet profound relation between the Creator and the creature,
> God and the soul, which makes possible his development;
> (c) to the predominant part played in that development by the
> free and prevenient action of the Supernatural—in theological
> language, by grace—as against all merely evolutionary or
> emergent theories of spiritual transcendence (*Mysticism*, p. vii).

This preface also makes the mainly defensive point that Christian
mystical experience by 1930 had been a good deal 'disentangled'
since 1911 from its strange or abnormal accompaniments thanks
to the work of scholars such as as Brémond, Maréchal, Cuthbert
Butler and others; also that many more and better mystical texts
had become available since then. But Evelyn also implicitly
suggests that her original option for a radical dualism in man's
spiritual experience accords not too badly with 'the recovery of
the concept of the supernatural' she associates with von Hugel.
Yet even as she offers an admirable summary of von Hugel's
doctrine one sees the distance between her early views and his.
The fundamental difference of outlook between them is in fact
understated by the later Evelyn, unwilling perhaps, or unable, to
think herself back into her old view point and remember how she
revelled in certain fashionable ambiguities. Her 1930 preface is
also unsatisfactory in not giving the reader any inkling of what

has happened to the original text in the pages which follow it, a topic which perhaps by rights should be left to some not too ambitious university thesis-writer but which cannot be entirely shirked here.

There are in fact a very large number of additions, subtractions and alterations to the text of the third edition. Some are only incidental, as when 'is' replaces 'seems', 'ineffable' replaces 'indicible' or 'called' stands in for 'denominated'. But others are more wide-ranging in their implications. Thus, writing of the impersonal metaphysical Absolute and the personal loving God as two aspects of Godhead which the mystics tend to reconcile in experience, she had written previously, 'Instinctive monists as they are, all the mystics feel . . . that these two aspects of Reality "are *One*".' In the final edition this becomes simply, 'All the mystics feel . . .' etc. (third ed. p. 410, twelfth ed. p. 344). Such an example of self-correction could be multiplied endlessly. In general the tendency is to bring the book into line with respectable orthodoxy, toning down absolutist enthusiasm with its heavy stress on immanence and diminishing the esoteric element. Rudolf Otto, Henri Brémond, Jacques Maritain, A. Poulain are authorities newly quoted among moderns while Arthur Waite, Rudolf Steiner, Arthur Machen, Henri Bergson and Rudolf Eucken have their contributions either curtailed or eliminated. Perhaps none suffers from this 'purge' so much as Waite, some five quotations from whom are omitted altogether, along with the corresponding laudatory mentions. With Waite inevitably wane other mystical signs and figures from those far-off days. The Ain Zoph is no longer mentioned; alchemy in general is less often referred to. Saint-Martin, the eighteenth-century mystical writer whom Waite had strenuously championed in days gone by, finds his contributions diminished by half while Madame Guyon, whom Waite had admired and whom Evelyn was formerly happy to quote at length, is much reduced. Passages from Eliphas Lévi are likewise curtailed, sometimes omitted, though a remarkable quantity of him manages to survive. To fill the gaps we now find rather more quotation from the New Testament, St Paul rather quaintly replacing Waite on one occasion (third ed. p. 111, twelfth ed. p. 93). We find Cusa, De Caussade, Grou, Malaval introduced for the first time, as well as additional material from Ruysbroeck and Saint John of the Cross. The defects of Algar Thorold's translation of Blessed Angela of Foligno having been realised, Evelyn prefers in the later edition to translate a French translation in default of a satisfactory original text. Rolt's translation of Dionysius the Areopagite replaces the one she originally used and the Benedictine translation of St Teresa is now preferred to that of David Lewis. In these respects as in a number of others, the look is improved by being brought up to date by the standards of 1930, although of course time has not stood still since then and fresh translations have superseded these improved ones.

So far as Evelyn's orthodoxy is concerned the change undergone by one passage alone must serve to illustrate her gradual evolution from 1911 to 1930 in the direction of a non-monist mystico-metaphysical psychology in which the parts of God and the human soul are clearly distinguished. In short, the three stages of her text here reveal, to express the matter crudely, monism, ambiguity and, finally, Christian dualism. The sentence in question occurs on page 371 of the first and third editions, page 311 of the twelfth. Evelyn is speaking of the three stages in the 'prayerful process', leading to union, given in Recollection, Quiet, and Contemplation. In the first edition she writes of these stages, or 'acts', that:

> they involve a progressive concentration of the mystic's powers, a gradual handing over of the reins from the surface intelligence to that inner and deeper mind whose growth constitutes the mystical life-process in man;

which becomes in the third edition:

> they involve a progressive concentration of the mystic's powers, a gradual handing over of the reins from the surface intelligence to the deeper mind, a progressive reception of the inflowing spirit of God.

Finally, in the twelfth edition, the sentence appears as:

> they require a progressive concentration of the mystic's powers, a gradual handing over of the reins from the surface intelligence to the deeper mind; that essential self which is capable of God.

Such changes as this entirely eclipse in importance the alteration, for example, of 'absorbed brooding' to 'dreamy pondering' as a description of meditation turning into recollection. It should not be forgotten in reading this section of Evelyn's book, the section on prayer, that 'orison' is the word for deep mystical prayer used by William James. Evelyn explains her reasons for adopting it in preference to 'prayer' in another of those rare embarrassed sentences which suffers a sea change in all three editions (first and third editions, p. 366, twelfth, p. 306).

Mysticism as Evelyn left it in 1930 remains a somewhat hybrid animal. The purist who reads it in part at least to relish its full 'period' flavour and personal fervency of tone will not be satisfied with any edition later than the eleventh, and finally prefer the first and so-called 'second' editions. Yet despite the modifications, despite its unsatisfactoriness from a scholarly point of view in, for instance, swallowing whole such an egregious character as Rulman Merswin, despite its eccentric account of some aspects of experience in prayer (Evelyn's account of the prayer of quiet, for example, betrays an undeveloped non-technical stage of discussion of the subject parallel to those of R. H. Benson), despite a bibliography now woefully out of date, it stands supreme as a kind of weathered masterpiece proudly displaying on a solid plinth of 'spiritual realism' the unmistakable outline of a very new (at the time) and very twentieth-century determination to test and prove even the allegedly 'supernatural' area of religious experience by a standard of fulfilment adequate to man's deepest and highest aspirations. Nor shall we, perhaps, feel inclined to blame her for expressing the idea that experience, authenticity, fulfilment have something to do with religion. This notion is a phantom constantly being driven from the doors of seemly religious premises. Yet it constantly returns despite the sharp supernatural forks which expel it, to claim that man's experience of God must be rich and actual as well as sacrificial and meritorious, that God 'felt of the heart' is at the centre of meaningful religious activity. The words of Plotinus describing the mystic quest as 'the flight of the alone to the Alone' are no longer for Evelyn in 1930, 'superb words' as they were in 1911; nevertheless, as her preface shows, she still could not bring herself entirely to renounce the way of experience; nor did she ever do so. On the other hand, there could be no question for her of diluting the essential religious quest with a social or merely philanthropic element. It was simply that the integrity of the quest itself required, on her later view, 'a wide spreading love to all in common',—a phrase constantly repeated in her later retreats and addresses. Once again one is confronted by von Hugel's fundamental distinction between 'inclusive' and 'exclusive' mysticism. One also turns again to the novels, in which the maxim: though he slay me, yet will I cleave to him' had been given dramatic form. What had been decided in principle in those early days of illumination had to wait some years to receive its perfect articulation. This final reconciliation of utmost personal adherence to God alone and total self-renunciation for all in common is the principle theme and achievement of Evelyn's later published work.

Since the greater part of Evelyn's work with which we now

have to deal consists of published retreat conferences it may be as well to say something about this side of her activity. It was the side which, together with spiritual counselling, she prized and felt most confidence about as she did not, for example, about addressing large ecclesiastical conferences or instructing the young. Early on she was accustomed to give seven retreat conferences, beginning with the first on Friday evening; later the number was reduced to five per retreat. She preferred a relatively small group of not more than twenty-four, and made herself available for consultations at least twice in the course of each day. Every retreat was given its key-note quotation or quotations, generally pinned to the chapel notice-board. If she wished to refer to a picture, a reproduction of that picture would also be pinned up. She herself chose the hymns which the retreat might have occasion to sing, the general awfulness of hymns being a sensitive point with her. She also liked it to be understood that she would act as sacristan in preparing the altar for the daily celebration of Holy Communion by the chaplain. A programme of a retreat given at Pleshey lists 'Prayers' at 12.30. Evelyn herself generally led these in the form of guided meditation on New Testament passages. Specimens of such meditations were published in the little book *Meditations and Prayers*. The period from two o'clock to four-thirty was given over to 'Rest and Recreation'.

Rest and recreation, renewal, re-birth, a recovery of quality and depth, a number of ideas suggest what Evelyn hoped her retreatants would gain from their temporary seclusion. Given that we are at the mercy of our surroundings, we lose, as she explains in an unpublished address on 'The Need of Retreat', all sense of proportion; we become 'fussy, restless, full of things that simply must be done, quite oblivious of the only reason why anything should be done'. We tend to become pragmatic, utilitarian, forget that the horizontal line of our lives, 'The chain of cause and effect which makes up human life', is bisected at every point by, as von

Hugel put it, a vertical line relating us and all we do to God. To recover our sense of the wider context within which we operate it is needful 'to dwell quietly and without self-occupation in the atmosphere of God'—no drama is necessary, no working up to a definitive choice, such as St Ignatius proposed as the climax of his 'spiritual exercises' (designed anyway for a quite different and specific purpose); rather we should let the Spirit operate and bring us to realise for a start, 'the chasm which separates deep from distracted prayer' and gain or recover a sense of quiet wonder, beauty, joy. It is the retreat giver's task to further the recovery of this atmosphere bearing in mind that 'nothing that he does here will be of the slightest use to his retreatants unless it proceeds from his own interior life with God'.

Evelyn might give as many as eight retreats in a year, using the same material throughout that 'season' so to speak. She visited a variety of retreat houses and communities on her rounds including Pleshey, in first place, St Michael's Home (Wantage), Little Compton, Water Millock (in the Lake District), Moreton, St Leonard's, Leiston Abbey, Glastonbury, Canterbury. Her audiences were mainly composed of women and would not have been helped by heavily philosophical or speculative discourses. On the other hand their faith could be assumed and Evelyn made it very much part of her task to try to increase her audiences' depth of wonder and confidence in the treasure already in their possession. These preliminary assumptions distinguish her retreat conferences from her more academic addresses on the one side and her broadcast talks on the other (see *The Spiritual Life*, 1937).

How then did Evelyn seek to relay 'the atmosphere of God' to her listeners at retreats, days of recollection and the like? The question concerns both her technique and her doctrine and must therefore be answered at both these levels, albeit briefly. So far as technique goes Evelyn generally cast her retreats as a whole using either the expedient of what one may call the enveloping metaphor or the more traditional method of glossing some well known prayer or constellation of related ideas. Examples of the former are *The House of the Soul* (1929) and *Light of Christ* (1932). *The Mount of Purification* which represents addresses delivered in 1931, partakes of both techniques since it is based on Dante's image of purification as a process of climbing the terraces of a mountain, the soul divesting itself at each terrace of one of the seven deadly sins. In *The House of the Soul*, as the title suggests, the guiding metaphor teaches that human life is multi-storied and requires both foundation and a roof, doors, windows and views. Each detail of the picture is expounded allegorically in the discourses. In *Light of Christ* the complex of the 'mysteries' of Christ's life—birth and childhood, Christ as healer, Christ as rescuer, Christ crucified and glorified, are linked as seven richly coloured windows of a cathedral through which streams God's own light. All the rest of Evelyn's published retreats are offered as expositions of, for example, the 'Golden Sequence' i.e. the Latin poem beginning *Veni, Sancte Spiritus* (*The Golden Sequence*, 1932), the Our Father (*Abba*, 1940—retreat given in 1934), St Paul's 'fruits of the Spirit' (*Fruits of the Spirit*, 1942—retreat given in 1936). *The School of Charity* (1934) represents addresses on the Creed given in 1933, and *The Mystery of Sacrifice* (1938) is based on the unfolding of the liturgy of the eucharist, a series of addresses originally delivered in 1935.

A complete account of Evelyn's doctrine at this period of her life would require not only that all the foregoing works should be duly analysed but also a number of important addresses collected in *Mixed Pastures* (1933) and *Collected Papers* (1946). The task would be worth doing but is out of place in a biographical introduction. The best we can attempt here is a succinct characterization of Evelyn's overall message as conveyed in all this material. In so doing we shall, at least in broad terms, be answering the question concerning her success in both counterbalancing the one-sided emphasis of *Mysticism* and working through the principles she laid down for herself in *The Column of Dust*. To keep our summary within bounds we shall restrict our examination of this teaching to three questions. First, what does she teach is the basic framework of Christian life? Second, what was the practical objective of her teaching? Third, to what in the Christian life does she finally assign priority?

The framework of Christian life adopted by Evelyn is first set out fully in *Man and the Supernatural* (1927) under the heading 'The Supernatural in Human Life' (pp. 204 ff.). She adopts there the threefold scheme of the early seventeenth-century founder of the Paris Oratory, Monsieur Olier, as expounded by Henri Brémond in his *Histoire Littéraire du sentiment religieux en France* (tome iii, pt i, pp. 105–6). M. Olier's scheme, which is a kind of codification of the doctrine he had received from the Cardinal de Bérulle, was intended by him to sum up all that is required for the completeness of prayer under three headings: Adoration, Communion, Co-operation. This outline Evelyn in *Man and the Supernatural* seizes upon as 'one of the best of all definitions of the spiritual life', making it as a matter of fact the frame of reference implicit or otherwise for most of her subsequent teaching. If it receives any modification at her hands this is chiefly in the direction of receiving an explicitly Trinitarian connotation which emerges fully fledged for example in *Worship* (pp. 62–3) and of tending to lose the middle term, Communion, aspects of which are more and more subsumed into each of the other two.

Despite the fact that this outline was not von Hugel's, it nevertheless lent itself to illustration from his writings and is close to his spirit. This is especially true of the first heading 'adoration' which finds many an echo in Evelyn's own works. As she put it in a paper of 1929 expounding the theme that 'the *sanctus* is the classic notion of all human worship', 'this note of solemn yet joyous adoration, which obliterates all thought of self, ought then to be the first point, both in public worship and in the private devotional life which supports that public worship and makes it real' (*Collected Papers*, pp. 69–70). The movement of Adoration is described in *The Mystery of Sacrifice* as 'the first step of self-transcendence' (pp. 31–2). It is the necessary preliminary to petition, as the Lord's prayer perfectly shows (*Abba*, pp. 50–51). It is the response of 'awe-struck love' to the overshadowing Reality of God, the 'first real response of the awakened creature' (*The Golden Sequence*, p. 158). Like the other headings, adoration gathers about it as it were a constellation of attendant concepts, that of spiritual smallness for example, an idea which she described in a correspondence with Middleton Murry in the columns of The Spectator as 'the corner-stone of my philosophy'. For adoration of God reveals to us the insignificance of the 'luggage' of life over which we make so much fuss, as it also cuts down to size our habitually inflated egoism. In adoration we acknowledge our Father, first, distinct, over-against the world. The only possible attitude before an adorable God is meekness, docility.

God is real; prayer is rooted in the reality of God from which it draws life. Prayer, she wrote for The Expository Times in 1931, 'is rooted in ontology. It is an appeal from the Successive to the Abiding, without which Succession has no meaning at all. It is a genuine communion with Reality, or nothing' (*Collected Papers*, p. 86). Prayer has as its soul adoration. But the God man adores is not 'out there', he is close, he is the medium in which man lives and moves and has his being:

Nothing in all nature is so lovely and so vigorous, so perfectly at home in its environment, as a fish in the sea. Its surroundings give to it a beauty, quality, and power which is not its own. We take it out, and at once a poor, limp, dull thing, fit for nothing, is gasping away its life. So the soul sunk in God, living the life of prayer, is supported, filled, transformed in beauty, by a vitality and a power which are not its own (*Golden Sequence*, p. 173).

But man communing with God is more acted upon than acting. True, there is a strong element of 'clinging' in this relationship and this heading is sometimes equated by Evelyn with 'adherence' (*Collected Papers*, p. 93; *Golden Sequence*, p. 175), illustrated by the 'monkey-way' taught in the Hindu 'bhakti' tradition:

> Those who follow the cat-way, say a soul should be as utterly abandoned to God as the kitten which the mother cat carries to safety in her mouth: the kitten does nothing about it at all. Those who follow the monkey-way, say the soul should rather be like a baby monkey, which knowing its helplessness if left alone in time of need puts forth all its efforts and clings to its mother with all its little might (*Golden Sequence*, p. 153; *Mount of Purification*, p. 29).

In the last analysis, communion is both God acting and man acting, for communion is essentially both putting on Christ and receiving his light (*Light of Christ*). It is thanks to communion with God in Christ that human life is transformed into a focus of divine presence and power in the world. Moulded by the Spirit in prayerful communion both priest and teacher for instance can hand on the 'contagion' of God—not otherwise (*Collected Papers*, pp. 122-3, 189-90).

Adoration and communion correspond in some degree to God apprehended as respectively transcendent and immanent by the worshipper. The third heading, co-operation, represents the corollary of divine presence, namely divine action in and through the worshipper's self-abandonment to that presence. Co-operation introduces the theme of the Christian's relationship with the world, that other environment embraced in the integrated but 'two-step philosophy' of von Hugel with its insistence on *both* 'the Reality of Finites' and 'the Reality of God' (*Mixed Pasture*, p. 211). If God moves men and women to adore him and, by the same token, consents to dwell with them and teach them in the innermost recesses of their being, this is not merely with the object of opening up new worlds to human experience or inducing pleasant sensations. God's action is as Evelyn frequently repeats '*purposive*'; God has an ulterior motive; as she puts it already in 1922, 'the ultimate object of all prayer is greater efficiency for God' (*Collected Papers*, p. 46). Her subsequent ample development of her doctrine under this heading is but an expansion of this idea. Thus co-operation also has its synonym in her vocabulary, namely 'action'. 'Action' in Eveylyn's sense is always and essentially the consummation of prayer. The whole scheme is put in a nutshell in such a way as almost to defy further exegesis in a passage from *The Golden Sequence* (pp. 182-3):

> The final purification in love of the human spirit, and the full achievement of its peculiar destiny as a collaborator in the Spirit's work, must go together: obverse and reverse of the unitive life. Then the soul's total prayer enters and is absorbed into, that ceaseless Divine action by which the created order is maintained and transformed. For by the prayer of self-abandonment, she enters another region; and by adherence is established in it. There the strange energy of will that is in us and so often wasted on unworthy ends, can be applied for the world's needs—sometimes in particular actions, sometimes by absorption into the pure act of God.

This last phrase, fully explained in what follows in its context, refers to the very real redemptive value of intercessory prayer as Evelyn understood it, a subject too large, regrettably, to be entered into here.

Having glanced briefly at some primary aspects of Evelyn's

teaching we are in a position to answer our second question concerning her practical objectives. First it should be obvious that she not only did not deploy a highly technical method in talking to people but did not in any sense set out to teach the Christian 'way' as some form of ascetical expertise dependent on an elaborate theological scheme. Her appropriation of the relatively straight—forward formula of the French Sulpician and her free and easy, not to say creative, use of it is ample evidence of her continuing preference for an elastic conceptual framework for her ideas. Brémond introducing Olier's trio of headings chooses the moment significantly to discuss the difference between the Sulpician's 'programme' and the Ignatian or Jesuit concept of an ascetical 'method'. Such a distinction would not be lost on Evelyn. Methods, as is well-known, generally pre-suppose stable metaphysical worlds of which they pose as the keys. Even in the domain of spirituality method suggests man can somehow dictate the conditions and timing of his own progress towards a clearly discernible goal; a programme on the other hand is purely procedural and contingent, its components can be argued about separately, added to and subtracted from; it is merely convenient for the time being. Evelyn taught a programme not a method; this fact and her programme itself adequately reflect her distrust of intellectual schemes and her respect for a universe radically open to divine initiative.

Evelyn set herself the specific objective of relaying to her retreatants 'the atmosphere of God'. Like those of many retreat-givers her opening discourse would generally harp on the gulf which the hustle and bustle of modern life puts between us and the realization of our deepest aspirations. Those who came on retreats, she could assume, would be those who felt some dislocation between reality and their ideal; this feeling she readily identified as a first stirring of God's action in the heart. Most of us in other words spend most of our lives like the fish out of water just described, spiritually extenuated, gasping, far from beautiful, far from effective. The remedy is to adopt the reality behind the term von Hugel consciously or unconsciously borrowed from Sir Thomas Browne, when he wrote:

> Man is incurably *amphibious*; he belongs to Two Worlds—to two sets of duties, needs and satisfactions—to the Visible or This World, and to the Invisible or the Other World. (*Essays and Addresses*, second series, pp. 246–47).

As a person becomes more and more surrendered to God's purposes or 'abandoned', so dualism is actually reduced and each of us attains to a relative harmonization of the warring powers he carries inside him, not by sacrificing a supposed 'lower' to a 'higher' nature but by transferring the affections of 'the whole' Godward. Only thus can our instinctive life turn 'away from self-fulfilment however noble, and towards entire self-mergence in God' (*Golden Sequence*, pp. 107–14). A man or woman so surrendered is then free to live in both worlds transforming each with the power derived from the other:

> our favourite distinction between the spiritual life and the practical life is false. We cannot divide them. One affects the other all the time: for we are creatures of sense and of spirit, and must live an amphibious life. . . . Most of our conflicts and difficulties come from trying to deal with the spiritual and practical aspects of our life separately instead of realising them as parts of a whole (*The Spiritual Life*, pp. 36–37).

As man carries 'up' all the sublimated energies of his 'jungle' nature so he transposes 'down' into the here and now all the wonder and attention and vitality of the life hidden with God in Christ. It was Evelyn's aspiration to introduce her retreatants to a new world, a fresh dimension, to insinuate the possibility of such a unified life. She did not spend her time laboriously plotting the way there and counting the cost.

Hence the priority of prayer which for Evelyn is an absolute priority:

> Prayer means turning to Reality, taking our part, however humble, tentative and half-understood, in the continual conversation, the communion of our spirits with the Eternal Spirit: the acknowledgement of our entire dependence, which is yet the partly free dependence of the child. For Prayer is really our whole life toward God: our longing for Him, our 'incurable God-sickness' as Barth calls it, our whole drive towards Him. It is the humble correspondence of the human spirit with the sum of all Perfection, the Fountain of Life. No narrower definition than this is truly satisfactory, or covers all the ground (*The Spiritual Life*, p. 61).

It is in and through prayer that the individual worshippers are brought to know God and their own condition as inhabitants of a borderland, whose rôle it is to mediate redemption between the two territories of which they are citizens. Thus they join the company of those who take up and use together both sides of our unbounded human inheritance, moving to and fro between the temporal world and the eternal world, between communion with God and communion with their fellow-men, as Christ did during his life on earth (*Collected Papers*, p. 107). It is essentially through prayer, Evelyn suggests, that God can operate effectively in the world; indeed, that is the ultimate rationale of all prayer, that God *shall* operate effectively in those whom he has stimulated this, 'man's fundamental spiritual activity'.

> Any study of it [prayer] which conceives it mainly so to speak, as the action of discrete spiritual individuals, surely misses its central truth; namely, the solidarity of that total and supernatural

action which is brought into existence by the Divine energy and exerted by God through and in the corporate activity of praying souls (*Collected Papers*, pp. 35, 82).

Such a summary account does not distinguish the nuances of development in Evelyn's teaching. A number of incidental points are of interest, as for example that the point of departure of the works and addresses of 1931-32 is to be found in *Mysticism*. Re-reading her 'big book' must have been a stimulating if also perhaps a depressing experience for her and it is not to be wondered at if parts of it remain strongly in her mind as she tackled her work of the early thirties. A remark she made about *The Golden Sequence* is especially revealing; 'A good bit of it is just what I've had to find out and live through' she told Elizabeth Rendel: a remark which seems to cry out for the appendage 'since I wrote Mysticism', as anyone who compares it with the middle section especially of that work (i.e. the first four chapters of Part II) can verify for himself. *The Golden Sequence* is the best book she wrote about the spiritual life in her Anglican period but we find in *Light of Christ*, also of 1932, the best concise commentary on her earlier work in her re-handling of Plato's celebrated parable of the cave. In *Mysticism* (Part II, chap. 3) the normal human universe was indeed the cave of illusions and bondage, and the only remedy—escape—lay along 'the mystic way': in *Light of Christ* the Platonic cave is rejected altogether as an appropriate metaphor; instead we are transported into a cathedral, dark certainly but bathed in divine light which floods through the mysterious transparent media of the Christian creed. It is curious, as the mysticism of Aldous Huxley and others shows, how a strongly immanentist even monist mystical emphasis only seems to accentuate the imperative need to 'escape', whereas a sacramental incarnational emphasis has no such consequence. Perhaps the malaise which afflicts such 'exclusive' mystics is the same as

that which overcame James Elroy Flecker's celebrated voyagers:
one world however divine really is too small for man:

They saw no ship that was not theirs.

And what of the mystics? Evelyn certainly never forgot them
or underrated mysticism. Only since they, on her final view,
occupy a relatively small corner of a pretty vast spectrum it would
be quite wrong to behave as if they and they alone mattered. We
have just glimpsed her opinion of a disproportionate interest in
'discrete spiritual individuals'. In a paper entitled 'What is
Mysticism?' (*Collected Papers*, pp. 105–20) of 1936 it is interesting
to see how 'those who move to and fro between the temporal
world and the eternal world . . . as Christ did . . . on earth' are
not, as one might suppose, the mystics. These belong in *another*
category, of those namely who are not interested in 'balance' but
always tend 'to swing out towards the Unseen'. Thus mysticism
is 'the passionate longing of the soul for God, the Unseen Reality,
loved, sought and adored in Himself for Himself alone', and a
mystic is 'the person who has a certain first-hand experience and
knowledge of God through love'. The mystic is thus still exemplary, revealing to us all what is mostly hidden to us, that
'something in man which longs for the Perfect and the Unchanging, and is sure, in spite of the confusion, the evils, the
rough and tumble of life, that the Perfect and the Unchanging
is the real'. All have the thirst: in the mystics its consequences in
terms of self-devotion and sacrifice are most apparent. Evelyn
never says that 'mystical experience' is the goal of us all but she
strongly implies that, properly understood, it is bound up in our
ultimate destiny to be God's instruments:

The mystics continually tell us that the goal of this prayer and
of the hidden life which shall itself become more and more of a
prayer, is union with God. We meet this phrase often: far too

often, for we lose the wholesome sense of its awfulness. What does union with God mean? Not a nice feeling which we enjoy in devout moments. This may or may not be a by-product of union with God: probably not. It can never be its substance. Union with God means such an entire self-giving to the Divine Charity, such identification with its interests, that the whole of our human nature is transformed in God, irradiated by His absolute light, His sanctifying grace. Thus it is woven up into the organ of His creative activity, His reedeming purpose; conformed to the pattern of Christ, heart, soul, mind and strength (*School of Charity*, 1954 ed., p. 49).

But the ultimate difference between the sheer single-hearted quest of the experience and the Christian view of union just summarised is given in Evelyn's last published commentary on 'the flight of the alone to the Alone' in the 1936 paper on *Mysticism*:

A non-Christian mystic, such as the great Plotinus, may describe his ecstatic experience of God as a solitary flight from this world with its demands, imperfections, and confusions and a self-loss in the peace and blessedness of eternity. The Christian mystic knows these wonderful moments too; but for him they are only wonderful moments. His experience of eternal life includes the Incarnation with its voluntary acceptance of all the circumstances of our common situation, its ministry of healing and enlightenment, its redemptive suffering. He cannot, therefore, contract out of existence with its tensions and demands. For him union with God means self-giving to the purposes of the divine energy and love (*Collected Papers*, pp. 114–15).

It is clear that for Evelyn as for all important Christian thinkers who have considered the subject, a Christian is in the last resort judged on his Christianity, not on his mysticism, but that the

mystical impulse is not a luxury in the church and is indeed a
talent, pearl or seed entrusted by our creator and redeemer to us
all. *Our* love of God probably does not rate the term 'mystical' in
Evelyn's sense. In which case we are in good company—as we
have seen. But love of God is none the less loving even when
innocent of certain degrees of intensity; as she wrote in *The
Fruits of the Spirit*:

> Meekness and temperance mean accepting our position,
> capacities, spiritual *attraits*, as an indication of God's will for
> me, and not fussing about the things other souls do or feeling
> despondent because I cannot do them! ... We are all rather
> inclined to be a bit romantic about religion. But God is a
> realist. He likes homegrown stuff. He asks me for a really good
> apple, not for a dubious South African peach. So, not lofty
> thoughts of God, remarkable powers of prayer or displays of
> devotional fervour or difficult virtues, but gentleness, long-
> suffering, faithfulness, meekness, a good quality of life, will
> prove I am growing the right way and producing as well as I
> can the homely fruits for which He asks (pp. 39–40).

It is difficult to imagine how anyone could be less guilty than the
mature Evelyn Underhill of debasing the mystical coinage, as she
is sometimes accused of doing: as she said:

> the limits within which each of us can realise and respond to
> Him are well-defined. Do not try to elude these limits or
> achieve something you have read about; it merely means your
> prayers will get puffy and out of shape. Let us rejoice in the
> great adoring acts and splendid heroism of God's great lovers
> and humbly do the little bit we can. We too have our place
> (p. 41).

Evelyn's third major preoccupation of the decade was *Worship*,
a book she was invited in 1933 to contribute to the series 'The

Library of Constructive Theology' by its editor, the then Dean of St Paul's, Dr W. R. Matthews. The work on this book displaced all her other activity, especially the giving of retreats. With Father Ward's warm approval she went so far as to cancel all retreat arrangements for 1935. Nonetheless the toll on her health and strength was very great as her friends bear witness. We who have only the finished work and are at leisure to admire its clear and spacious outline, its almost irreproachable harmony of theological, historical, devotional and purely practical themes, are given no glimpse of the labour it must have cost her to produce, for she was not especially well-versed in the enormously intricate and mine-strewn learned literature of liturgical scholarship and vehemently deprecated the theological animosities generated in the course of church polemics over such matters.

Perhaps this is in part the reason for the book's excellence. Evelyn as she approached sixty had nothing if not a sense of distance from the purely human ingredient in man's perennial attempts to articulate God to himself. She who had agonised enough over the possibility of self-suggestion, yet had responded with fervour to the suggestion of ritual and incantation, had re-learnt the language of the Christian Sacraments which acknowledge simultaneously both man's utter dependence upon and need of the historical, socially conditioned media of sensible signs, and his thirst for the transcendent 'other than himself', was almost, it might seem, inevitably predestined to do the work which the Dean placed in her hands. She had long in fact been thinking and writing about 'worship'. She knew the subject from 'the inside' as few of her contemporaries. It remained only for her to engage sympathetically with the several chief traditions which go to compose the spectrum of Christian worship. Such a sympathetic re-articulation of the past for the enlightenment of the present has long been a glory of women writers, historians or historical novelists in this country, and Evelyn deserves, on the strength of both *Mysticism* and *Worship*, to be counted among their number.

In its general plan *Worship* resembles *Mysticism* in being divided into a preliminary defining section and a second which is chiefly historical. In the first part she establishes what for her are the abiding theological first principles of Christian worship regarded in both its public and its private dimension, both in general and in relation to such particular Christian concepts and institutions as sacrifice, the sacraments, the liturgical year, the liturgy itself. In the second part she gives a brief account of and situates, using the principles and definitions earlier established, the several traditions of worship within Christianity, beginning with Jewish worship in Chapter X and ending with 'The Anglican Tradition' in Chapter XV. In this part particularly Evelyn relied for information upon such learned collaborators as Bishop Frere, Dr Nicholas Zernov, and others whose help is duly acknowledged in her Preface; but the judgements are evidently very much her own.

Thoroughly analysed, the book's clarity of outline could lead one to suppose it no more than an arid digest or a scholastic summary of the subject. Nothing could be further from the truth. Although in the first section there is a great deal about man in general, the nature of worship, ritual and symbol, the book is throughout thoroughly personal both in the sense that the author is fully engaged as a Christian believer working for her fellows, and in the sense that it is about people who are faced with and have adopted definite options for perfectly explicable motives. It is a book which well embodies its writer's fully Catholic principle that:

Christian worship in its fulness should include and harmonise all the various phases of our human experience. It has room for the extremes of awestruck adoration and penitent love, humble demand and inward assurance. All levels of life and action are relevant to it: for they are covered and sanctified by the principle of incarnation (p. 71).

The points of interest in the work which could be singled out are too numerous to mention here. Of them all none perhaps is so important as the quite transcendent fact that for Evelyn the liturgy of the Church *is* supremely important. The Church, said Waite, had failed significantly to change the selfish egocentric nature of humanity because the Church had failed to help man to lose his egoism in that love of God which the mystical life perfectly exemplifies. We do not know whether Evelyn would have agreed with Waite as to the substance of his judgement but one thing is certain: she did believe that it was the task of the Church to stimulate, arouse, foster and lead on that deeper self in man which ever thirsts for God. She also believed that the Church's chief, if not its only, means to achieve this with God's help is the liturgy. From this point of view the liturgy which articulates the worship of any given body or tradition of Christians is clearly at the very centre of the Church's redemptive mission and, she implies, should be in the very centre of its preoccupations. The Church's worship does not justify itself, it, too, is 'purposive' and the purpose in question is to make 'saints' (cf. pp. 79, 330). The most perfect expression of worship is then the eucharist in which the Christian joins his self-offering to that of Christ in his body the Church, loses self, becomes what he is, or should be, a free and open channel for divine redemptive action in the world. In Christian worship at its summit:

> the individual must lose his life to find it: the longing for personal expression, personal experience, safety, joy, must more and more be swallowed up in Charity. For the goal of Christian sanctification and Christian worship is the ceaseless self-offering of the Church, in and with Christ her head, to the increase of the glory of God (p. 82).

Worship is inextricably rooted in life and life in prayer, prayer and life issue in practical love, the Holy Spirit in a world to be redeemed. One can pay Evelyn's book no higher compliment than to say that she never loses sight of these facts.

Worship is also personal in the sense that it expresses judgements and preferences of its author. These sometimes appear almost prophetic in relation to subsequent developments, but sometimes also the perspective could seem disconcerting to fashionable preconceptions of the present day. We, for example, are now well-placed to agree with her that it is a tragedy of Christian life that almost from the first the prophetic and sacramental tempers have tended to separate (p. 89). These two aspects of the Christian tradition which are elsewhere (pp. 233–34) contrasted as the 'sacramental' and the 'pneumatic', she divides roughly as old church against Protestant reformers, order again spontaneity, personality against tradition, enthusiasm versus mystery, pro-phecy versus sacrifice, liturgy facing liberty. But both these contrasting series are required, she maintains, for fullness. As we advance through the book we become aware that on the whole her sympathies lie with the tradition of worship which she characterizes as 'objective', 'liturgic', that type of worship which tends to lift the worshipper away from him- or herself into that supra-sensible world into which attendant signs and symbols, rhythms, poetry and ceremonial are designed to introduce him. But the issue is not clear-cut. Evelyn's treatment raises questions which any student of these matters can afford to meditate upon. What value does she set, for example, on 'spiritual realism', what *is* it for her? 'Spiritual realism' characterises the worship of the New Testament and the religion of Jesus as well as that of early reformers and is clearly desirable: and yet it is opposed precisely to 'the objective', the 'detached' attitude of so much that she also admires. Yet again, how can she describe the liturgy of the Eastern churches as 'non-objective' and based on 'realistic apprehensions', a liturgy in which characteristically, as she says, 'something really happens'? (*Worship*, pp. 233, 220, 276, 308, 262–63, 256, 323).

If Evelyn does not show herself a revolutionary pioneer in liturgical matters her perferences do nonetheless anticipate the shape of things to come as, for example, in her endorsement of a 'corporate' type of service over against both the purely hieratic— 'the splendid ceremony in which all is done by a few professionals' —and the silence of corporate worship devoid of representative actions save for extempore prayer. On her view:

> the corporate service—the concerted action in which all take a real part—is a more complete act of adoration, more congenial to the Christian spirit, and also more efficacious for the common life than the alternatives (p. 97).

Evelyn deprecates High Mass without communion, the loss of the intercessions from the Roman mass, the loss of the offertory from the Anglican liturgy; she foresees much good from the movement for liturgical reform then strongly stirring in the churches. It is perhaps unnecessary to stress that Evelyn would have been unable to conceive of a Christian eucharist not sacrificial in meaning or that she had strong feelings about inferior hymnody; in regard to the last point she went so far as to forbid in her will that any hymns 'of a mournful or lugubrious kind' should be sung at her funeral.

A word should perhaps be added about her final chapter on the 'Anglican tradition' in which in general she adheres to the Anglican *via media* as conceived and put into effect by the tractations, not because she wished to champion a 'high' view of ritual as such—her anathema for 'ritualism' is early declared in the book (p. 34)—but because such 'churchmanship', to use the Anglican word, was for her 'the outward sign and necessary concomitant of an inner orientation'. In fact she believed that while the worship of the Church of England leaned more 'to the prophetic and Biblical than to the liturgic and sacramental side of the Christian cultus' (p. 318) *both* sides were represented in its borders, *both*

an almost complete Evangelicalism: grave, Biblical, prophetic, devoted, based on the preaching and hearing of the Word, suspicious of ceremonial acts and sensible signs, emphasising the personal relation of the soul to God, greatly concerned with man, his needs, problems and duties . . .

and

a sacramental, objective, and theocentric worship: emphasising the holiness, authority and total action of the Church, her call to adoration and vocation of sacrifice—reverencing her traditions and her saints, using all the resources of symbolic expression (p. 323).

As to the English Eucharistic liturgy in particular, i.e. the rite of 1662, despite 'certain unfortunate dislocations and omissions' she finds much to be thankful for and we do not recognise the Evelyn who many years previously had written to Margaret Robinson:

I regard Cranmer's editing of the Consecration prayer as one of the great crimes of humanity. He there effected a break with tradition so violent that no 'Anglo-Catholic' fiddlings and adjustments can ever make it right.[3]

Worship was welcomed at the time it was published and is still appreciated by those who remember it and have time to read it.

3. Letter of 2 August 1907: this section omitted in *Letters*, p.67.

Blackfriars made up for its harsh treatment of *Mystics of the Church* by according it a brief but wholly approving article in the issue of February 1937. 'Depth of learning' 'comprehensive sympathy', 'theological soundness' 'the traditional Catholic teaching', 'redolent of the spirit of Baron von Hugel', all beautiful phrases perhaps but such as cannot have fallen altogether unpleasantly on the ear of the somewhat exhausted author. Maurice Nédoncelle, reviewing the book for Irénikon (mars–avril, 1937), hailed it as a valuable 'oeuvre de synthèse' of significant originality and singled out for admiration the chapters on the Latin and Orthodox liturgies.

Many aspects of Evelyn's life, work and interests remain to be examined, none perhaps more pressingly than her work as pastor and director of souls. This important aspect of her achievement has to some extent been summarised by Bishop Lumsden Barkway writing in Theology in 1954. The Bishop of St Andrews went so far as to say that this 'pastoral ministry' was indeed her 'vocation', and one who follows his account and reads her letters can only agree with him. This was indeed the 'purpose' for which she had been trained and purified and set to work in the world. It is however an aspect of her life which has its theoretical and spiritual foundations in the works and attitudes which we have already examined but which otherwise is exceedingly difficult to come to grips with, consisting as it does so largely in particular counsels designed to help a varied collection of individuals to 'get out of their own light'. The director of souls is typically a *removens prohibens*, one who endeavours single-heartedly to keep the minds and hearts of his 'family' uncluttered and receptive to the Spirit, seeking always to help them on *their* way as God seems to be revealing it to them. Such certainly was Evelyn's style, soothing the tense and over-excited, trying to coax out of themselves the self-preoccupied, broadening the horizon of the restricted, urging to desirable objectives the docile and eager. In such work her own experience is always implicitly, sometimes explicitly, in the background. Restraining one penitent she reveals that she too indulged in excessive mortifications in the past; as she attempts to remind the Quaker, W.Y., of the implications of an incarnational religion her history, too, is to some extent rehearsed; as it is in her dealings with the fearfully intense and exalted, then depressed, Lucy Menzies. Echoes of von Hugel and Chapman are frequent as we should expect, the latter especially after the publication of his *Spiritual Letters* for he was the man 'who knew more *really* about prayer than anyone I ever met' (*Letters*, pp. 244, 245). Evelyn taught the perennial guide-lines; she could also on occasion put her foot down. At least one 'spiritual daughter' survives to tell how in a moment of doubt and difficulty a letter from Evelyn resolved the issue in the direction of overcoming all to follow Christ.

Towards the end of Evelyn's life one has a sense of a decrease of activity but not of alertness. Confined to bed for weeks on end early in 1938 she was in no state to go to Aberdeen that autumn to receive in person the honorary doctorate in theology which the University wished to confer on her. Shortly before war began she and her husband went to stay with Roland and Marjorie Vernon at their house called Highden, near Washington on the Sussex downs. It is characteristic of Evelyn that a letter written from there soon afterward should complain of guilt feelings about such relative security in a world grown anything but safe for the bulk of the population in the south-east of England. She did not return to 50, Campden Hill Square, which was closed down when the Stuart Moores finally decided to move in with the Vernons in their London home, Lawn House, Hampstead in mid-1940.

But Evelyn did not cease from her work: there was yet another book of retreat addresses to see through the press (*Abba*, 1940), there were the children in the village near Highden who needed instruction—a job she found 'terrifying'; there was also the prayer-group, formed by her friend Agatha Norman, which had asked her to help them both by talking to their meetings and, later, when her physical attendance became impossible and the members had dispersed, by sending them periodical letters of encouragement and prayers suitable to the times.

We have seen how Evelyn was loath on principle to make a public stand which might divide her on party lines from those she might otherwise be able to help. But the cause of pacifism proved an exception to this rule and Evelyn made no bones about taking her stand from the very start of hostilities in total opposition to all forms of international armed conflict. She did not and had never opposed legitimate self-defence and forceful police action when necessary, but the catastrophe of a new world war seemed to escape the argumentative force of all lesser analogies and to enter a category of dreadfulness which could be countered only by an exceptional and heroic sacrifice on the part of Christian love.

Her views were set out in two small publications in 1939-40 issued by the Christian Literature Association in a pamphlet published on behalf of the Fellowship of Reconciliation, and in a collective work entitled *Into the Way of Peace*, assembling the pacifist witness of a number of Anglican communicants under the editorship of Percy Harill. Evelyn's contribution, entitled 'Postcript', was shortly afterwards published separately under the title *The Church and War* by the Anglican Pacifist Fellowship. Her views had been long maturing. In 1930 she had warmly welcomed in The Spectator the Lambeth Report's trenchant declaration that 'the Christian conscience is now called upon to condemn war'. In 1932 one can see the way the wind is blowing in a favourable review of a pacifist work in The Spectator, as in the fact that the pacifist view was alone allowed to hold the floor twice in the series 'Problems of the Christian Conscience', run by her in that year. On 19 February 1932 a letter to Margaret Cropper states that she has tried without success to persuade the Sorella Maria to join the Disarmament Prayer Group (*Letters*, p. 201). In 1936 she definitely feels Aldous Huxley is on the right side in his pacifist pamphlet, *What are you going to do about it?* (*Letters*, p. 253) and she is a member of the Peace Pledge Union and the Anglican Pacifist Fellowship in these years.

Evelyn conceded that the practical arguments for waging war could appear overwhelming and yet to reject the principle that love can find a way and adopt the argument that war is 'the only alternative' was unacceptable to her. War quite simply was not Christian: it was answering sin with sin, hate with hate, grasping selfishness with all the spontaneous reactions of just the same disease. She developed her views briefly in the pamphlets we have mentioned and in her letters, emphasising again and again that Christian love must find a better way:

> It is because our Christianity is so impoverished, so second-hand and non-organic, that we now feel we are incapable of the transformation of life which is needed to get humanity out of its present mess . . . (*Letters*, pp. 296–97).
> I think Hitler is a 'real scourge of God', the permitted judgment of our civilization; and there are only two ways of meeting him—war, or the Cross. And only a very small number are ready for the Cross, in the full sense of loving and unresisting abandonment to the worst that may come (12 May 1941; *Letters*, p. 308).

Evelyn's unpopular position on waging war was in a sense the natural outcome of her belief that the fervent practice of Christian love and prayer can really bring something new into the world, something requiring the 'supernatural' as its only adequate explanation. Von Hugel had seen such super-human novelty in the self-sacrificing devotion of heroic individuals like Damian who gave his life to tending lepers, as also in the unbroken ranks of soldiers who lined the decks of the sinking 'Birkenhead'. It was this that Evelyn demanded and it could or should have been an expected flowering of the seed of contemplation. Such heroism as the war *did* bring out, like the coming together of Christians which it also occasioned, were, she hoped, signs that a new age would yet be born from the appalling Armageddon. Hope was always possible for, as she wrote in *Abba* (1940):

the coming of the Kingdom is perpetual. Again and again, freshness, novelty, power from beyond the world break in by unexpected paths, bringing unexpected change. Those who cling to tradition and fear all novelty in God's relation with his world deny the creative activity of the Holy Spirit, and forget that what is now tradition was once innovation; that the real Christian is always a revolutionary, belongs to a new race, and has been given a new name and a new song. God is with the future (*Abba*, pp. 33-34).

We know only a little about how Evelyn occupied her last months. Her father had died in June 1939 but she herself does not seem to have been given a great deal of extra work as a consequence. Hubert, who had devoted many of his leisure hours before the war to working on the naval training ship, The Implacable, found himself with rather too much time on his hands after war had broken out, and returned to his old work in the Surgical Supply Workshop, devoting himself to turning out splints, bed-tables and so forth. Both he and Evelyn also did what she describes as ' a little Red Cross sewing'. Otherwise she read: C. S. Lewis, E. I. Watkin, Maisie Spens, all of whom she knew—and Søren Kierkegaard, a relatively new and much admired star in her firmament. She wrote letters and prepared her homilies for the Prayer Group. She gladly espoused the cause of the Abbé Couturier's Reunion Movement, championed by her friend,

Maisie Spens, and which set great store by the invisible union of
Christians in prayer, an idea long precious to Evelyn also.

Evelyn's last writings speak much of trust and abandonment.
We may imagine her feeling to have been much like that of St
Francis de Sales as he journeyed in a small boat on a lake and
reflected how narrow a width of plank separated him from his
Creator. Evelyn once illustrated a similar thought with the tale
she told about a visitor to Iona who, on her return from the
island, was asked by an old Scotsman where she had been. 'When
she told him, he said "Ah! Iona is a very thin place!" She asked
him what he meant by a thin place, and he answered, "There's
very little between Iona and the Lord!" (*Collected Papers*, p. 196).
Evelyn's point was that to 'the eyes of worship' the whole of the
visible world is rather 'thin'. So, too, we may imagine, was
Evelyn's world at the end, as the bombers droned or whined about
their business overhead and her asthma tightened its grip and made
work impossible.

The only description at present available of her last illness up to
the day of her death on the 15 June 1941 suggests that she died of
a thrombosis. It is found in a pencilled memorandum on a scrap
of paper inserted in a book by her which was happily encountered recently in a second-hand bookshop in London. Unfortunately the writer's identity is not known for certain and one word
(the last) is difficult to decipher. But the passage rings true in an
extraordinary way, revealing to us an Evelyn, as we should expect,
fully engaged with her world, suffering with it and for it, and in
travail over it, after the fashion of Constance Tyrrel on the eve
of Christ's nativity in the 1909 *Column of Dust*. Even the 'violent
oscillation' here described seems characteristic of Evelyn as we
have come to know her; and yet again, clearly, we are faced here
by no private emotional storm but by an outward-facing passion,
absorbing and rending, but weighted with love and fruitful.
Beyond all cliché it seems true to say that the circumstances of

Evelyn's death according to this account sum up and consummate the meaning and tendency of her life as we have been able to study it. The description reads:

She had four weeks final illness with a swelling in her neck caused by a clot of blood. She had a good bit of pain and she set herself with great fortitude to face the situation. She had some deep laid scheme to combat pain by means of prayer but she sent messages to many people asking for prayers for all sufferers, for union of Christian Churches. She went through a good bit of pain which reached a climax when the distress seemed to be spiritual rather than physical. She was very strange and we thought she was dying. Then next morning she became radiantly happy and remained all day in an ecstasy of triumph, from what she said she knew that something had been accomplished and the sufferers would not be disappointed. She was rejoicing in God and Christ in a way which was very different from her normally rather austere devotion. She fell asleep very peacefully. We watched the course of events with the greatest interest and (?) exhilaration.

She was buried in the churchyard of St John's parish church, Hampstead, in the same grave in which her husband also was buried some ten years later.

Although the memory of Evelyn Underhill has long been cherished by those who knew her personally and her name and fame respected by the very great many who read her books, it was perhaps inevitable that she should gradually pass out of public view. She would have been the first to accept her displacement as a spiritual guide by fresh teachers with a new language and outlook who, nonetheless, owe her more perhaps than she in her modesty would have anticipated or they themselves are sometimes prepared to acknowledge. The contemplative outlook on life of which she became a principal spokesman for her genertaion, is not a luxury followers of Christ can dispense with, and it is likely that the reputation of Evelyn Underhill will stand high wherever the Christian philosophy of the contemplative life is taken seriously as a basis for Christian action. That her own understanding and teaching of that philosophy was entirely practical in its aims and its consequences is demonstrated by the fact that she herself not only believed in it but practised it in her life.

Bibliography

The list of Evelyn Underhill's publications which follows, is far from complete. It omits almost entirely her book-reviews and contributions to several daily newspapers, weeklies and more obscure religious journals, as well as some longer less accessible articles. It is offered as evidence of her activity over the years. None more complete has yet appeared and we look forward to the comprehensive bibliography being prepared by Mrs Joan Gartland of the University of Detroit Library. Juvenilia are not included nor are verses separately published.

We list here books, articles, stories, reviews etc. Where any of these has been collected the short title and page number of the relevant book is also given.

1902 *A Bar-Lamb's Ballad Book*. London: Kegan, Paul, Trench, Trubner & Co. Comic verse occasioned by English legal processes.

1904 *The Grey World*. London: William Heinemann. New York: The Century Company. Novel.
The Death of a Saint. The Horlicks Magazine vol. 2, pp. 173–177.
The Ivory Tower. The Horlicks Magazine vol. 2, pp. 207–211.
Our Lady of the Gate. The Horlicks Magazine vol. 2, pp. 243–247.
The Mountain Image. The Horlicks Magazine vol. 2, pp. 375–380.
A Green Mass. The Horlicks Magazine vol. 2, pp. 445–448.

1905 *The Miracles of Our Lady St Mary Brought Out of Divers Tongues and Newly Set Forth by Evelyn Underhill*. London: William Heinemann. A free translation of twenty-five medieval legends concerning the Virgin Mary.

Two Miracles of Our Lady. The Fortnightly Review September, pp. 496–506.

1907 *The Lost Word*. London: William Heinemann. Novel.
A Defence of Magic. The Fortnightly Review November, pp. 754–765.

1908 '*The Cant of Unconventionality*'—*A Rejoinder to Lady Robert Cecil by Evelyn Underhill*. The National Review No. 299, January, pp. 751–60.

1909 *The Column of Dust*. London: Methuen & Co. Novel.

1910 *The Mirror of Simple Souls* [Extracts]. Introduction by Evelyn Underhill, pp. 2–4. The Porch [Series] Vol. 1, no. 8.
The Fountain of Life: An Iconographical Study. The Burlington Magazine no. 86 April, pp. 99–109. With an illustration.

1911 *Mysticism. A Study of the Nature and Development of Man's Spiritual Consciousness*. London: Methuen & Co. Ltd. First published 2 March 1911; third edition revised January 1912; twelfth edition revised 1930 and reprinted nine times to 1967.
The Path of Eternal Wisdom. A Mystical Commentary on the Way of the Cross. By John Cordelier [Evelyn Underhill]. London: John M. Watkins.
The Cloud of Unknowing. The Seeker vol. 6, no. 24, February, pp. 215–24.
The Mirror of Simple Souls. The Fortnightly Review no. 78, February, pp. 345–54.
Discussions: Theology and the Subconscious. The Hibbert Journal vol. 9 no. 8, April, pp. 644–46.
The Message of Ruysbroeck, Part 1. The Seeker vol. 7 no. 26, August, pp. 65–82.
The Message of Ruysbroeck, Part 2. The Seeker vol. 7 no. 27, November, pp. 137–53.

1912 *The Spiral Way. Being Meditations upon the Fifteen Mysteries of the Soul's Ascent*. By John Cordelier [Evelyn Underhill]. London: John M. Watkins. New Edition revised 1922.

Immanence. A Book of Verses. London: J. M. Dent & Sons Ltd. Reprinted 1913.
The Cloud of Unknowing. Edited, with an Introduction by Evelyn Underhill. Introduction pp. 5–37. London: John M. Watkins. Second edition 1922.
A Franciscan Mystic of the Thirteenth Century: The Blessed Angela of Foligno. In *Franciscan Studies* by Paul Sabatier and others. Aberdeen: The University Press, pp. 88–107.
An Indian Mystic. The Nation vol. 12, November, pp. 320–22. Review of *Gitanjali* by Rabindranath Tagore.

1913 *The Mystic Way. A Psychological Study in Christian Origins.* London: J. M. Dent & Sons Ltd.
The Place of Will, Intellect and Feeling in Prayer. The Interpreter vol. 9 no. 3, April, pp. 241–56. (*The Essentials*, pp. 99–115.)
The Mystic as Creative Artist. The Quest vol. 4, July, pp. 629–52. (*The Essentials*, pp. 64–85.)
The Circle and the Centre. The Nation vol. 13, 13 December, pp. 499–500; review of *Sadhana: The Realization of Life* and *The Crescent Moon*, both by Rabindranath Tagore.

1914 *Practical Mysticism.* London: J. M. Dent & Sons. New York: E. P. Dutton & Co. (Everyman series).
The Autobiography of Maharshi Devendranath Tagore. Translated from the original Bangali by Satyendranath Tagore and Indira Devi. Introduction by Evelyn Underhill, pp. ix–xlii. London: Macmillan & Co. Ltd.
The Fire of Love or Melody of Love. etc Translated by Richard Misyn from the *Incendium Amoris* . . . of Richard Rolle. Edited . . . by Frances M. M. Comper. With an Introduction by Evelyn Underhill. Introduction, pp. vii–xxv. London: Methuen & Co. Ltd. Second edition 1922.
Mysticism and the Doctrine of the Atonement. The Interpreter vol. 10 no. 4, January, pp. 131–48. (*The Essentials*, pp. 44–63.)
Kabir the Weaver Mystic. The Contemporary Review no. 578, February, pp. 193–200.

1915   *Ruysbroeck.* London: G. Bell & Sons.
One Hundred Poems of Kabir. Translated by Rabindranath Tagore. Assisted by Evelyn Underhill. Introduction by Evelyn Underhill, pp. 1–18. London: Macmillan & Co. Ltd. Sixteen times reprinted to 1972; Macmillan pocket Tagore edition 1973.
Mysticism and War. The Quest vol. 6 no. 2, January, pp. 207–19. Reprinted the same year 'Revised and Enlarged' as a pamphlet by John M. Watkins.
The Mystic and the Corporate Life. The Interpreter vol. 11 no. 2, January, pp. 143–60. (*The Essentials*, pp. 25–43.)
Charles Peguy: In Memoriam. The Contemporary Review no. 592, April, pp. 472–78. (*The Essentials*, pp. 228–45.)
Problems of Conflict. The Hibbert Journal vol. 13 no. 3, April, pp. 497–510.
The Prayer of Silence. The Challenge vol 3 no. 59, 11 June, p. 126 (a letter from Evelyn Underhill appears on p. 124 of this number).

1916   *Theophanies. A Book of Verses.* London: J. M. Dent & Sons. Reprinted 1926.
John of Ruysbroeck. The Adornment of the Spritual Marriage. The Sparkling Stone. The Book of Supreme Truth. Translated from the Flemish by C. A. Wynschenk Dom. Edited with an Introduction and Notes by Evelyn Underhill. Introduction, pp. xi–xxxii. London: J. M. Dent & Sons.
The Education of the Spirit. The Parents' Review vol. 28 no. 10, October, pp. 753–61.
Review of J. W. Buckham: *Mysticism and Modern Life* and of W. F. Cobbs: *Mysticism and the Creed.* The Harvard Theological Review vol 9 no. 2, April, pp. 234–38.

1918   *The Future of Mysticism.* Everyman vol. 12 no. 301, 20 July, pp. 335–36.
The Mysticism of Plotinus. The Quaterly Review vol. 231 no. 459, pp. 479–97. Review of W. R. Inge's *The Philosophy of Plotinus* etc. (*The Essentials*, pp. 116–40.)

1919   *Jacopone da Todi Poet and Mystic 1228–1306. A Spritiual Biography*
       By Evelyn Underhill. With a selection . . . by Mrs Theodore
       Beck. London: J. M. Dent & Sons.

1920   *Julian of Norwich*. St Martin-in-the-Fields Monthly Review
       no. 35, May, pp. 10–15. (*The Essentials*, pp. 183–98.)
       The Essentials of Mysticism and Other Essays. London & Toronto:
       J. M. Dent & Sons. Reprinted in the Everyman series by E. P.
       Dutton & Co., New York 1960.
       The Confessions of Jacob Boehme. Compiled and edited by W.
       Scott Palmer. With an introduction by Evelyn Underhill.
       Introduction, pp. xi–xxxv. London: Methuen & Co. Ltd.
       Second edition 1954.
       The Essentials of Mysticism. The Quest vol. 11 no. 2, January,
       pp. 145–66. (*The Essentials*, pp. 1–24.)
       A Modern Saint [St Theresa of Lisieux]. The Fortnightly
       Review no. 644 (N.S.), August, pp. 279–89. (*The Essentials*,
       pp. 199–214.)

1921   *Sources of Power in Human Life*. The Hibbert Journal vol. 19 no.
       3, April, pp. 385–400.

1922   *The Life of the Spirit and the Life of To-day*. London: Methuen.
       Lectures delivered in Oxford in 1921.
       The Degrees of Prayer. Lecture for the Guild of Health published
       as a pamphlet. (*Collected Papers*, pp. 35–53.)

1923   *The Scale of Perfection*. By Walter Hilton Canon of Thurgarton.
       Newly Edited . . . With an Introduction by Evelyn Underhill.
       Introduction, pp. v–liv. London: John M. Watkins.
       Some Implicits of Christian Social Reform. The Pilgrim vol 3 no. 2,
       January, pp. 141–157. (*Mixed Pasture*, pp. 63–83.)

1924   *Christian Fellowship: Past and Present*. The Interpreter vol. 20
       no. 3, July, pp. 171–81.
       The Will of the Voice. The Pilgrim vol. 4 no. 4, July, pp. 373–81.
       (*Mixed Pasture*, pp. 84–94.)

1925   *The Mystics of the Church*. London: James Clarke [1925]. In a
series 'The Living Church'.
Our Two-Fold Relation to Reality. The Hibbert Journal vol. 23
no. 2, January, pp. 218–30.

1926   *Concerning the Inner Life*. London: Methuen. Retreat addresses
to clergy. Three editions in 1926 after publication on 15 July.
The Authority of Personal Religious Experience. Theology vol. 10
no. 55, January, pp. 8–18. Paper read in July 1924.
The House of Three Windows. By Eva Gore-Booth, With a Portrait, and an Introduction by Evelyn Underhill. Introduction,
pp. v–xi. London: Longmans Green & Co.
Baron Friedrich von Hugel. The Spectator 13 November, p. 862.
Review of *Essays and Addresses on the Philosophy of Religion by*
von Hugel.

1927   *Man and the Supernatural*. London: Methuen.
A Scholar-Saint. The Spectator 30 April, p. 766. Review of
Baron Friedrich von Hugel: Selected Letters.
The Hill of the Lord. The Spectator 19 November, pp. 869–70.

1928   *The Teacher's Vocation*. Address of 1927 published as pamphlet
by St Christopher's Press. (*Collected Papers*, pp. 157–71.)
The Spirit of Malines. The Spectator 28 January, p. 121. Review
article.
A Franciscan Hermitage. The Spectator 11 February, pp. 183–84.
Life as Prayer. Address published by the Publications Depart-
ment of the Church of Scotland. (*Collected Papers*, pp. 54–63.)
Ricardus Heremita. The Dublin Review no. 367, October, pp.
176–87. (*Mixed Pasture*, pp. 169–87 entitled *Richard the Hermit*.)
The Essence of von Hugel. The Spectator 1 December, pp. 822–23.
Review of *Letters from Baron von Hugel to a Niece* and *Readings
from Friedrich von Hugel* edited by Algar Thorold.
Nicholas of Cusa: The Vision of God. Translated by Emma
Gurney Salter. With an Introduction by Evelyn Underhill.
Introduction, pp. vii–xvii. London: J. M. Dent & Sons.

1929   *The House of the Soul*. London: Methuen. Reprinted with *Concerning the Inner Life* in one vol. by the same publishers in 1959.

Worship. Lecture delivered 12 January 1929. London: A. R. Mowbray. (*Collected Papers*, pp. 64–80.)

In Defence of the Faith. The Spectator 15 June, pp. 923–24 (anon.).

1930 *Pax Domini.* The Spectator 27 December, pp. 1003–1004.

1931 *Thoughts on Prayer and the Divine Immanence.* The Expository Times vol. 42 no. 9, June, pp. 405–409.

Churches in the Wilderness. The Spectator 1 August, pp. 146–47.

The Inside of Life. Address broadcast 13 December, published as pamphlet by A. R. Mowbray. (*Collected Papers*, pp. 94–104.)

A Simple Method of Raising the Soul to Contemplation in the Form of a Dialogue. By Francois Malaval 1627–1719. Translated by Lucy Menzies. With an Introduction by Evelyn Underhill. Introduction, pp. v–xx. London & Toronto: J. M. Dent & Sons.

1932 *The Golden Sequence. A Four-Fold Study of the Spiritual Life.* London: Methuen. New York: Harper Brothers (Torch book series) 1960.

The Meaning of Sanctity. The Spectator 23 January, p. 102. (*Mixed Pasture*, pp. 29–40 entitled *What is Sanctity?*)

Finite and Infinite. A Study of Friedrich von Hugel. The Criterion vol 11 no. 43, January, pp. 183–97. (*Mixed Pasture*, pp. 209–28.)

Father Wainright. The Spectator 9 April, pp. 502–503.

A Christian's Faith. The Spectator 2 December, pp. 781–82.

Medieval Mysticism. Chapter XXVI of *The Cambridge Medieval History* vol. 7, pp. 777–812. Cambridge: at the University Press.

1933 *Mixed Pasture. Twelve Essays and Addresses.* London: Methuen.

The Ideals of the Ministry of Women. Theology vol. 26 no. 151, January, pp. 37–42. (*Mixed Pasture*, pp. 113–22.)

The Spiritual Significance of the Oxford Movement. The Hibbert Journal vol 31 no. 3, April, pp. 401–12. (*Mixed Pasture*, pp. 123–46.)

1934 *The School of Charity.* London: Longmans Green. Reprinted with *The Mystery of Sacrifice* in one volume by the same publishers in 1954.

The Spiritual Life of the Teacher. Address published as pamphlet. (*Collected Papers*, pp. 172–87.)

1935 Review of *The Spiritual Letters of Dom John Chapman*. The Criterion vol. 14 no. 57, July, pp. 641–44.
Review of *The Spiritual Letters of Dom John Chapman. Theology* vol. 30 no. 180, June, pp. 371–73.

1936 *Worship.* London: Nisbet. In the Series *The Library of Constructive Theology*, general editors: W. R. Matthews and H. Wheeler Robinson. Reprinted New York: Harper Brothers 1957 (Torchbook series).
What is Mysticism? Address broadcast early 1936 (cf. *Life*, p. 193), published as pamphlet by A. R. Mowbray. (*Collected Papers*, pp. 105–20.)
The Parish Priest and the Life of Prayer. Theology vol. 33 no. 198, December, pp. 326–36. (*Collected Papers*, pp. 121–38.)

1937 *The Spiritual Life. Four Broadcast Talks.* London: Hodder & Stoughton. New York: Harper Brothers.
The Training of the People in Prayer. Theology vol. 34 no. 200, February, pp. 83–91. (*Collected Papers*, pp. 138–56 entitled *The Life of Prayer in the Parish*.)

1938 *The Mystery of Sacrifice. A Meditation on the Liturgy.* London: Longmans Green. Reprinted in one volume with *The School of Charity* 1954.

1939 *Eucharistic Prayers from the Ancient Liturgies.* Chosen and arranged by Evelyn Underhill. London: Longmans Green [1939].
Letters of Direction. Thoughts on the Spiritual Life from the letters of the Abbé de Tourville. With an Introduction by Evelyn Underhill. Introduction, pp. 7–10. London: Dacre Press. Twelve times reprinted to 1972.
The Spiritual Life in War-Time. Christian Literature Association pamphlet.
A Service of Prayers for Use in War-Time. Christian Literature Association pamplet.

1940 *Abba. Meditations Based on the Lord's Prayer.* Longmans Green. Addresses dating from 1934.
Into the Way of Peace. By Communicants of the English Church. Edited by Percy Harill. London: James Clark. *Postscript* by Evelyn Underhill, pp. 187–92; separately published as *The Church and War.*

Posthumous publications

1942 *The Fruits of the Spirit.* Part 1: retreat address from May 1936. Part 2: letters to the prayer group 1940–41. London: Longmans Green. Reprinted in one volume with *Light of Christ* and *Abba* by the same publishers in 1960.

1943 *The Letters of Evelyn Underhill.* Edited with an Introduction by Charles Williams. London: Longmans Green.

1944 *Light of Christ.* Retreat addresses of May 1932. Reprinted with *The Fruits of the Spirit* etc. 1960. London: Longmans Green.

1946 *Collected Papers.* Edited by Lucy Menzies with an Introduction: *Evelyn Underhill in her Writings* by Bishop Lumsden Barkway. Contains the first printed bibliography of Evelyn Underhill's writings. London: Longmans Green. Reprinted in *The Mount of Purification.*

1947 *Spiritual Life and Influence [of Walter Howard Frere].* Contributed to *Walter Howard Frere Bishop of Truro. A Memoir* by C. S. Phillips and others. Chapter X, pp. 175–82 (previously printed?). London: Faber & Faber.

1948 *Meditations and Prayers.* Privately printed by Ronald Harrington Hutson [1948]; four times reprinted and included in *The Mount of Purification* (see below).

1949 *Shrines and Cities of France and Italy.* Edited by Lucy Menzies from an early diary, 1901–7. Written and Illustrated by Evelyn Underhill. London: Longmans Green.

1953 *The Spiritual and the Secular*. Contributed to *Politics and the Faith* edited by Maurice B. Reckitt, pp. 11–24 (previously printed?). Published by The Church Union ('Beacon Books' series) [1953].

1960 *The Mount of Purification*. Retreat addresses of 1931 published in one volume with *Meditations and Prayers* and *Miscellaneous Papers* i.e. *Collected Papers* (as above).

Anthologies

Evelyn Underhill. In Benn's Augustan Books of Poetry 1932.

The Wisdom of Evelyn Underhill: an Anthology from her writings, compiled by J. Stobbart. With decorations by Sylvia Green. London 1951. Booklet.

An Anthology of the Love of God from the Writings of Evelyn Underhill. Edited by Lumsden Barkway and Lucy Menzies. London 1953.

The Evelyn Underhill Reader. Compiled by T. S. Kepler. New York [1962].

Lent With Evelyn Underhill. Selections from her writings. Edited by G. P. Mellick Belshaw. New York and London 1964.

Studies

Geoffrey Curtis C.R.: *Evelyn Underhill*. The Community of the Resurrection Chronicle no. 155, Michaelmas 1941, pp. 7–14.

Charles Williams: *Introduction*, pp. 7–45 in *The Letters of Evelyn Underhill* (1943)—see above.

Lucy Menzies: *Evelyn Underhill: Memoir* in *Light of Christ* (1944)—see above.

Lumsden Barkway: *Evelyn Underhill in her Writings* in *Collected Papers* (1946) pp. 7–30—see above. Reprinted in *The Mount of Purification* (1960) pp. 135–58—see above.

Lumsden Barkway: *Evelyn Underhill*. Theology vol. 56 no. 400, October 1953, pp. 368–72. (In a series, *Great Pastors*.)

Margaret Cropper: *Evelyn Underhill*. London: Longmans Green, 1958.

Marjorie Vernon, article in *The Dictionary of National Biography 1941–1950*. Edited by L. G. Wickham Legg and E. T. Williams. Oxford University Press 1959, pp. 897–98.

E. I. Watkin: *Evelyn Underhill*. The Month vol. 22, January 1959, pp. 45–50.

Valerie Pitt: *Clouds of Unknowing*. Prism vol. 3, no. 3, June 1959, pp. 7–12.

Sister Mary Xavier Kirby S.S.J.: *The Writings of Evelyn Underhill. A Critical Analysis*. Unpublished Ph.D. dissertation deposited in University of Pennsylvania (copies held by Evelyn Underhill's literary executor and Pleshey Retreat House).

Olive Wyon: *Desire for God*. A Study of Three Spiritual Classics. Collins: Fontana Books 1966. The third section pp. 81–116 is devoted to Evelyn Underhill.